REVIEWING

2013 New World Translation of Jehovah's Witnesses

Examining the History of the Watchtower
Translation and the Latest Revision

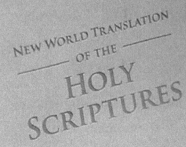

EDWARD D. ANDREWS

REVIEWING

2013 New World Translation of Jehovah's Witnesses

Examining the History of the Watchtower Translation and the Latest Revision

Edward D. Andrews

Christian Publishing House

Cambridge, Ohio

Professional Christian Publishing of the Good News

REVIEWING 2013 New World Translation of Jehovah's Witnesses: Examining the History of the Watchtower Translation and the Latest Revision by Edward D. Andrews

ISBN-13: 978-1-945757-78-5

ISBN-10: 1-945757-78-7

Table of Contents

INTRODUCTION

REVIEWING 2013 New World Translation of Jehovah's Witnesses is going to challenge your objectivity. Being **objective** means that personal feelings or opinions do not influence you in considering and representing facts. Being **subjective** means that your understanding is based on or influenced by personal feelings, tastes, or ideas. If the reader finds these insights offense, it might be a little mind control at work from years of being told the same misinformation repeatedly, so ponder things objectively. We can also have **preconceived** ideas that have been a part of our thinking for so long; we do not question them. Preconceived is an idea or opinion that is formed before having the evidence for its truth. If we are to be effective, we must season our words, so that they are received well. Then there is the term **preconception**, which means a preconceived idea or prejudice. Seasoned words, honesty, and accuracy are distinctive features of effective apologetic evangelism.

CHAPTER 1 History of the Jehovah's Witnesses Printing and Distributing of the Bible

The 2013 year of the Jehovah's Witnesses was the biggest since 1914. While they made many doctrinal adjustments this year, it is their 2013 revision of their New World Translation of the Holy Scriptures that was most shocking, to both Witnesses and non-Witnesses alike. The Witnesses have used a literal translation from the beginning in their evangelism work. Setting aside doctrinal differences, the Witnesses are notorious for their dedication to the commission of Matthew 28:1-20.

Below you will find the history of the Bible publishing and printing endeavors of the Jehovah's Witnesses over the past 125 years. You will notice first and foremost that they have always cherished literal translations. They have written on this subject quite extensively and have always raved about how literal translations get you closer to what God said. However, being that I have read many of their articles on the differences between literal and dynamic equivalent translation philosophies, and how to pick a good translation, or what makes up a good translation, I can say that their position has been that literal is preferred, but the dynamic equivalent has its place. They have written about the strengths and the weaknesses of both translation philosophies. Below the history of their Printing and distrusting of the Bible, you will find a complete quote from Appendix A and B of their newly revised 2013 New World Translation. You will recognize my comments because they will be within bold square brackets [............].

History of the Jehovah's Witnesses Printing and Distributing of the Bible

- As early as 1890, according to available evidence, the Society arranged for a special printing, bearing its own name, of the Second Edition of *The New Testament Newly Translated and Critically Emphasised,* as prepared by the British Bible translator Joseph B. Rotherham. Why this translation? Because of its literalness ...

- In 1902 a special printing of the Holman Linear Parallel Edition of the Bible was made by the arrangement of the Watch Tower Society.

- That same year, the Watch Tower Society came into possession of the printing plates for *The Emphatic Diaglott,* which includes J. J. Griesbach's Greek text of the Christian Greek Scriptures (the 1796-1806 edition) along with an English interlinear translation.

- Four years later, in 1907, the Bible Students Edition of the *King James Version* was published.

- It was 36 years after it first undertook publishing Bibles that the Watch Tower Bible and Tract Society *printed* and *bound* a Bible in its own factory. The first one thus produced was *The Emphatic Diaglott,* the plates for which had been owned by the Society for 24 years. In December 1926 this Bible was printed on a flatbed press in the Society's Concord Street factory in Brooklyn.

- Sixteen years later, in the midst of World War II, the Society undertook the printing of the entire Bible. To this end, plates for the *King James Version* with marginal references were purchased in 1942 from the A. J. Holman Company, of Philadelphia, Pennsylvania.

- The Witnesses wanted to help people to get to know the personal name, as well as the purpose, of its divine author, Jehovah God. There was a translation in English—the *American Standard Version* of 1901—that used the divine name in the more than 6,870 places where it appeared in the sources from which the translators worked. In 1944, after a number of months of negotiations, the Watch Tower Society purchased the right to make a set of key plates for this Bible from plates and type supplied by Thomas Nelson and Sons, of New York.

- Steven Byington, of Ballard Vale, Massachusetts, U.S.A., had also made a modern-English translation of the Bible that gave the divine name its rightful place. The Watch Tower Society came into possession of his unpublished manuscript in 1951 and acquired the sole right of publication in 1961. That complete translation was printed in 1972.

- Jehovah's Witnesses wanted a translation that embodied the benefits of the latest scholarship, one that was not colored by the creeds and traditions of Christendom, a literal translation that faithfully presented what is in the original writings and so could provide the basis for continued growth in knowledge of divine truth, a translation that would be clear and understandable to modern-day readers. The *New World Translation of the Christian Greek Scriptures,* released in 1950, filled that need—at least for that part of the Bible.

- After that, the Hebrew Scriptures were translated into English and were released progressively, in five separate volumes, beginning in 1953.

- Since the one-volume edition of 1961 was published, four additional up-to-date revisions have been issued. The most recent of these was in 1984 when a large-print edition with an extensive appendix, 125,000 marginal references, 11,400 enlightening footnotes, and a concordance was published.[1]

Below we will take a deeper dive into the history of the New World Translation. We have allowed them to tell their own history. If there is some that the author disagrees with in that he feels they are misleading or misinforming, he will interject his comments right in between their material. It will look like this: **REVIEW**: ....

Printing and Distributing God's Own Sacred Word

Image 1 Taken from jw.org

---

[1] Jehovah's Witnesses—Proclaimers of God's Kingdom chap. 27 p. 605 -611 Printing and Distributing God's Own Sacred Word

ON THE outside of the principal factory complex at their world headquarters, Jehovah's Witnesses have for decades displayed a sign that urges everyone: "Read God's Word the Holy Bible Daily."

They themselves are diligent students of God's Word. Over the years they have made use of scores of different Bible translations in an endeavor to ascertain the exact sense of the original inspired Scriptures. Every Witness is encouraged to have a personal program of daily Bible reading. In addition to their topical study of God's Word, they progressively read and discuss the Bible itself in their congregation meetings. Their objective is not to search out texts to support *their* ideas. They recognize the Bible as *God's* own inspired Word. They realize that it gives reproof and discipline, and they earnestly endeavor to conform their thinking and conduct to what it says.—2 Tim. 3:16, 17; compare 1 Thessalonians 2:13.

Because of their conviction that the Bible is God's own sacred Word and because they know the glorious good news that it contains, Jehovah's Witnesses are also zealous publishers and distributors of the Bible.

A Bible-Publishing Society

It was in 1896 that direct reference to the Bible was *officially* included in the name of the legal corporation then being used by the Bible Students in their publishing work. At that time Zion's Watch Tower Tract Society became legally known as Watch Tower *Bible* and Tract Society.[2] The Society did not immediately become a *printer* and *binder* of Bibles, but it was an active *publisher* of them, working out specifications, providing valuable supplementary features, and then arranging with commercial firms to do the printing and binding.

Even prior to 1896, the Society was doing much as a Bible distributor. Not for commercial gain but as a service to its readers, it drew attention to various Bible translations that were available, bought them in large quantities so as to obtain good rates, and then made them available for a price that was sometimes only 35 percent of the list price. Included among these were numerous editions of the *King James Version* that were easy to carry and use, also larger 'Teachers' Bibles' (*King James Version* with such helps as a concordance, maps, and marginal references), *The Emphatic Diaglott* with its Greek-to-English interlinear rendering, Leeser's translation that placed the English text alongside the Hebrew, Murdock's translation from ancient Syriac, *The Newberry Bible* with its marginal references that drew attention to

---

[2] As shown by the *Watch Tower* of July 15, 1892 (p. 210), the name Watch Tower Bible and Tract Society had been used for a number of years before that name was legally registered. A tract published in 1890 in the *Old Theology* series identified the publishers as Tower *Bible* and Tract Society.

occurrences of the divine name in the original language as well as other valuable details reflected in the Hebrew and Greek text, Tischendorf's *New Testament* with its footnote references to variant readings in three of the most complete ancient Greek Bible manuscripts (Sinaitic, Vatican, and Alexandrine), the Variorum Bible with its footnotes that set out not only variant readings of ancient manuscripts but also various translations of portions of the text by eminent scholars, and Young's literal translation. The Society also made available such helps as *Cruden's Concordance* and Young's *Analytical Concordance* with its comments on the original Hebrew and Greek words. In the years that followed, around the globe Jehovah's Witnesses frequently obtained from other Bible societies many thousands of Bibles in whatever languages were available and distributed these.

As early as 1890, according to available evidence, the Society arranged for a special printing, bearing its own name, of the Second Edition of *The New Testament Newly Translated and Critically Emphasised,* as prepared by the British Bible translator Joseph B. Rotherham. Why this translation? Because of its literalness and its endeavor to benefit fully from research that had been done to establish a more accurate Greek text and because the reader was helped by devices employed by the translator to identify which words or expressions were given special emphasis in the Greek text.

In 1902 a special printing of the Holman Linear Parallel Edition of the Bible was made by arrangement of the Watch Tower Society. It contained wide margins in which were printed references to places in Watch Tower publications where various verses were explained, also an index listing scores of subjects along with Scripture citations and helpful references to the Society's publications. This Bible contained the wording of two translations—the *King James* rendering above that of the *Revised Version* where there was any difference. It also included an extensive concordance that alerted the user to various meanings of original-language words.

That same year, the Watch Tower Society came into possession of the printing plates for *The Emphatic Diaglott,* which includes J. J. Griesbach's Greek text of the Christian Greek Scriptures (the 1796-1806 edition) along with an English interlinear translation. Alongside this was the rendering of the text by British-born Benjamin Wilson, who had taken up residence in Geneva, Illinois, U.S.A. Those plates and the sole right of publication had been purchased and then given as a gift to the Society. After copies already in stock had been sent out, arrangements were made by the Society for more to be produced, and those became available in 1903.

Four years later, in 1907, the Bible Students Edition of the *King James Version* was published. The "Berean Bible Teachers' Manual" was bound with it, as an appendix. This included concise comments on verses from all parts

12

of the Bible, along with references to Watch Tower publications for fuller explanation. An edition with an enlarged appendix was published about a year later.

These Bibles were ordered from the printers and binders in lots of between 5,000 and 10,000 at a time, in order to keep the cost down. The Society was desirous of making a variety of Bible translations and related research tools readily available to as many people as possible.

Then, in 1926 the Watch Tower Society took a major step forward in its involvement in Bible publishing.

Printing the Bible on Our Own Presses

It was 36 years after it first undertook publishing Bibles that the Watch Tower Bible and Tract Society *printed* and *bound* a Bible in its own factory. The first one thus produced was *The Emphatic Diaglott,* the plates for which had been owned by the Society for 24 years. In December 1926 this Bible was printed on a flatbed press in the Society's Concord Street factory in Brooklyn. To date, 427,924 of these have been produced.

Sixteen years later, in the midst of World War II, the Society undertook the printing of the entire Bible. To this end, plates for the *King James Version* with marginal references were purchased in 1942 from the A. J. Holman Company, of Philadelphia, Pennsylvania. This translation of the complete Bible into English was produced, not from the Latin *Vulgate,* but by scholars who were able to compare earlier translations with the original Hebrew, Aramaic, and Greek. A concordance, prepared by more than 150 collaborating servants of Jehovah, was added. This was specially designed to help Jehovah's Witnesses find appropriate texts quickly when in the field ministry and thus use the Bible effectively as "the sword of the spirit," to cut away and expose religious falsehood. (Eph. 6:17) In order to make the Bible available to people everywhere at a low cost, it was printed on a web rotary press—something that had never been attempted by other Bible printers. As of 1992, a total of 1,858,368 of these Bibles had been produced.

The desire of Jehovah's Witnesses went beyond getting copies of the Bible, the book itself, into the hands of people. The Witnesses wanted to help people to get to know the personal name, as well as the purpose, of its divine author, Jehovah God. There was a translation in English—the *American Standard Version* of 1901—that used the divine name in the more than 6,870 places where it appeared in the sources from which the translators worked. In 1944, after a number of months of negotiations, the Watch Tower Society purchased the right to make a set of key plates for this Bible from plates and type supplied by Thomas Nelson and Sons, of New York. During the next 48 years, 1,039,482 copies were produced.

Steven Byington, of Ballard Vale, Massachusetts, U.S.A., had also made a modern-English translation of the Bible that gave the divine name its rightful place. The Watch Tower Society came into possession of his unpublished manuscript in 1951 and acquired the sole right of publication in 1961. That complete translation was printed in 1972. Down till 1992, there had been 262,573 produced.

In the meantime, however, another development was taking place.

Producing the *New World Translation*

It was early in October 1946 that Nathan H. Knorr, who was then the president of the Watch Tower Society, first proposed that the Society produce a fresh translation of the Christian Greek Scriptures. Actual work on the translation got under way on December 2, 1947. The complete text was carefully reviewed by the entire translation committee, all of them spirit-anointed Christians. Then, on September 3, 1949, Brother Knorr convened a joint meeting of the boards of directors of the Society's New York and Pennsylvania corporations. He announced to them that the New World Bible Translation Committee had completed work on a modern-language translation of the Christian Greek Scriptures and had turned it over to the Society for publication.[3] This was a fresh translation from the original Greek.

Was there really need for another translation? Already at that time, the complete Bible had been published in 190 languages, and at least part of it had been translated into 928 additional languages and dialects. Jehovah's Witnesses have at various times used most of these translations. But the fact is that most of these were made by clergymen and missionaries of Christendom's religious sects, and to varying degrees their translations were influenced by the pagan philosophies and unscriptural traditions that their religious systems had inherited from the past as well as by the bias of higher criticism. Furthermore, older and more reliable Bible manuscripts were becoming available. The Greek language of the first century was becoming more clearly understood as a result of archaeological discoveries. Also, the languages into which translations are made undergo changes over the years.

Jehovah's Witnesses wanted a translation that embodied the benefits of the latest scholarship, one that was not colored by the creeds and traditions of Christendom, a literal translation that faithfully presented what is in the original writings and so could provide the basis for continued growth in knowledge of divine truth, a translation that would be clear and

---

[3] This translation was assigned to the Watch Tower Bible and Tract Society of Pennsylvania for publication, with the request that the names of the translators never be published. They wanted all honor to go to Jehovah God, the Divine Author of his inspired Word.

understandable to modern-day readers. The *New World Translation of the Christian Greek Scriptures,* released in 1950, filled that need—at least for that part of the Bible. As Jehovah's Witnesses began to use it, many were thrilled not simply because they found its modern-day language easier to read but because they realized that they were getting a clearer understanding of the sense of God's inspired Word.

One of the outstanding features of this translation is its restoration of the divine name, the personal name of God, Jehovah, 237 times in the Christian Greek Scriptures. This was not the first translation to restore the name.[4] But it may have been the first to do it consistently in the main text from Matthew through Revelation. An extensive discussion of this matter in the foreword showed the sound basis for what was done.

Thereafter, the Hebrew Scriptures were translated into English and were released progressively, in five separate volumes, beginning in 1953. As had been done with the Christian Greek Scriptures, care was exercised to convey as literally as possible what was in the original-language text. Special attention was given to making the renderings uniform, conveying accurately the action or state expressed in the verbs, and using simple language that would be readily understood by modern-day readers. Wherever the Tetragrammaton appeared in the Hebrew text, it was appropriately rendered as the personal name of God, instead of being replaced by some other term as had become common in many other translations. Appendix articles and footnotes in these volumes enabled careful students to examine the basis for the renderings used.

On March 13, 1960, the New World Bible Translation Committee completed its final reading of the text of the portion of the Bible that was

---

[4] Some earlier translations into Hebrew, German, and English restored the divine name in the Christian Greek Scriptures, as did many missionary versions.

15

designated for the fifth volume. That was 12 years, 3 months, and 11 days after actual translation of the Christian Greek Scriptures had begun. A few months later, that final volume of the Hebrew Scriptures, in printed form, was released for distribution.

Rather than disband after that project was completed, the translation committee continued to work. A comprehensive review of the entire translation was made. Then, the complete *New World Translation of the Holy Scriptures,* a revised edition in one volume, was published by the Watch Tower Society in 1961. It was made available for distribution for just one dollar (U.S.) so that everyone, regardless of his economic situation, would be able to obtain a copy of God's Word.

Two years later a special students' edition was published. This combined under one cover all the original individual volumes, unrevised, with their thousands of valuable textual footnotes, as well as foreword and appendix discussions. It also retained the valuable cross-references that directed readers to parallel words, parallel thoughts or events, biographic information, geographic details, fulfillments of prophecies, and direct quotations in or from other parts of the Bible.

Since the one-volume edition of 1961 was published, four additional up-to-date revisions have been issued. The most recent of these was in 1984, when a large-print edition with an extensive appendix, 125,000 marginal references, 11,400 enlightening footnotes, and a concordance was published. The features of this edition help students to understand why various texts need to be rendered in a certain way in order to be accurate, as well as when texts can be correctly rendered in more than

"A Text With Instant Vocabulary"

In "The Classical Journal," Thomas N. Winter of the University of Nebraska wrote a review of "The Kingdom Interlinear Translation of the Greek Scriptures" in which he said: "This is no ordinary interlinear: the integrity of the text is preserved, and the English which appears below it is simply the basic meaning of the Greek word. Thus the interlinear feature of this book is no translation at all. A text with instant vocabulary more correctly describes it. A translation in smooth English appears in a slim column at the right-hand margin of the pages. . . .

"The text is based on that of Brooke F. Westcott and Fenton J. A. Hort (1881, repr.), but the translation by the anonymous committee is thoroughly up-to-date and consistently accurate."— April-May issue of 1974, pp. 375-6.

16

one manner. The cross-references also help them to appreciate the interlocking harmony between the various Bible books.

As part of the earnest effort of the New World Bible Translation Committee to help lovers of God's Word to get acquainted with the contents of the original Koine (common Greek) text of the Christian Greek Scriptures, the committee produced *The Kingdom Interlinear Translation of the Greek Scriptures.* This was first published by the Watch Tower Society in 1969 and then updated in 1985. It contains *The New Testament in the Original Greek,* as compiled by B. F. Westcott and F. J. A. Hort. At the right-hand side of the page appears the *New World Translation* text (the 1984 revision in the updated edition). But then, between the lines of Greek text, there is another translation, a very literal, word-for-word rendering of what the Greek actually says according to the basic meaning and grammatical form of each word. This enables even students who cannot read Greek to find out what is actually in the original Greek text.

Was this work on the *New World Translation* going to benefit only those who could read English? In many places Watch Tower missionaries were finding it difficult to obtain enough local-language Bibles to distribute to people who longed for a personal copy of God's Word. It was not uncommon, in some parts of the world, for these missionaries to be the principal distributors of Bibles printed by other Bible societies. But that was not always viewed favorably by religious personnel who represented those Bible societies. Further, some of these Bibles were not the best of translations.

Translation Into Other Languages

The year that the complete *New World Translation* first appeared in a single volume, that is, 1961, a group of skilled translators was assembled to render the English text into six other widely used languages—Dutch, French, German, Italian, Portuguese, and Spanish. Retranslation from English, supplemented by comparison with the Hebrew and the Greek, was possible because of the literal nature of the English translation itself. The translators worked as an international committee in association with the New World Bible Translation Committee, at the Society's headquarters in Brooklyn, New York. In 1963 the Christian Greek Scriptures was printed and released in all six languages.

By 1992 the complete *New World Translation of the Holy Scriptures* was available in 12 languages—Czech, Danish, Dutch, English, French, German, Italian, Japanese, Portuguese, Slovak, Spanish, and Swedish. The Christian Greek Scriptures was available in two more languages. That meant that this translation was available in the native tongues of some 1,400,000,000 persons, or upwards of one fourth of the world's population, and many more were benefiting from it through the translation of excerpts from it into 97 other languages in *The Watchtower*. Those reading these 97 languages, however, were anxious to have the full *New World Translation* in their own tongue. As of 1992, arrangements were already under way to produce this translation in 16 of those languages and to complete the Hebrew Scriptures in the 2 languages that had only the Christian Greek Scriptures.

Since the publishing of these Bibles was done in the Society's own factories by volunteer workers, it was possible to make them available at minimal cost. In 1972 when an Austrian Witness showed a bookbinder the *New World Translation* in German and asked him how much he thought it would cost, the man was amazed to learn that the suggested contribution was only one tenth of the price he named.

Some examples illustrate the impact of this translation. In France the Catholic Church had for centuries prohibited possession of the Bible by the laity. Catholic translations that had become available were relatively expensive, and few homes had these. The *New World Translation of the Christian*

18

Greek Scriptures was released in French in 1963, followed by the complete Bible in 1974. By 1992 a combined total of 2,437,711 copies of the *New World Translation* had been shipped out for distribution in France; and the number of Jehovah's Witnesses in France increased 488 percent during that same period, reaching a total of 119,674.

The situation was similar in Italy. The people had long been forbidden to have a copy of the Bible. After the release of the Italian edition of the *New World Translation* and down till 1992, there were 3,597,220 copies distributed; the vast majority of these were the complete Bible. People wanted to examine for themselves what God's Word contains. Interestingly, during that same period, the number of Jehovah's Witnesses in Italy rose sharply—from 7,801 to 194,013.

When the *New World Translation of the Christian Greek Scriptures* was made available in Portuguese, there were just 30,118 Witnesses in Brazil and 1,798 in Portugal. During the following years, down till 1992, a total of 213,438 copies of the Christian Greek Scriptures and 4,153,738 copies of the complete Bible in Portuguese were sent out to individuals and congregations in these lands. What were the results? In Brazil, over 11 times as many active praisers of Jehovah; and in Portugal, 22 times as many. Tens of thousands of people who had never had a Bible were grateful to get one, and others appreciated having a Bible that used words they could understand. When the *New World Translation of the Holy Scriptures—With References* was made available in Brazil, the news media pointed out that it was the most complete version (that is, with more cross-references and footnotes) available in the country. It also noted that the initial printing was ten times as great as that for most national editions.

The Spanish edition of the *New World Translation of the Christian Greek Scriptures* was also released in 1963, followed in 1967 by the complete Bible. There were 527,451 copies of the Christian Greek Scriptures published, and thereafter, down to 1992, a total of 17,445,782 copies of the complete Bible in Spanish. This contributed to an outstanding increase in the number of praisers of Jehovah in Spanish-speaking lands. Thus, from 1963 to 1992, in predominantly Spanish-speaking lands where Jehovah's Witnesses carry on their ministry, their numbers grew from 82,106 to 942,551. And in the United States, in 1992, there were another 130,224 Spanish-speaking Witnesses of Jehovah.

It was not only in the realm of Christendom that the *New World Translation* was enthusiastically received. In the first year of publication of the Japanese edition, the branch office in Japan received orders for half a million copies.

As of 1992 the printing of the complete *New World Translation of the Holy Scriptures,* in the 12 languages then available, numbered 70,105,258 copies. In addition to that, 8,819,080 copies of portions of the translation had been printed.

Making the Bible Available in Many Forms

Computerization of the Watch Tower Society's operations, starting in 1977, has assisted in Bible production, as it has in other aspects of publishing activity. It has helped translators to achieve greater consistency in their work; it has also made it easier to print the Bible in a variety of forms.

After the full text of the Bible was entered into the computer, it was not difficult to use an electronic phototypesetter to print out the text in a variety of sizes and forms. First, in 1981, came a regular-sized edition in English with a concordance and other helpful appendix features. This was the first edition to be printed by the Watch Tower Society on a web *offset* press. After the benefits of revision had been incorporated into the text stored in the computer, a large-print edition in English was issued in 1984; this included many valuable features for research. A regular-size English edition of that same revision was also made available that year; cross-references and a concordance were included, but not footnotes; and its appendix was designed for field ministry instead of for deeper study. Then, for the benefit of those who wanted a very small pocket edition, this was published in English in 1987. All these editions were quickly published in other languages too.

In addition, attention was given to assisting those with special needs. To help those who could see but who needed very large print, the complete English-language *New World Translation* in four large volumes was published in 1985. Soon that same edition was printed in German, French, Spanish, and Japanese. Before that, in 1983, the *New World Translation of the Christian Greek Scriptures,* in four volumes, had been made available in grade-two English Braille. Within another five years, the complete *New World Translation* had been produced in English Braille in 18 volumes.

Would some people be helped if they could listen to a recording of the Bible? Definitely. So the Watch Tower Society undertook the production of this too. The first audiocassette recording was *The Good News According to John,* in English, released in 1978. In time the entire *New World Translation* in English was made available on 75 audiocassettes. What began as a small operation soon mushroomed into a major project. Quickly, it became available in other languages. By 1992 the *New World Translation,* the whole or part, was available on audiocassettes in 14 languages. At first, some of the branches had the work done by commercial companies. Down till 1992, on their own equipment, the Watch Tower Society had turned out over 31,000,000 of such audiocassettes.

The benefits from the Bible audiocassettes and the uses to which they were put far exceeded original expectations. In all parts of the earth, people were using cassette players. Many who could not read were helped in this way to benefit personally from God's sacred Word. Women were able to listen to the audiocassettes while doing their housework. Men listened to them on tape decks while commuting to work by automobile. The teaching ability of individual Witnesses was enhanced as they listened regularly to God's Word and took note of the pronunciation of Bible names and the manner in which passages of Scripture were read.

As of 1992, various editions of the *New World Translation* were being printed on the Society's presses in North and South America, Europe, and the Orient. A total of 78,924,338 volumes had been produced and made available for distribution. In Brooklyn alone, there were three huge high-speed web offset presses largely devoted to Bible production. Combined, these presses can produce the equivalent of 7,900 Bibles per hour, and at times it has been necessary for them to run an extra shift.

However, Jehovah's Witnesses offer people more than a Bible that might simply be put on the shelf. They also offer to anyone who is interested in the Bible—whether he obtains a copy from Jehovah's Witnesses or not—a free home Bible study. These studies do not continue indefinitely. Some students take to heart what they learn, become baptized Witnesses, and then share in teaching others. After some months, if reasonable progress is not made in applying what is learned, studies are often discontinued in favor of other people who are genuinely interested. As of 1992, Jehovah's Witnesses were providing 4,278,127 individuals or households with this free Bible study service, usually on a weekly basis.

Thus, in a manner unmatched by any other organization, Jehovah's Witnesses are publishers and distributors of the Bible and are teachers of God's sacred Word.

The 2013 Revision of the New World Translation

OVER the years, the *New World Translation of the Holy Scriptures* has been revised a number of times, but the 2013 revision was by far the most extensive. For example, there are now about 10 percent fewer English words in the translation. Some key Biblical terms were revised. Certain chapters were changed to poetic format, and clarifying footnotes were added to the regular edition. It would be impossible in this article to discuss all the changes, but let us consider a few of the main adjustments.

Which key Biblical expressions were changed? As was mentioned in the preceding article, the renderings for "Sheol," "Hades," and "soul" were revised. Additionally, though, a number of other terms were adjusted.

For example, "impaled" was changed to "executed on a stake" or "nailed to the stake" to avoid giving a wrong impression about how Jesus was executed. (Matt. 20:19; 27:31) "Loose conduct" was adjusted to "brazen conduct," which conveys the contemptuous attitude embodied in the Greek term. The expression "long-suffering," as previously used, could be misunderstood to mean suffering for a long time; "patience" better conveys the right sense. "Revelries" was replaced with "wild parties," which would be better understood today. (Gal. 5:19-22) In place of "loving-kindness," the thought is accurately rendered "loyal love." That captures the meaning of a Bible term often used in parallel with "faithfulness."—Ps. 36:5; 89:1.

Some terms that had consistently been translated with one expression are now translated according to context. For example, the Hebrew 'oh·lam', previously rendered "time indefinite," can have the sense of "forever." Compare how this affects the rendering of such verses as Psalm 90:2 and Micah 5:2.

The Hebrew and Greek terms translated "seed" appear often in the Scriptures, both in an agricultural sense and with the figurative meaning of "offspring." Past editions of the *New World Translation* consistently used "seed," including at Genesis 3:15. However, using the term "seed" in the sense of "offspring" is no longer common in English, so the revision uses "offspring" at Genesis 3:15 and related verses. (Gen. 22:17, 18; Rev. 12:17) Other occurrences are translated according to context.—Gen. 1:11; Ps. 22:30; Isa. 57:3.

Why have many literal renderings been adjusted? Appendix A1 of the 2013 revision says that a good Bible translation will "communicate the correct sense of a word or a phrase when a literal rendering would distort or obscure the meaning." When the original-language idioms make sense in other languages, they are rendered literally. Following this approach, the expression "searches the . . . hearts" at Revelation 2:23 makes sense in many languages. However, in the same verse, "searches the kidneys" may not be readily understood, so "kidneys" was revised to "innermost thoughts," thus reflecting the original sense. Similarly, at Deuteronomy 32:14, the literal idiom "the kidney fat of wheat" is rendered more clearly as "the finest wheat." For a similar reason, "I am uncircumcised in lips" is not nearly as clear in most languages as "I speak with difficulty."—Ex. 6:12.

Why are the expressions "sons of Israel" and "fatherless boys" now translated "Israelites" and "fatherless children"? In Hebrew, the masculine gender or the feminine gender usually identifies whether the reference is to a male or to a female. However, some masculine terms may include both males and females. For example, the context of some verses suggests that "the sons of Israel" included both men and women, so this expression is now usually rendered "the Israelites."—Ex. 1:7; 35:29; 2 Ki. 8:12.

Along the same lines, the Hebrew masculine term meaning "sons" at Genesis 3:16 was translated "children" in earlier editions of the *New World Translation*. But at Exodus 22:24, the same word has now been revised to read: "Your *children* [Hebrew, "sons"] will be fatherless." Applying this principle in other cases, "fatherless boy" has been changed to "fatherless child" or "orphan." (Deut. 10:18; Job 6:27) That is similar to the rendering in the Greek *Septuagint*. This also resulted in the phrase "the days of your youth" instead of "the days of your young manhood" at Ecclesiastes 12:1.

Why has the rendering of many Hebrew verbs been simplified? The two main Hebrew verb states are the imperfect, denoting continuous action, and the perfect, denoting completed action. Past editions of the *New World Translation* consistently rendered Hebrew imperfect verbs with a verb and an auxiliary term, such as "proceeded to" or "went on to" in order to show continuous or repeated action. Emphatic expressions such as "certainly," "must," and "indeed" were used to show the completed action of perfect verbs.

In the 2013 revision, such auxiliary expressions are not used unless they add to the meaning. For example, there is no need to emphasize that God repeatedly said, "Let there be light," so in the revision the imperfect verb "say" is not rendered as continuous. (Gen. 1:3) However, Jehovah evidently called to Adam repeatedly, so this is still highlighted at Genesis 3:9 with the rendering "kept calling." Overall, verbs are rendered in a simpler way, focusing on the action rather than on the incomplete or complete aspects reflected in the Hebrew. A related benefit is that this helps to recapture, to an extent, the terseness of the Hebrew.

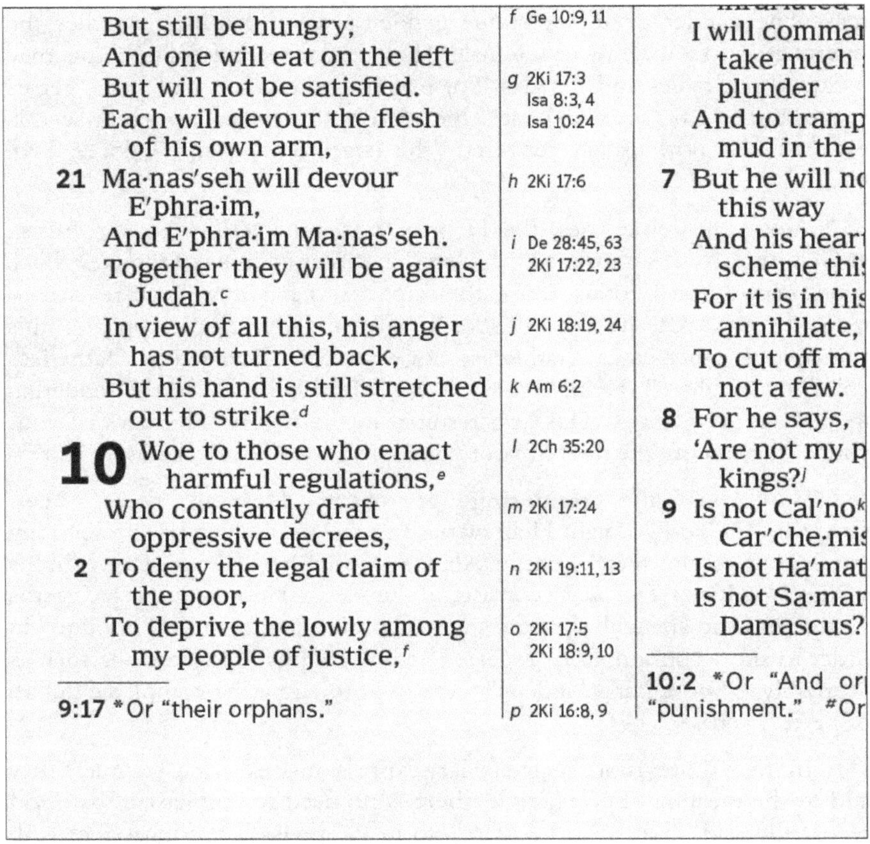

But still be hungry;
And one will eat on the left
But will not be satisfied.
Each will devour the flesh
 of his own arm,
21 Ma·nasʹseh will devour
 Eʹphra·im,
And Eʹphra·im Ma·nasʹseh.
Together they will be against
 Judah.c
In view of all this, his anger
 has not turned back,
But his hand is still stretched
 out to strike.d

10 Woe to those who enact
 harmful regulations,e
Who constantly draft
 oppressive decrees,
2 To deny the legal claim of
 the poor,
To deprive the lowly among
 my people of justice,f

9:17 *Or "their orphans."

f Ge 10:9, 11

g 2Ki 17:3
  Isa 8:3, 4
  Isa 10:24

h 2Ki 17:6

i De 28:45, 63
  2Ki 17:22, 23

j 2Ki 18:19, 24

k Am 6:2

l 2Ch 35:20

m 2Ki 17:24

n 2Ki 19:11, 13

o 2Ki 17:5
  2Ki 18:9, 10

p 2Ki 16:8, 9

I will comma
 take much
 plunder
And to tramp
 mud in the
7 But he will n
 this way
And his hear
 scheme thi
For it is in hi
 annihilate,
To cut off ma
 not a few.
8 For he says,
 'Are not my p
 kings?'j
9 Is not Calʹnok
 Carʹche·mi
Is not Haʹmat
Is not Sa·mar
Damascus?

10:2 *Or "And or
"punishment." #Or

Image 2 In keeping with the poetic writing style of the original text, more chapters are now in poetic format

Why are more chapters now in poetic format? Many parts of the Bible were originally written as poetry. In modern languages, poetry is often distinguished by rhyme, whereas in Hebrew poetry, the most important formal elements are parallelism and contrast. Rhythm is achieved in Hebrew poetry, not by rhyming words, but by the logical order of the thoughts.

Previous editions of the *New World Translation* formatted Job and Psalms in verse format to show that they were originally meant to be sung or recited. This format highlights the poetic elements for emphasis and serves as a memory aid. In the 2013 revision, Proverbs, Song of Solomon, and many chapters of the prophetic books are also now in verse format to show that the passages were written as poetry and to highlight the parallelism and contrasts. An example of this is Isaiah 24:2, where each line contains a

24

contrast, and one line builds on another to emphasize that no one would be excluded from God's judgment. Recognizing such passages as poetry shows the reader that the Bible writer was not simply repeating himself; rather, he was using a poetic technique to emphasize God's message.

The distinction between Hebrew prose and poetry may not always be clearly evident, so there are differences among Bible translations as to which passages are poetic. The translators' judgment is involved in deciding which verses are printed as poetry. Some contain prose that is poetic in wording, freely using pictorial language, wordplay, and parallelism to drive home a point.

A new feature, the Outline of Contents, is especially useful in identifying the frequent change of speakers in the ancient poem The Song of Solomon.

How did study of the original-language manuscripts affect the revision? The original *New World Translation* was based on the Hebrew Masoretic text and the respected Greek text by Westcott and Hort. The study of ancient Bible manuscripts has continued to advance, shedding light on the reading of certain Bible verses. Readings from the Dead Sea Scrolls have become available. More Greek manuscripts have been studied. Much updated manuscript evidence is available in computer format, making it easier to analyze the differences between manuscripts to determine which reading of the Hebrew or Greek text is best supported. The New World Bible Translation Committee took advantage of these developments to study certain verses, resulting in some changes.

For example, at 2 Samuel 13:21, the Greek *Septuagint* contains the equivalent of the words: "But he would not hurt the feelings of Amnon his son, because he loved him, for he was his firstborn." Earlier versions of the *New World Translation* did not include these words because they are not in the Masoretic text. However, the Dead Sea Scrolls do contain these words, which are now included in the 2013 revision. For similar reasons, God's name was restored five times in the book of First Samuel. Study of Greek texts also resulted in a change in the order of ideas at Matthew 21:29-31. Thus, some changes were based on the weight of manuscript evidence rather than on the strict adherence to a single master Greek text.

These are but a few of the changes that have enhanced reading and understanding for many who view the *New World Translation* as a gift from the God of communication.

CHAPTER 2 NWT: History, Translation, Features, Critical Review, and Controversial Passages

The **New World Translation of the Holy Scriptures (NWT)** is a translation of the Bible published by the **Watch Tower Bible and Tract Society**.[5] The New Testament portion was released in 1950,[6] as The New World Translation of the Christian Greek Scriptures, with the complete Bible released in 1961;[7] it is used and distributed by Jehovah's Witnesses.[8] Though it is not the first Bible to be published by the group, it is their first original translation of ancient **Biblical Hebrew**,[9] **Koine Greek**,[10] and **Old Aramaic**[11] biblical texts.[12] As of March 2, 2020, the Watch Tower Society has published more than 240 million copies of the New World Translation

---

[5] The Watch Tower Bible and Tract Society of Pennsylvania is a non-stock, not-for-profit organization headquartered in Warwick, New York. It is the main legal entity used worldwide by Jehovah's Witnesses to direct, administer and disseminate doctrines for the group and is often referred to by members of the denomination simply as "the Society."

[6] Scorgie, Strauss & Voth 2009, pp. 185. Geisler & Nix 2012, pp. 455.

[7] Gordon 2010, pp. 280.

[8] Torres-Pruñonosa, Jose; Plaza-Navas, Miquel-Angel; Brown, Silas (2022). "Jehovah's Witnesses' adoption of digitally-mediated services during Covid-19 pandemic". Cogent Social Sciences. 8 (1). doi:10.1080/23311886.2022.2071034. S2CID 248581687. Retrieved 7 May 2022.

[9] Biblical Hebrew (עִבְרִית מִקְרָאִית, (Ivrit Miqra'it) or לְשׁוֹן הַמִּקְרָא, (Leshon ha-Miqra)), also called Classical Hebrew, is an archaic form of the Hebrew language, a language in the Canaanite branch of Semitic languages spoken by the Israelites in the area known as the Land of Israel, roughly west of the Jordan River and east of the Mediterranean Sea. The term "Hebrew" (ivrit) was not used for the language in the Bible, which was referred to as שְׂפַת כְּנַעַן (sefat kena'an, i.e.

[10] Koine Greek (UK: ; Modern Greek: Ελληνιστική Κοινή, romanized: Ellinistikí Kiní, lit. 'Common Greek'; Greek: [elinisti'ci ci'ni]), also known as Alexandrian dialect, common Attic, Hellenistic, or Biblical Greek, was the common supra-regional form of Greek spoken and written during the Hellenistic period, the Roman Empire and the early Byzantine Empire. It evolved from the spread of Greek following the conquests of Alexander the Great in the fourth century BC and served as the lingua franca of much of the Mediterranean region and the Middle East during the following centuries.

[11] Old Aramaic refers to the earliest stage of the Aramaic language, known from the Aramaic inscriptions discovered since the 19th century. Emerging as the language of the city-states of the Arameans in the Levant in the Early Iron Age, Old Aramaic was adopted as a lingua franca, and in this role was inherited for official use by the Achaemenid Empire during classical antiquity.

[12] Geisler & Nix 2012, pp. 456.

in whole or in part in 210 languages.[13] Though commentators have said a scholarly effort went into the translation, critics have described it as biased.[14]

History of the New World Translation

Until the release of the New World Translation, Jehovah's Witnesses in English-speaking countries primarily used the King James Version.[15] According to the publishers, one of the main reasons for producing a new translation was that most Bible versions in common use, including the Authorized Version (King James), employed archaic language.[16] The stated intention was to produce a fresh translation, free of archaisms.[17] Additionally, over the centuries since the King James Version was produced, more copies of earlier manuscripts of the original texts in the Hebrew and Greek languages have become available. According to the publishers, better manuscript evidence had made it possible to determine with greater accuracy what the original writers intended, particularly in more obscure passages,

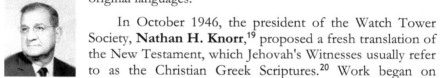

allowing linguists to better understand certain aspects of the original languages.[18]

In October 1946, the president of the Watch Tower Society, **Nathan H. Knorr**,[19] proposed a fresh translation of the New Testament, which Jehovah's Witnesses usually refer to as the Christian Greek Scriptures.[20] Work began on

---

[13] "Online Bible." Watch Tower Society. (https://www.jw.org/en/library/bible/) "Jehovah's Witnesses Reach Translation Milestone With Bible Release in Mozambique". Watch Tower Bible and Tract Society of Pennsylvania. Retrieved March 2, 2021.

[14] Chryssides 2016, pp. 140.

[15] *The Watchtower*, 1 November 1959, p. 672: "Up until 1950 the teachings of Jehovah's witnesses were based mainly upon the King James Version of the Bible" Botting, Heather; Gary Botting (1984). The Orwellian World of Jehovah's Witnesses. University of Toronto Press. p. 99. ISBN 978-0-8020-6545-2. "The King James Bible was used by the Witnesses prior to the release of their own version, which began with the Greek Scriptures, in 1950." Gordon 2010, pp. 280.

[16] Chryssides 2009, pp. lx.

[17] "Announcements." The Watchtower, August 1, 1954, p. 480

[18] "Bible Knowledge Made Plain Through Modern Translation," *The Watchtower*, October 15, 1961, p. 636

[19] Nathan Homer Knorr (April 23, 1905 – June 8, 1977) was the third president of the incorporated Watch Tower Bible and Tract Society, becoming so on January 13, 1942, replacing Joseph Franklin Rutherford, who had served in the position since 1917.

[20] "Part Three—How the Bible Came to Us", *The Watchtower*, October 15, 1997, p. 11, "With this objective, associates of the Society set out in 1946 to produce a fresh translation of the Scriptures. A translation committee of experienced anointed Christians was organized to produce the New World Translation of the Holy Scriptures in English." Mattingly 1951, pp. 439.

December 2, 1947, when the "New World Bible Translation Committee" was formed, composed of Jehovah's Witnesses who professed to be **anointed**.[21] The Watch Tower Society is said to have "become aware" of the committee's existence a year later. The committee agreed to turn over its translation to the Society for publication[22] and on September 3, 1949, Knorr convened a joint meeting of the board of directors of both the Watch Tower Society's New York and Pennsylvania corporations where he again announced to the directors the existence of the committee[23] and that it was now able to print its new modern English translation of the Christian Greek Scriptures. Several chapters of the translation were read to the directors, who then voted to accept it as a gift.[24]

The New World Translation of the Christian Greek Scriptures was released at a Jehovah's Witness convention at **Yankee Stadium, New York, on August 2, 1950**.[25] The translation of the Old Testament, which Jehovah's Witnesses refer to as the Hebrew Scriptures, was released in five volumes in 1953, 1955, 1957, 1958, and 1960. The complete New World Translation of the Holy Scriptures was released as a single volume in 1961,[26] and has since undergone various revisions.[27] Cross references which had appeared in the six separate volumes were updated and included in the complete volume in the 1984 revision, which is often referred to as the Reference Bible.[28]

In 1961, the Watch Tower Society began to translate the New World Translation into Dutch, French, German, Italian, Portuguese, and Spanish; the New Testament in these languages was released simultaneously in July 1963 in Milwaukee, Wisconsin. By 1989, the New World Translation was translated into eleven languages, with more than 56,000,000 copies printed.[29]

---

[21] Jehovah's Witnesses believe salvation is a gift from God attained by being part of "God's organization" and putting faith in Jesus' ransom sacrifice. They do not believe in predestination or eternal security. "Stand Complete and With Firm Conviction—The New World Translation Appreciated by Millions Worldwide," The Watchtower, November 15, 2001, p. 7. How the Governing Body Differs From a Legal Corporation:, The Watchtower, January 15, 2001, p. 30. Chryssides 2016, pp. 137.

[22] "New Bible Translation Completed, Released," The Watchtower, October 1, 1960, p. 599.

[23] "New World Translation of the Christian Greek Scriptures," The Watchtower, September 15, 1950, p. 315.

[24] "New Bible Translation Completed, Released," The Watchtower, October 1, 1960, p. 599.

[25] Chryssides 2009, pp. 100.

[26] Gordon 2010, pp. 280. Paul 2003, pp. 85.

[27] Paul 2003, pp. 85. Watchtower October 1st, 1960 p. 601 para. 13

[28] Foreword, *New World Translation of the Holy Scriptures*, 1984.

[29] All Scripture is Inspired of God and Beneficial 1990 p. 331

Translators of the New World Translation

The New World Translation was produced by the New World Bible Translation Committee, formed in 1947. This committee is said to have comprised unnamed members of multinational background.[30] The committee requested that the Watch Tower Society not publish the names of its members,[31] stating that they did not want to "advertise themselves but let all the glory go to the Author of the Scriptures, God,"[32] adding that the translation, "should direct the reader, not to the translators, but to the Bible's Author, Jehovah God."[33] The publishers stated that "the particulars of [the New World Bible Translation Committee's members] university or other educational training are not the important thing" and that "the translation testifies to their qualification."[34]

Former high-ranking Watch Tower staff have identified various members of the translation team. Former governing body member **Raymond Franz**[35] listed **Nathan H. Knorr,**[36] **Fredrick W. Franz,**[37] **Albert D. Schroeder, George D. Gangas,** and **Milton G. Henschel**[38] as members of the translation team, adding that only Frederick Franz had sufficient

---

[30] New York Times, August 3, 1950, p. 19.

[31] The Watchtower, September 15, 1950, p. 320. Walsh vs Honorable James Latham, Court of Session Scotland, 1954, cross examination of Frederick Franz pp. 90–92

[32] The Watchtower, November 15, 1950, p. 454

[33] The Watchtower, December 15, 1974, p. 768.

[34] IBID.

[35] Raymond Victor Franz (May 8, 1922 – June 2, 2010) was a member of the Governing Body of Jehovah's Witnesses from October 20, 1971, until his removal on May 22, 1980, and served at the organization's world headquarters for fifteen years, from 1965 until 1980. Franz stated the request for his resignation and his subsequent disfellowshipping resulted from allegations of apostasy.

[36] Nathan Homer Knorr (April 23, 1905 – June 8, 1977) was the third president of the incorporated Watch Tower Bible and Tract Society, becoming so on January 13, 1942, replacing Joseph Franklin Rutherford, who had served in the position since 1917.

[37] Frederick William Franz (September 12, 1893 – December 22, 1992) was an American religious leader who served as president of the Watch Tower Bible and Tract Society of Pennsylvania, the legal entity used to administer the work of Jehovah's Witnesses. He had previously served as vice president of the same corporation from 1945 until 1977 when he replaced Nathan H. Knorr as president.

[38] Milton George Henschel (August 9, 1920 – March 22, 2003) was a member of the Governing Body of Jehovah's Witnesses and succeeded Frederick W. Franz as president of the Watch Tower Society in 1992.

knowledge in biblical languages.[39] Referring to the identified members, evangelical minister **Walter Ralston Martin**[40] said, "The New World Bible translation committee had no known translators with recognized degrees in Greek or Hebrew exegesis or translation... None of these men had any university education except Franz, who left school after two years, never completing even an undergraduate degree." Fredrick Franz had stated that he was familiar with not only Hebrew, but with Greek, Latin, Spanish, Portuguese, German, and French for the purpose of biblical translation.[41]

Translation Services Department

In 1989, a Translation Services Department was established at the world headquarters of Jehovah's Witnesses, overseen by the Writing Committee of the Governing Body. The goal of the Translation Services Department was to accelerate Bible translation with the aid of computer technology.

---

[39] Raymond V. Franz, Crisis of Conscience (Atlanta: Commentary Press, 1983), p. 50. Tony Wills, M.A., A People For His Name—A History of Jehovah's Witnesses and An Evaluation, Lulu, 2006. Originally published in 1967 by Vantage Press. "[Frederick] Franz is a language scholar of no mean ability—he supervised the translation of the Bible from the original languages into the New World Translation, completed in 1961." (p. 253)

[40] Walter Ralston Martin (September 10, 1928 – June 26, 1989), was an American Baptist Christian minister and author who founded the Christian Research Institute in 1960 as a para-church ministry specializing as a clearing-house of information in both general Christian apologetics and in countercult apologetics. As the author of the influential The Kingdom of the Cults (1965), he has been dubbed the "godfather of the anti-cult movement." Some opponents have made claims that Martin did not have a valid doctorate. Mr. and Mrs. Robert Brown of Arizona, two members of The Church of Jesus Christ of Latter-day Saints, have stated that California Western University, now known as California Coast University (CCU) was not accredited at the time the degree was awarded. In addition some opponents of Martin claim he purchased his doctorate from CCU, which they claim was a degree mill. It must be noted[original research?] that Martin completed all the coursework at New York University, which is also an accredited school. Furthermore, California Coast University also offers fully accredited programs, being approved by the State of California since 1974. Such approval is currently granted by the California Bureau for Private Postsecondary Education. It, however, received national accreditation only in 2005, from the Distance Education and Training Council (DETC). It obtained this status after a study by the US General Accounting Office (GAO), which sought to provide national accreditation to schools that offered high-quality education, which concluded that CCU was never a diploma mill and never committed wrongdoing.

[41] Walter Martin, *Kingdom of the Cults—Expanded Anniversary Edition*, October 1997, Bethany House Publishers, p. 123-124. "the New World Bible translation committee had no known translators with recognized degrees in Greek or Hebrew exegesis or translation. While the members of the [NWT] committee have never been identified officially by the Watchtower, many Witnesses who worked at the headquarters during the translation period were fully aware of who the members were. They included Nathan H. Knorr (president of the Society at the time), Frederick W. Franz (who later succeeded Knorr as president), Albert D. Schroeder, George Gangas, and Milton Henschel.'" Penton, M. James (1997). Apocalypse Delayed: The Story of Jehovah's Witnesses (2nd ed.). University of Toronto Press. p. 174.

Previously, some Bible translation projects lasted twenty years or more. Under the direction of the Translation Services Department, translation of the Old Testament in a particular language may be completed in as little as two years. During the period from 1963 to 1989, the New World Translation became available in ten additional languages. Since the formation of the Translation Services Department in 1989, there has been a significant increase in the number of languages in which the New World Translation has been made available.[42]

2013 Revision of the NWT

At the Watch Tower Society's annual meeting on October 5, 2013, a significantly revised translation was released. Referring to the new revision, the publishers stated, "There are now about 10 percent fewer English words in the translation. Some key Biblical terms were revised. Certain chapters were changed to poetic format, and clarifying footnotes were added to the regular edition."[43]

The Pericope Adulterae (John 7:53 – 8:11) and the Short and Long Conclusions of Mark 16 (Mark 16:8–20)—offset from the main text in earlier editions—were removed.[44] The new revision was also released as part of an app called JW Library.[45] As of April 2020, the 2013 edition of the New World Translation has been translated into 200 languages.[46]

Translation Philosophy

According to the Watch Tower Society, the New World Translation attempts to convey the intended sense of original-language words according to the context. The original New World Translation employs nearly 16,000 English expressions to translate about 5,500 biblical Greek terms, and over 27,000 English expressions to translate about 8,500 Hebrew terms. The

---

[42] A Milestone for Lovers of God's Word (Watchtower October 15, 1999 pp. 30–31) 2012 Yearbook of Jehovah's Witnesses, p. 26

[43] JW.org, "The 2013 Revision of the New World Translation"

[44] Chryssides 2016, pp. 142. The Removal of these two major interpolations is justified because they were not in the originals. However, they should have provided a footnote explaining why. See NTTC JOHN 7:53–8:11: Where Did Those Verses Go of Jesus and the Woman Caught In Adultery? (https://bit.ly/3G3lqG3) See also NTTC Was the Woman Caught in Adultery John 7:53-8:11 In the Original and What Was Being Taught? (https://bit.ly/38DbmHE). See also NTTC MARK 16:9-20: Were These Twelve Verses Written by Mark? (https://bit.ly/3Nni03l)

[45] "Jehovah's Witnesses distribute free Bibles," The Daytona Beach News-Journal, October 26, 2013

[46] "Jehovah's Witnesses Reach Translation Milestone With Bible Release in Mozambique." Watch Tower Bible and Tract Society of Pennsylvania. Retrieved March 2, 2021.

translators state that, where possible in the target language, the New World Translation prefers literal renderings and does not paraphrase the original text.[47]

Textual Basis of the NWT

The master text used for translating the Old Testament into English was **Kittel's Biblia Hebraica**.[48] The Hebrew texts, **Biblia Hebraica Stuttgartensia**[49] and **Biblia Hebraica Quinta**,[50] were used for preparing the latest version of this translation. Other works consulted in preparing the translation include **Aramaic Targums**,[51] the **Dead Sea Scrolls**,[52] the

---

[47] How Can You Choose a Good Bible Translation? (Watchtower May 1, 2008, pp. 18–22)

[48] Biblia Hebraica refers primarily to the three editions of the Hebrew Bible edited by Rudolf Kittel. When referenced, Kittel's Biblia Hebraica is usually abbreviated BH, or BHK (K for Kittel).

[49] The Biblia Hebraica Stuttgartensia, abbreviated as BHS or rarely BH4, is an edition of the Masoretic Text of the Hebrew Bible as preserved in the Leningrad Codex, and supplemented by Masoretic and text-critical notes. It is the fourth edition in the Biblia Hebraica series started by Rudolf Kittel and is published by the Deutsche Bibelgesellschaft (German Bible Society) in Stuttgart.

[50] The Biblia Hebraica Quinta Editione, abbreviated as BHQ or rarely BH5, is the fifth edition of the Biblia Hebraica and when complete will supersede the fourth edition, the Biblia Hebraica Stuttgartensia (BHS).

[51] A targum (Aramaic: תרגום 'interpretation, translation, version') was an originally spoken translation of the Hebrew Bible (also called the Tanakh) that a professional translator (מְתוּרגְמָן məturgəmān) would give in the common language of the listeners when that was not Hebrew. This had become necessary near the end of the first century BCE, as the common language was Aramaic and Hebrew was used for little more than schooling and worship.

[52] The Dead Sea Scrolls (also the Qumran Caves Scrolls) are ancient Jewish and Hebrew religious manuscripts discovered in 1946/47 at the Qumran Caves in what was then Mandatory Palestine, near Ein Feshkha in the West Bank, on the northern shore of the Dead Sea. Dating from the 3rd century BCE to the 1st century CE, the Dead Sea Scrolls are considered to be a keystone in the history of archaeology with great historical, religious, and linguistic significance because they include the oldest surviving manuscripts of entire books later included in the biblical canons, along with deuterocanonical and extra-biblical manuscripts which preserve evidence of the diversity of religious thought in late Second Temple Judaism.

Samaritan Torah,[53] the **Greek Septuagint**,[54] the **Latin Vulgate**,[55] the **Masoretic Text**,[56] the **Cairo Codex**,[57] the **Aleppo Codex**,[58] Christian David Ginsburg's **Hebrew Text**,[59] and the **Leningrad Codex**.[60]

---

[53] The Samaritan Pentateuch, also known as the Samaritan Torah (Samaritan Hebrew: ⵠⵠⵠⵠⵠ ⵠⵠⵠⵠⵠ Tōrā 'Shamaeriym; Hebrew: תורה שֶׁמְרִים torah shamarim), is a text of the Torah, written in the Samaritan script and used as sacred scripture by the Samaritans. It dates back to one of the ancient versions of the Hebrew Bible that existed during the Second Temple period, and constitutes their entire biblical canon.Some six thousand differences exist between the Samaritan and the Rabbinic Masoretic Text.

[54] The Greek Old Testament, or Septuagint (, US also ; from the Latin: septuaginta, lit. 'seventy'; often abbreviated 70; in Roman numerals, LXX), is the earliest extant Greek translation of books from the Hebrew Bible. It includes several books beyond those contained in the Masoretic text of the Hebrew Bible as canonically used in the tradition of mainstream Rabbinical Judaism.

[55] The Vulgate (; also called Biblia Vulgata, Latin: [ˈbɪbli.a wʊlˈɡaːta]) is a late-4th-century Latin translation of the Bible. The Vulgate is largely the work of Jerome of Stridon who, in 382, had been commissioned by Pope Damasus I to revise the Vetus Latina Gospels used by the Roman Church.

[56] The Masoretic Text (MT or 𝔐; Hebrew: נוסח המסורה, romanized: Nusakh Ham'mas'sora) is the authoritative Hebrew and Aramaic text of the 24 books of the Hebrew Bible (Tanakh) in Rabbinic Judaism. The Masoretic Text defines the Jewish canon and its precise letter-text, with its vocalization and accentuation known as the mas'sora.

[57] The Codex Cairensis (also: Codex Prophetarum Cairensis, Cairo Codex of the Prophets) is a Hebrew manuscript containing the complete text of the Hebrew Bible's Nevi'im (Prophets). It has traditionally been described as "the oldest dated Hebrew Codex of the Bible which has come down to us", but modern research seems to indicate an 11th-century date rather than the 895 CE date written into its colophon.

[58] The Aleppo Codex (Hebrew: כֶּתֶר אֲרָם צוֹבָא, romanized: Keter Aram Tzova, lit. 'Crown of Aleppo') is a medieval bound manuscript of the Hebrew Bible.

[59] Christian David Ginsburg (Hebrew: 25, כריסטיאן דוד גינצבורג December 1831 – 7 March 1914) was a Polish-born British Bible scholar and a student of the Masoretic tradition in Judaism. He was born to a Jewish family in Warsaw but converted to Christianity at the age of 15.

[60] The Leningrad Codex (Latin: Codex Leningradensis, the "codex of Leningrad") is the oldest complete manuscript of the Hebrew Bible in Hebrew, using the Masoretic Text and Tiberian vocalization. According to its colophon, it was made in Cairo in 1008 CE (or possibly 1009).Some have proposed that the Leningrad Codex was corrected against the slightly earlier Aleppo Codex. "All Scripture is Inspired of God and Beneficial" 1990 pp. 305-314. How the Bible Came to Us, Appendix A3 of 2013 REVISION

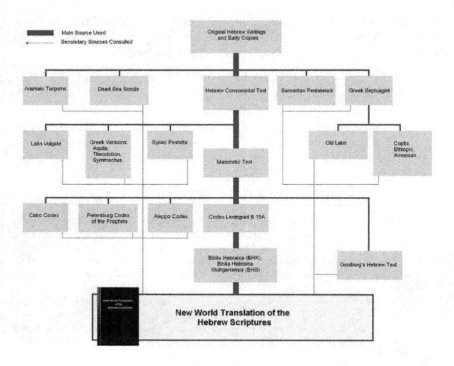

New World Translation of the Hebrew Scriptures

The Greek master text by the Cambridge University scholars **B. F. Westcott**[61] and **F. J. A. Hort**[62] (1881) was used as the basis for translating the New Testament into English.[63] The committee also referred to the **Novum Testamentum Graece**[64] (18th edition, 1948) and to works by Jesuit scholars José M. Bover (1943),[65] and Augustinus Merk (1948).[66] The **United Bible Societies'**[67] text (5th ed. 2014) and the **Nestle-Aland** text (28th ed. 2012) were used to update the footnotes in the 1984 version. Additional works consulted in preparing the New World Translation include the **Armenian Version,**[68] **Coptic Versions,**[69] the **Latin Vulgate, Sistine and Clementine Revised Latin Texts,**[70] **Textus Receptus,**[71] the **Johann**

---

[61] Brooke Foss Westcott (12 January 1825 – 27 July 1901) was an English bishop, biblical scholar and theologian, serving as Bishop of Durham from 1890 until his death. He is perhaps most known for co-editing The New Testament in the Original Greek in 1881.

[62] Fenton John Anthony Hort (1828–1892), known as F. J. A. Hort, was an Irish-born theologian and editor, with Brooke Foss Westcott of a critical edition of The New Testament in the Original Greek.

[63] Paul 2003, pp. 85.

[64] Novum Testamentum Graece (The New Testament in Greek) is a critical edition of the New Testament in its original Koine Greek, forming the basis of most modern Bible translations and biblical criticism. It is also known as the Nestle–Aland edition after its most influential editors, Eberhard Nestle and Kurt Aland.

[65] Paul 2003, pp. 85.

[66] IBID

[67] The United Bible Societies (UBS) is a global fellowship of around 150 Bible Societies operating in more than 240 countries and territories. It has working hubs in England, Singapore, Nairobi and Miami.

[68] The Armenian Bible is due to Saint Mesrob's early-5th-century translation. The first monument of Armenian literature is the version of the Holy Scriptures.

[69] There have been many Coptic versions of the Bible, including some of the earliest translations into any language. Several different versions were made in the ancient world, with different editions of the Old and New Testament in five of the dialects of Coptic: Bohairic (northern), Fayyumic, Sahidic (southern), Akhmimic and Mesokemic (middle).

[70] The Sixto-Clementine Vulgate or Clementine Vulgate (Latin: Vulgata Clementina) is the edition promulgated in 1592 by Pope Clement VIII of the Vulgate—a 4th-century Latin translation of the Bible that was written largely by Jerome. It was the second edition of the Vulgate to be authorised by the Catholic Church, the first being the Sixtine Vulgate.

[71] In Christianity, the term Textus Receptus (Latin for "received text") refers to all printed editions of the Greek New Testament from Erasmus' Novum Instrumentum omne (1516) to the 1633 Elzevir edition. It was the most commonly used text type for Protestant denominations.

Jakob Griesbach's Greek[72] text, the **Emphatic Diaglott**,[73] and various papyri.[74]

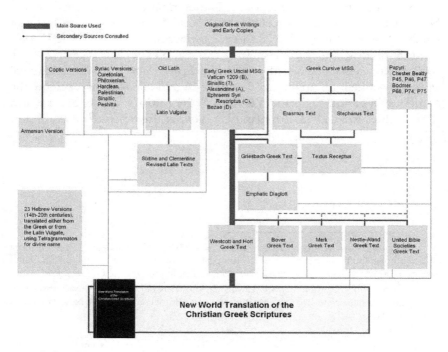

Other Languages

Translation into other languages is based on the English text, supplemented by comparison with the Hebrew and Greek.[75] The complete New World Translation has been published in more than one hundred languages or scripts, with the New Testament available in more than fifty additional languages.

---

[72] Johann Jakob Griesbach (4 January 1745 – 24 March 1812) was a German biblical textual critic. Griesbach's fame rests upon his work in New Testament criticism, in which he inaugurated a new epoch.

[73] The Emphatic Diaglott is a diaglot, or two-language polyglot translation, of the New Testament by Benjamin Wilson, first published in 1864. It is an interlinear translation with the original Greek text and a word-for-word English translation in the left column, and a full English translation in the right column.

[74] "All Scripture is Inspired of God and Beneficial" 1990 pp. 305-314

[75] Jehovah's Witnesses—Proclaimers of God's Kingdom (1993) Chap. 27 p. 611, subheading Translation Into Other Languages.

When the Writing Committee approves the translation of the Bible into a new language, it appoints a group of baptized Jehovah's Witnesses to serve as a translation team. Translators are given a list of words and expressions commonly used in the English New World Translation with related English words grouped together (e.g. atone, atonement or propitiation). A list of vernacular equivalents is then composed. A database of Greek and Hebrew terms is available where a translator has difficulty rendering a verse. The vernacular terms are then applied to the text in the target language. Further editing and translation is then performed to produce a final version.[76]

Features of the NWT

The layout resembles the 1901 edition of the **American Standard Version**.[77] The translators use the terms "Hebrew-Aramaic Scriptures" and "Christian Greek Scriptures" rather than "Old Testament" and "New Testament," stating that the use of "testament" was based on a misunderstanding of 2 Corinthians 3:14.[78] Headings were included at the top of each page to assist in locating texts; these have been replaced in the 2013 revision by an "Outline of Contents" introducing each Bible book. There is also an index listing scriptures by subject.

Square brackets [ ] were added around words that were inserted editorially but were removed as of the 2006 printing. Double brackets were used to indicate text considered doubtful. The pronoun "you" was printed in small capitals (i.e., YOU) to indicate plurality, as were some verbs when plurality may be unclear. These features were discontinued in the 2013 release. The New World Translation attempts to indicate progressive rather than completed actions, such as "proceeded to rest" at Genesis 2:2 instead of "rested." The 2013 release indicates progressive verbs only where considered contextually important.

The name *Jehovah* is a translation of the Tetragrammaton (Hebrew: יהוה, transliterated as JHVH. The Tetragrammaton (; from Ancient Greek τετραγράμματον (tetragrámmaton) '[consisting of] four letters'), or Tetragram, is the four-letter Hebrew theonym יהוה (transliterated as YHWH), the name of the national god of Israel. The four letters, written and read from

---

[76] A Milestone for Lovers of God's Word (Watchtower October 15, 1999 pp. 30–31)

[77] The American Standard Version (ASV), officially Revised Version, Standard American Edition, is a Bible translation into English that was completed in 1901 with the publication of the revision of the Old Testament. The revised New Testament had been released in 1900.

[78] Chryssides 2009, pp. 100. Appendix 7E in the New World Translation reference edition

right to left, are yodh, he, waw, and he. The New World Translation uses the name Jehovah 6,979 times in the Old Testament.[79] According to the Watch Tower Society, the Tetragrammaton appears in "the oldest fragments of the Greek Septuagint."[80] In reference to the Septuagint, biblical scholar Paul E. Kahle stated, "We now know that the Greek Bible text as far as it was written by Jews for Jews did not translate the Divine name by Kyrios, but the Tetragrammaton written with Hebrew or Greek letters was retained in such MSS (manuscripts). It was the Christians who replaced the Tetragrammaton by Kyrios, when the divine name written in Hebrew letters was not understood any more."[81] However, according to professor Albert Pietersma, since pre-Christian times adonai and the Tetragrammaton were considered equivalent to the Greek term kyrios. Pietersma stated, "The translators felt no more bound to retain the tetragram in written form than they felt compelled to render distinctively Hebrew el, elohim or shaddai."[82] He also considers that old manuscripts containing the tetragram, like the papyrus Fouad 266, "is evidence of a secondary stage."[83] Regardless of the modern arguments, the fact is God gave us his personal name, a personal name that is still found in every translation when you look at the personal name of the kings.

many Hebrew kings and others used by God personally in Bible times used part of the Father's personal name in their name, like **Jeho**ash, **Jeho**ram, **Jeho**iakim, **Jeho**iachin, **Jeho**ram, **Jeho**hanan, **Jeho**nada b, **Jeho**ahaz, and even the wife of High Priest **Jeho**iada; daughter of King **Jeho**ram of Judah, **Jeho**sheba, among many more. We notice that the beginning of the Father's personal name is used in every one of these cases. Does anyone find it a bit troubling that the Bibles (JB, LEB, HCSB), which choose to use the so-called scholarly "Yahweh" rendering still spell the above names with Jeho? Why do these same translations not spell **Jeho**ash "**Yah**ash"? We will look at how the Holman Christian Standard Bible (and the HCSB revision, the 2017 Christian Standard Bible) and the Lexham English Bible render the Father's personal name and how they render **Jeho**sheba, **Jeho**ram, and **Jeho**ash.

---

[79] Revised New World Translation of the Holy Scriptures Archived 2013-11-01 at the Wayback Machine. Accessed 14 October 2013.

[80] Insight on the Scriptures, Vol. II p. 9, 1988; Watchtower Bible and Tract Society of Pennsylvania

[81] The Cairo Geniza, Basil Blackwell, Oxford, 1959, p. 222

[82] De Septuaginta: Studies in Honour of John William Wevers on His Sixty-Fifth Birthday, Albert Pietersma, 1984, pages 98-99

[83] *De Septuaginta: Studies in Honour of John William Wevers on His Sixty-Fifth Birthday*, Albert Pietersma, 1984, pages 99-100

There have been myths perpetuated for far too long that just are not true. There was a "J" in biblical Hebrew. Unlike Yiddish, which modern Jews speak, the Hebrew language that was spoken by Abraham and Moses and that is preserved in the Scriptures does have the "j" sound. From ancient times, the "j" sound has been represented by the letter jod (in ancient Hebrew , and in Biblical Hebrew י). Although Ashkenazi Jews have changed the pronunciation of jod to the "y" sound, the Sephardic Jews have retained the original pronunciation of jod as "j." The Sephardic phonetic system is acknowledged by scholars as to the most accurate representation of the ancient Hebrew. Sephardi Hebrew is the pronunciation system used by most Biblical Hebrew grammars.

The myth that there was no "J" until 500 years ago is also false. The first symbol representing both "I" and "j" appeared around 800 A.D. This symbol was invented by French monks, who adapted it from Roman writings. In 1066 the symbol was transported to Saxon England by William the Conqueror. Thus the first symbol representing the "j" sound was introduced to the English-speaking peoples more than nine hundred years ago—nearly five centuries before Tyndale's transliteration of יְהֹוָה (JHVH) as Iehouah (pronounced Jehovah). About 1200 A.D., the lowercase "j" was developed by tweaking the bottom of the lowercase "i," in order to distinguish the "i" sound from the "j" sound. Capital "J" was not invented until the late 1500s or early 1600s. In Tyndale's day, capital "I," when used before a vowel at the beginning of a word, still represented the consonant sound of "J."

The myth that the name "Jehovah" was invented is untrue as well. In arguing against the use of Jehovah, sacred namers [those preferring Yahweh] claim that this name was unknown in Biblical times. They insist that the name Jehovah is a recent invention, concocted in the 1500s by a Catholic priest. They quote well-known Biblical writers and editors who support this view. The scholarly community today has inherited a myth from the past. Historical records bear ample evidence that the name Jehovah was not invented by Galatinus. [The statement still commonly repeated that it originated with Petrus Galatinus (1518) is erroneous; "Jehova" occurs in manuscripts at least as early as the 14th century. (1911 Encyclopædia Britannica/Jehova)] The pronunciation of the divine name JHVH as Jehovah was used by European scholars as early as the 10th century A.D. This fact confirms that the vowel points of JHVH were accepted as a legitimate part of the Hebrew text during this period of history. The pronunciation of JHVH as Jehovah predates Galatinus, Tyndale, Reuchlin and Buechelin (Fagius) to the time when the Levitical families began migrating to Spain from Palestine with their pointed Masoretic Texts. These texts had been consistently pointed since the 400's

A.D. There is no historical evidence to support the claim that the Masoretes had falsified the vowel points in the text.

When the Ben Asher text was finally sealed by 980 A.D. and the work of the Masoretes became the standard Hebrew text for all time, the divine name JHVH was pointed to be pronounced Jehovah. When Fagius, or Buechelin, supported the name Jehovah, he was following the vowel markings that he had learned from the Hebrew text of Ben Asher. When Tyndale translated JHVH to be pronounced as Jehovah, he was following the vowel markings that he had learned from the Hebrew text of Ben Asher.

Contrary to the claims of sacred namers, the name Jehovah was not invented by Galatinus. The records of history testify to all who are willing to examine them that Jehovah is the true pronunciation of the divine name JHVH.

The myth that Jehovah was pointed with the vowel markings of Adonai is simply untrue as well. The divine name יהוה (JHVH) is used some six thousand eight hundred and twenty-three times in the Masoretic Text. Six thousand five hundred and eighteen times the name is marked to be pronounced יְהֹוָה (Hebrew) J'hōh-vāh' 3068). Three hundred and five times the name is marked to be pronounced יֱהֹוִה (Hebrew Jehōh-vih' 3069). Not once is the divine name JHVH marked to be pronounced in any other way.[84]

How Does the Father Feel About His Own Personal Name?

Isaiah 42:8 American Standard Version (ASV)

8 I am Jehovah, that is my name; and my glory will I not give to another, neither my praise unto graven images.

Malachi 3:16 American Standard Version (ASV)

16 Then they that feared Jehovah spake one with another; and Jehovah hearkened, and heard, and a book of remembrance was written before him, for them that feared Jehovah, and that thought upon his name.

Micah 4:5 American Standard Version (ASV)

5 For all the peoples walk everyone in the name of his god; and we will walk in the name of Jehovah our God for ever and ever.

Proverbs 18:10 American Standard Version (ASV)

10 The name of Jehovah is a strong tower; The righteous runs into it, and is safe.

---

[84] http://www.cbcg.org/ By © Carl D. Franklin December 9, 1997

Joel 2:32 American Standard Version (ASV)

32 And it shall come to pass, that whosoever shall call on the name of Jehovah shall be delivered; for in mount Zion and in Jerusalem there shall be those that escape, as Jehovah hath said, and among the remnant those whom Jehovah doth call.

The *New World Translation* also uses the name *Jehovah* 237 times in the New Testament where the extant texts use only the Greek words *kyrios* (*Lord*) and *theos* (*God*).[85] The use of *Jehovah* in the New Testament is very rare, but not unique to the *New World Translation*.[86] Walter Martin, an evangelical minister, wrote, "It can be shown from literally thousands of copies of the Greek New Testament that not once does the tetragrammaton appear."[87] However, the translators of the *New World Translation* believed that the name *Jehovah* was present in the original manuscripts of the New Testament when quoting from the Old Testament, but replaced with the other terms by later copyists. Based on this reasoning, the translators consider to have "restored the divine name", though it is not present in any extant manuscripts.[88]

John McRay, in his book Archaeology and the New Testament, writes,

> This whole issue becomes even more intriguing when we consider the possibility that the New Testament autographs, written almost entirely by Jewish Christians (the possible exception being Luke-Acts), may have preserved the Jewish custom and retained the divine name in Aramaic script in quotations from the Old Testament. Thus they may have followed the lead of some Jewish authors who used one script for the divine name when they quoted Scripture and another when they themselves referred to God. Similarly, it was customary at Qumran to use the Tetragram freely when one was either copying or introducing Scripture

---

[85] Gutjahr 2017, pp. 655–656. Bowman, Robert M. Understanding Jehovah's Witnesses. Grand Rapids: Baker Book House. 1991. p. 114

[86] Translations in English with similar renderings include A Literal Translation of the New Testament ... From the Text of the Vatican Manuscript (Heinfetter, 1863); The Emphatic Diaglott (Benjamin Wilson, 1864); The Epistles of Paul in Modern English (George Stevens, 1898); St. Paul's Epistle to the Romans (Rutherford, 1900); The Christian's Bible — New Testament (LeFevre, 1928) and The New Testament Letters (Wand, 1946).

[87] Walter Martin, The Kingdom of the Cults Revised, Updated, and Expanded Anniversary Edition, Bethany House Publishers, Minneapolis, Minnesota 1997, p. 125.

[88] The Watchtower, August 1, 2008. Brooklyn, New York: Watch Tower Bible and Tract Society of Pennsylvania. 2008. pp. 18–23. "Lord". Insight on the Scriptures. Vol. 2. p. 267.

quotations into a commentary, but to use El ("God") in original material written for a commentary.[89]

Having references to Yahweh clearly indicated would be of enormous help, for any verses that refer to "the Lord" are unclear as to whether Christ or God (Yahweh) is meant. For example, Peter's quotation (in Acts 2:34) of David, "The Lord said to my Lord," is unclear until the Hebrew original (Ps. 110:1) is read: "Yahweh says to my Adonai." Such verses that quote the Old Testament would be clearer if YHWH (the Tetragram) were used in the New Testament.

Another case in point is Romans 10:16, which quotes Isaiah 53:1, "Lord, who has believed our report?" "Lord" would seem to refer to Christ, for "the word of Christ" is a reading which appears in the most recent New Testament texts of verse 17, even though many of the ancient witnesses have "the word of God."[90] Actually, the word Lord does not appear in the Hebrew text of Isaiah 53:1, although it does appear in the Greek text, which Paul quotes, as κυριε. Since this word became a surrogate in Christian copies of the Septuagint for YHWH, it is natural to assume that κυριε in the Septuagint of Isaiah 53:1 refers to YHWH. It undoubtedly slipped into the Septuagint from an early Hebrew lemma (in commentaries, the setting forth of a text prior to its discussion) which led to the inference that the YHWH mentioned in the second part of Isaiah 53:1 is the person being addressed in the first part of that verse. Since this verse is Scripture rather than commentary, Jewish scribal practice would have dictated the use of "Yahweh" rather than "Adonai." The verse would then have read, "Yahweh, who has believed our report?"[91] This is the way Paul would have understood the Septuagint. Contrary to current textual criticism, then, the reading in Romans 10:17 should probably be "the word of God" rather than "the word of Christ." Rudolf Bultmann's argument that "the unmodified expression 'the Lord' is unthinkable (nicht denkbar)" in Jewish usage (and thus

---

[89] Howard ("Tetragram and the New Testament," 66-67) presents two illustrations: 1 QpHab 10:6-7 (equals Hab. 2:13) and 1 QpHab 11: 10 (equals Hab. 2:16).

[90] See the discussion in Bruce M. Metzger, A Textual Commentary on the Greek New Testament (New York: United Bible Societies, 1971), 525.

[91] Other examples are discussed by Howard, "Tetragram and the New Testament," 76-83

unthinkable in Isa. 53:1a)[92] is now rebutted by several Palestinian Aramaic texts which have the word Mare or Marya ("Lord") as a title for God. Thus, pre-Christian Jews did refer to God in an absolute sense as "the Lord."[93]

While Dr. John McRay is correct in all that he says, the earliest New Testament papyri does not contain the Tetragrammaton or a replacement of some sort. However, we do have the Nomina Sacra (Sacred Names) This Greek text, especially with the early dating of 150 C.E., evidences a scribal custom that had recently developed. The scribes used suspensions (IH XP. Ἰησοῦς Χριστὸς [*Jesus Christ*]) or contractions (ΘΣ, Θεός, Theos, God), to which he would place a bar over the entire name (O͞K͞C), for sacred names and words (*nomina sacra*). **Nomina Sacra** (singular: *nomen sacrum* from Latin *sacred name*): In early Christian scribal practices (how early we cannot know), there was the abbreviation of several frequently occurring divine names or titles within the Greek manuscripts. The very earliest copyists used a special form for the divine names: *kurios* (Lord), *Iēsous* (Jesus), *Christos* (Christ), *theos* (God), and *pneuma* (Spirit). In time, the list grew to fifteen names or words.

This practice by the Christian scribes followed the custom of the Jewish scribes and their rendering of the Tetragrammaton or sacred name יהוה [JHVH] in Greek by the words *kyrios* ("Lord") without the definite article and *theos* ("God") with only the first and last letters written and a stroke above them. However, P4+P64+P67 dates to (150-175 C.E.), P32 dates to (150-200 C.E.), P46 dates to 150 C.E.), P66 dates to about (150 C.E.),

---

[92] Rudolph Bultmann, Theology of the New Testament, 2 vols. (London: SCM, 1952), 1.51 equals Theologie des Neuen Testaments (Tübingen: Mohr, 1948), 52.

[93] Joseph A. Fitzmyer, "The Aramaic Language and the Study of the New Testament," JBL 99 (1980): 13. See McRay, John (2008-02-01). Archaeology and the New Testament (Kindle Locations 5515-5582). Baker Academic. Kindle Edition.

P75 dates to about (175 C.E.), and P90 dates to (150-200 C.E.). This means that the nomina sacra for Lord, Jesus, Christ, God, and Spirit are standard by 150 C.E. Which would suggest that, after the death of the last apostle John died in about 100 C.E., more than just division started to set in, as the apostles had really served as a restraint against the great apostasy that was about to come. Now, this little excursion into an area that might seem totally unrelated is just to say, we cannot know what the authors penned in their autographs, nor the first generation of copyists, based on mid-late second-century manuscripts. Why? The phenomena of the standardization of the nomina sacra only need about fifty-years to take place. Of course, John wrote his Gospel and three letters between 96-98 C.E. so we can say that his writings would have been closest. The other books all date prior to 70 C.E.

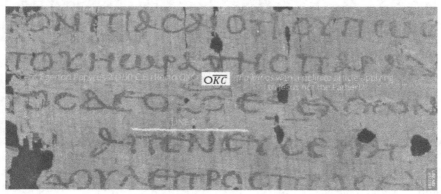

gain, the first four nominal sacra were ('Jesus,' 'God,' 'Lord,' and 'Christ') in the earliest extant manuscripts that we have. It is possible that the personal name of the Father, Jehovah, could be designated in the Greek as $\overline{KC}$ and $\overline{\theta C}$ and were the first attempts at the nomina sacra.[2] The Christian scribes soon thereafter expanded the list of abbreviations that included the following: $\overline{OKC}$ *ho kyrios* with a definite article applying to Jesus, not the Father? Followed by $\overline{IH}$ (*Iesous*, Jesus). Was the initial attempt with $\overline{KC}$ the title for the father replacing the Tetragrammaton or sacred name יהוה in Greek without the definite article? Also, $\overline{\theta C}$, the title for the father replacing the Tetragrammaton or sacred name יהוה in Greek? In addition, we have $\overline{\Pi PA}$ (*patera,* father) and $\overline{M\omega}$ (*Mojses,* Moses).[94] It is certainly an anomaly that we find Moses' name abbreviated by suspension (the first two letters) here in P Egerton 2 similar to how Jesus' name is treated. Comfort writes, "Scattered across the pages of nearly every extant Greek New

---

[94] *Fragments of an Unknown Gospel,* by Bell and Skeat, p. 2.

44

Testament manuscript can be seen the following nomina sacra."
(Encountering the Manuscripts, 2005, 199). The contraction or suspended
word would have a bar over it.

ΚΣ for κυριος (Kurios) = Lord
IH or IHΣ for ιησους (Iēsous) = Jesus
XP or XΣ or XPΣ for χριστος (Christos) = Christ
ΘΣ for θεος (theos) = God
ΠΝΑ for πνευμα (pneuma) = Spirit

Take a look at the image below at "1 verso" and note $\overline{\Pi P A}$ in line
12, $\overline{M\omega}$ in line 13 and $\overline{\vartheta C}$ in line 16. Next look at "1 recto" and note $\overline{OKC}$ in
line 9 and $\overline{\Pi I}$ in line 12. However, we do not have *Kyrios* without the definite
article, which would apply to the Father in the fragments. Really, we can say
that it is likely that 150 C.E. was entering the time of standardization of the
nomina sacra that would grow in sacred names and words.

Egerton Gospel Translation

**The Unknown Gospel Egerton Papyrus 2 + Cologne Papyrus 255
Fragment 1: Verso (?)**

. . . ? And Jesus said] unto the lawyers, [? Punish] every wrongdoer and
transgessor, and not me; . . . . . And turning to the rulers of the people he
spake this saying, Search the scriptures, in which ye think that ye have life;
these are they which bear witness of me. [John 5:39.] Think not that I came to
accuse you to my Father; there is one that accuseth you, even Moses, on
whom ye have set your hope. [John 5:45] And when they said, We know well that
God spake unto Moses, but as for thee, we know not whence thou art, [John
9:29] Jesus answered and said unto them, Now is your unbelief accused ...

Fragment 1: Recto (?)

... ? they gave counsel to] the multitude to [? carry the] stones together
and stone him. [John 8:59; 10:31] And the rulers sought to lay their hands on him
that they might take him and [? hand him over] to the multitude; and they
could not take him, because the hour of his betrayal was not yet come. [John
7:30] But he himself, even the Lord, going out through the midst of them,
departed from them. [Luke 4:30] And behold, there cometh unto him a leper and
saith, Master Jesus, journeying with lepers and eating with them in the inn I
myself also became a leper. If therefore thou wilt, I am made clean. The Lord
then said unto him, I will; be thou made clean. And straightway the leprosy
departed from him. [And the Lord said unto him], Go [and shew thyself]
unto the [priests . . .

Fragment 2: Recto (?)

45

... coming unto him began to tempt him with a question, saying, Master Jesus, we know that thou art come from God, [John 3:2; Matt. 22:16] for the things which thou doest testify above all the prophets. [John 10:25] Tell us therefore: Is it lawful [? to render] unto kings that which pertaineth unto their rule? [Shall we render unto them], or not? [Matt. 22:17] But Jesus, knowing their thought, [Matt. 9:4] being moved with indignation, said unto them, Why call ye me with your mouth Master, when ye hear not what I say? [Luke 6:46] Well did Isaiah prophesy of you, saying, This people honour me with their lips, but their heart is far from me. In vain do they worship me, [teaching as their doctrines the] precepts [of men] [Matt. 15:7-9] ...

Fragment 2: Verso (?)

... shut up ... in ... place ... its weight unweighed? And when they were perplexed at his strange question, Jesus, as he walked, stood still on the edge of the river Jordan, and stretching forth his right hand he ... and sprinkled it upon the ... And then ... water that had been sprinkled ... before them and sent forth fruit ... Translation reprinted from: H.I. Bell and T.C. Skeat, Fragments of an Unknown Gospel and Other Early Christian Papyri (London: Oxford University Press, 1935).

The date of the manuscript, AKA the Unknown Gospel, is established on paleography alone. When the Egerton fragments were first published its date was estimated at around 150 CE;[95] implying that of early Christian papyri it would be rivaled in age only by P[52], the John Rylands Library fragment of the *Gospel of John*.

In short, concerning the sayings of Jesus that were not part of the canonical Gospels, they can be viewed with mere curiosity because they were not preserved for us through inspiration by NT authors Matthew, Mark, Luke, and John when the canonical Scriptures were being written. They contain no value that would be binding on Christians.

---

[95] Bell, Idris and Skeat, T.C. *Fragments of an Unknown Gospel and other Early Christian Papyri.* Oxford, OUP, 1935.

Nevertheless, there is a great value in Egerton Papyrus 2 fragments just as it true with P[52]. They serve as an aid in undermining the Bible critics. These critics have long argued that John's Gospel was not written until 150 C.E. This would mean that it could not have been written by the apostle John who died fifty years earlier in 100 C.E. Since Egerton Papyrus 2 fragments have so many parallel expressions found in John's Gospel, it strongly indicates that whoever wrote Egerton Papyrus 2 fragments, he was using John's writing as a source. Then, we have P[52], a fragment of John's Gospel, which has been dated to 100-150 C.E. Thus, the Gospel of John must have been written earlier than 150 C.E. in order for it to have been circulating down in Egypt where the Egerton Papyrus 2 fragments were written about 150 C.E. Therefore, Egerton Papyrus 2 fragments bolstered by the discovery in 1935 of the fragment P[52] of John's Gospel (Papyrus Rylands Gk 457), which also dates likely 110-150 C.E. to give it time to be found in Egypt, confirm the date of the writing of John's Gospel to be about 96 C.E.

Editions of the NWT

In 1984, a Reference edition of the New World Translation was released in addition to a revision of the regular volume.[96] The regular edition includes several appendices containing arguments for various translation decisions, maps, diagrams and other information; and over 125,000 cross references. The reference edition contains the cross references and adds footnotes about translation decisions and additional appendices that provide further detail relating to certain translation decisions and doctrinal views.[97] The Reference edition is out of print as of the release of the 2013 revision of the New World Translation.

Kingdom Interlinear Translation of the Greek Scriptures

The New World Bible Translation Committee included the English text from the New World Translation in its 1969 and 1985 editions of The **Kingdom Interlinear Translation of the Greek Scriptures**.[98] It also incorporates the Greek text published by **Westcott**[99] and **Hort**[100] in The

---

[96] "Announcements", *Our Kingdom Ministry*, September 1988, p. 4. *Jehovah's Witnesses—Proclaimers of God's Kingdom*, published by Jehovah's Witnesses, p. 614

[97] "Study—Rewarding and Enjoyable," *The Watchtower*, October 1, 2000, p. 16

[98] The Kingdom Interlinear Translation of the Greek Scriptures is an interlinear translation of the New Testament, published by the Watchtower Bible and Tract Society of New York, Inc. and translated by the New World Bible Translation Committee.

[99] Brooke Foss Westcott (12 January 1825 – 27 July 1901) was an English bishop, biblical scholar and theologian, serving as Bishop of Durham from 1890 until his death. He is perhaps most known for co-editing The New Testament in the Original Greek in 1881.

[100] Fenton John Anthony Hort (1828–1892), known as F. J. A. Hort, was an Irish-born theologian and editor, with Brooke Foss Westcott of a critical edition of The New Testament in the Original Greek.

New Testament in the Original Greek[101] and a literal word-for-word translation.[102]

Non-Print Editions

In 1978, the Watch Tower Society began producing recordings of the New World Translation on audio cassette,[103] with the New Testament released by 1981[104] and the Old Testament in three albums released by 1990.[105] In 2004, the NWT was released on compact disc in MP3 format in major languages.[106] Since 2008, audio downloads of the NWT have been made available in 18 languages in MP3 and AAC formats, including support for podcasts.

In 1983, the English Braille edition of the New World Translation's New Testament was released;[107] the complete English Braille edition was released by 1988.[108] NWT editions have since become available in several additional Braille scripts.[109] Production of the NWT in American Sign Language began in 2006; the New Testament was made available by 2010,[110] and the complete ASL edition was released in February 2020.[111]

In 1992, a digital edition of the New World Translation of the Holy Scriptures—With References was released on floppy disk. Since 1994, the New World Translation of the Holy Scriptures—With References has been included in the Watchtower Library on CD-ROM.[112] Both editions of the New World Translation are available online in various languages and digital

---

[101] The New Testament in the Original Greek is a Greek-language version of the New Testament published in 1881. It is also known as the Westcott and Hort text, after its editors Brooke Foss Westcott (1825–1901) and Fenton John Anthony Hort (1828–1892).

[102] Paul 2003, pp. 127. Jehovah's Witnesses—Proclaimers of God's Kingdom, published 1993 by Jehovah's Witnesses, "Chapter 27: Printing and Distributing God's Own Sacred Word", p. 610. "Between-the-Lines" Translations of the Bible," The Watchtower, November 15, 1969, p. 692.

[103] Our Kingdom Ministry, September 1978, p. 3

[104] Our Kingdom Ministry, October 1981, p. 7

[105] The Watchtower, February 15, 1990, p. 32

[106] Watchtower Publications Index 1986–2007, "Compact Discs"

[107] Our Kingdom Ministry, August 1983, pp. 3–4

[108] Jehovah's Witnesses—Proclaimers of God's Kingdom, published 1993 by Jehovah's Witnesses, "Chapter 27: Printing and Distributing God's Own Sacred Word", pp. 614–615

[109] Awake!, November, 2007 p. 30

[110] 2007 Yearbook of Jehovah's Witnesses, published by Jehovah's Witnesses, pp. 21–22. Sign Language Connection on jw.org

[111] The Complete New World Translation of the Bible Is Available in ASL

[112] "The Compact Disc—What Is It All About?", Awake!, April 22, 1994, p. 23. Our Kingdom Ministry, September 2007, p. 3.

formats.[113] Since 2015, a Study Edition of the New World Translation has been gradually released online starting with the books of the New Testament, based on the 2013 revision with additional reference material.[114]

Critical Review of the NWT

In its review of Bible translations released from 1955 to 1985, The HarperCollins Bible Dictionary listed the New World Translation as one of the major modern translations.[115]

In 1993, in his book, How to Read the Bible for All Its Worth, Pentecostal theologian Gordon Fee refers to the New World translation as being an "extremely literal translation" filled with "heretical doctrines."[116] This is definitely an extreme over-exaggeration. First, Fee is a serious advocate for interpretive translations, so for any literal translation, he is going to say that it is an "extremely literal translation." The primary purpose is to give the Bible readers what God said by way of his human authors, not what a translator thinks God meant in its place. The primary goal is to be accurate and faithful to the original text. The meaning of a word is the responsibility of the interpreter (i.e., reader), not the translator. Second, is it supposedly filled with "heretical doctrines"? Really? There are maybe 100 verses that are under suspicion of being rendered based on their theological bias. There are 31,102 verses in the Bible. Does that sound like it is filled with "heretical doctrines"? And if we are being honest, some of those 100 verses has mixed messages because some renowned Greek-English grammars side with the NWT rendering, and some do not. So, let's try and be balanced. Is it balanced by Fee to not mention all Bible translations are guilty of some theological bias in their translation choices? Every translator would openly admit this.

In 2004, Anthony Byatt and Hal Flemings published their anthology 'Your Word is Truth,' Essays in Celebration of the 50th Anniversary of the New World Translation of the Holy Scriptures (1950, 1953). They included

---

[113] "Watch Tower Online Library". Watch Tower Bible and Tract Society. Retrieved 2014-11-07. "Online Bible-Jehovah's Witnesses: jw.org". Watch Tower Society. Retrieved 2012-10-27. "JW Library APP-Jehovah's Witnesses". Watch Tower Society. Retrieved 2012-10-27.

[114] JW.org, "New World Translation of the Holy Scriptures (Study Edition)" https://www.jw.org/en/publications/bible/study-bible/title-page-nwt/

[115] Robert G. Bratcher, "English Bible, The" The HarperCollins Bible Dictionary (revised and updated edition of Harper's Bible Dictionary, 1st ed. c1985), HarperCollins Publishers/The Society of Biblical Literature, 1996, p. 292.

[116] Gordon D. Fee and Douglas K. Stuart, How to Read the Bible for All Its Worth, 3rd ed. (Grand Rapids, MI: Zondervan Publishing House, 1993), 52.

essays responding to criticism of the New World Translation from non-Witnesses and a bibliography of reviews of the work.[117]

Old Testament

Regarding the New World Translation's use of English in the 1953 first volume of the NWT (Genesis to Ruth), biblical scholar **Harold Henry Rowley**[118] was critical of what he called "wooden literalism" and "harsh construction." He characterized these as "an insult to the Word of God," citing various verses of Genesis as examples. Rowley concluded, "From beginning to end this [first] volume is a shining example of how the Bible should not be translated."[119] He added in a subsequent review that "the second volume shows the same faults as the first."[120] This author, the Chief Bible translator of the Updated American Standard Version (UASV), finds Rowley's comments more over-exaggeration because the NWT is no more "wooden" with so-called "harsh constructions" than 1901 ASV, the early NASB, and the KJV, which many people praise. If one wants what God said over what a translator thinks God meant by what he said, he will want a literal translation. A former member of the Jehovah's Witnesses, Rolf Furuli, a former professor in Semitic languages, said that a literal translation that follows the sentence structure of the source language rather than the target language must be somewhat wooden and unidiomatic. Furuli added that Rowley's assessment based on his own preference for idiomatic translations ignores the NWT's stated objective of being as literal as possible.[121] Furuli was very upset when the 2013 NWT edition came out that was a more interpretive translation, along the lines of the NIV, as he felt the NWT had abandoned the correct translation philosophy, literal.

Samuel Haas, in his 1955 review of the 1953 first volume of the New World Translation of the Hebrew Scriptures, in the Journal of Biblical Literature, states: "this work indicates a great deal of effort and thought as well as considerable scholarship, it is to be regretted that religious bias was

---

[117] Williams, J. T. (June 2006). "'Your Word is Truth': Essays in Celebration of the 50th Anniversary of the New World Translation of the Holy Scriptures (1950, 1953)". Journal for the Study of the Old Testament. 30 (5): 54. – via EBSCO's Academic Search Complete (subscription required)

[118] Harold Henry Rowley (24 March 1890 – 4 October 1969) was an English Old Testament scholar from the Baptist tradition.

[119] H.H. Rowley, How Not To Translate the Bible, The Expository Times, 1953; 65; 41

[120] Gruss, Edmond C. (1970). Apostles of Denial: An Examination and Exposé of the History, Doctrines and Claims of the Jehovah's Witnesses. Presbyterian and Reformed Publishing Co. pp. 212–213. ISBN 978-0-87552-305-7.

[121] Furuli, Rolf (1999). "An evaluation of NWT's critics". The Role of Theology and Bias in Bible Translation. Huntington Beach, California: Elihu books. pp. 293–294.

allowed to colour many passages."[122] Yes, we have the same regret over all translations that slip off into theological bias in their preferred renderings, ignoring grammar or textual evidence.

In 1981, biblical scholar **Benjamin Kedar-Kopfstein**[123] stated that the Old Testament work is largely based upon the formal structure of biblical Hebrew.[124] In 1989, Kedar-Kopfstein said, "In my linguistic research in connection with the Hebrew Bible and translations, I often refer to the English edition of what is known as the 'New World Translation.' In so doing, I find my feeling repeatedly confirmed that this work reflects an honest endeavor to achieve an understanding of the text that is as accurate as possible. Giving evidence of a broad command of the original language, it renders the original words into a second language understandably without deviating unnecessarily from the specific structure of the Hebrew. ... Every statement of language allows for a certain latitude in interpreting or translating. So the linguistic solution in any given case may be open to debate. But I have never discovered in the 'New World Translation' any biased intent to read something into the text that it does not contain." In 1993 Kedar-Kopfstein said that the NWT is one of his occasionally quoted reference works.[125] Kopfstein said, But I have never discovered in the 'New World Translation' any biased intent to read something into the text that it does not contain." Well, just as I called out the other side, this is a bit of an exaggeration as well. They do have their theological bias moments, which are a bit obvious, John 14:14 being an example where they ignore textual evidence that they would otherwise have followed.

New Testament

Edgar J. Goodspeed,[126] the translator of the New Testament in An American Translation, positively criticized the New World translation.[127] According to the editors of the Watchtower, Goodspeed wrote in a letter dated December 8, 1950, to the Watch Tower Society: "I am interested in the

---

[122] Haas, Samuel S. (December 1955). "Reviewed Work: New World Translation of the Hebrew Scriptures, Vol. I by New World Bible Translation Committee". Journal of Biblical Literature. 74 (4): 282–283. doi:10.2307/3261681. JSTOR 3261681.

[123] Benjamin Kedar-Kopfstein (1 August 1923 – 2013) was an Israeli professor emeritus and scholar of Biblical Hebrew at the University of Haifa.

[124] Kedar-Kopfstein 1981, pp. 262.

[125] Kedar-Kopfstein 1994, pp. 17.

[126] Edgar Johnson Goodspeed (October 23, 1871 – January 13, 1962) was an American theologian and scholar of Greek and the New Testament, and Ernest DeWitt Burton Distinguished Service Professor of the University of Chicago until his retirement. He taught for many years at the University of Chicago, whose collection of New Testament manuscripts he enriched by his searches.

[127] Chryssides 2019, pp. 232.

mission work of your people, and its worldwide scope, and much pleased with the free, frank and vigorous translation. It exhibits a vast array of sound serious learning, as I can testify."[128]

In 1952, religious writer **Alexander Thomson** wrote of the New World Translation: "The translation is evidently the work of skilled and clever scholars, who have sought to bring out as much of the true sense of the Greek text as the English language is capable of expressing. ... We heartily recommend the New World Translation of the Christian Greek Scriptures, published in 1950 by the Watch Tower Bible and Tract Society."[129] In 1959, Thomson added that the version was quite a good one, even though it was padded with many English words that had no equivalent in the Greek or Hebrew.[130]

In 1953, former American Bible Society board member **Bruce M. Metzger**[131] concluded that "on the whole, one gains a tolerably good impression of the scholarly equipment of the translators,"[132] but identified instances where the translation has been written to support Jehovah's Witness doctrines, with "several quite erroneous renderings of the Greek."[133] Metzger said there were a number of "indefensible" characteristics of the translation, including its use of "Jehovah" in the New Testament.

In 1954, Unitarian theologian **Charles F. Potter**[134] stated about the New World Translation: "Apart from a few semantic peculiarities like translating the Greek word stauros as "stake" instead of "cross," and the often startling use of the colloquial and the vernacular, the anonymous translators have certainly rendered the best manuscript texts, both Greek and

---

[128] "Loyally advocating the Word of God," The Watchtower (15 March 1982), p. 23.

[129] Alexander Thomson, The Differentiator, 1952, 55, 57 Nos. 2, 6

[130] The Differentiator (June 1959), cited in Ian Croft, "The New World Translation of the Holy Scriptures: Does It Really Have the Support of Greek Scholars?", Perth, Western Australia, Concerned Growth Ministries, 1987, p. 2

[131] Bruce Manning Metzger (February 9, 1914 – February 13, 2007) was an American biblical scholar, Bible translator and textual critic who was a longtime professor at Princeton Theological Seminary and Bible editor who served on the board of the American Bible Society and United Bible Societies. He was a scholar of Greek, New Testament, and New Testament textual criticism, and wrote prolifically on these subjects.

[132] Paul 2003, pp. 85. UBS Metzger, Bruce M, The New World Translation of the Christian Greek Scriptures, The Bible Translator 15/3 (July 1964), p. 151.

[133] Bruce M. Metzger, "Jehovah's Witnesses and Jesus Christ," Theology Today, (April 1953 p. 74); see also Metzger, "The New World Translation of the Christian Greek Scriptures,".

[134] Charles Francis Potter (October 28, 1885 – October 4, 1962) was an American Unitarian minister, theologian, and author. In 1923 and 1924, he became nationally known through a series of debates with John Roach Straton, a fundamentalist Christian.

Hebrew, with scholarly ability and acumen."[135] Actually, the Greek word (σταυρός stauros) rendered "stake" in the NWT is a mixed bag because the evidence is split.

F. E. Mayer wrote: "It is a version that lends support to denial of doctrines which the Christian churches consider basic, such as the co-equality of Jesus Christ with the Father, the personhood of the Holy Spirit, and the survival of the human person after physical death. It teaches the annihilation of the wicked, the non-existence of hell, and the purely animal nature of man's soul."[136] The first part of Mayer's statement is true about the Trinity doctrine. However, there is no such place as hell, eternal torment.

Hades: (*hades*) Hades (**ᾅδης hadēs**) is the standard transliteration of the Greek into English, which occurs ten times in the UASV. (Matt. 11:23; 16:18; Lu 10:15; 16:23; Ac 2:27, 31; Rev. 1:18; 6:8; 20:13, 14.) It has the underlying meaning of 'a place of the dead, where they are conscious of nothing, awaiting a resurrection, for both the righteous and the unrighteous.' (John 5:28-29; Acts 24:15) It corresponds to "Sheol" in the OT. It does not involve torment and punishment. Adam was told, "in the day that you eat from it you **shall surely die**." (Gen. 2:17) The Bible says, "the soul that sins **will die**." (Eze 18:4, 20) The apostle Paul says, "the wages of sin **is death**." (Rom. 6:23) Paul also said, "those who do not know God and on those who do not obey the gospel of our Lord Jesus. These ones will pay the penalty of **eternal destruction**, from before the Lord." – 2 Thessalonian 1:8-9.

Sheol: (שְׁאוֹל sheol) Sheol occurs sixty-six times in the UASV. The Greek Septuagint renders Sheol as Hades. It is the grave. It has the underlying meaning of a place of the dead, where they are conscious of nothing, awaiting a resurrection, for both the righteous and the unrighteous. (Gen. 37:35; Psa. 16:10; Ac 2:31; John 5:28-29; Acts 24:15) It corresponds to "Hades" in the NT. It does not involve torment and punishment.

Gehenna: (γέεννα geenna) occurs twelve times and is the Greek name for the Valley of Hinnom, southwest of Jerusalem (Jer. 7:31), where the horrendous worship of Moloch took place, and it was prophetically said that this was where dead bodies would be thrown. (Jer. 7:32; 19:6) It was an incinerator where trash and dead bodies were destroyed, not a place to be burned alive or tormented. Jesus and his disciples used Gehenna to symbolize

---

[135] The faiths men live by, Kessinger Publishing, 1954, 239.

[136] Mayer, Frederick E. (1954). The Religious Bodies of America (1st edition) (1961 Revised ed.). Concordia Publishing House. p. 469. Gruss, Edmond C. (1970). Apostles of Denial: An Examination and Exposé of the History, Doctrines and Claims of the Jehovah's Witnesses. Presbyterian and Reformed Publishing Co. p. 210.

eternal destruction, annihilation, or the "second death," an eternal punishment of death.

Tartarus: (ταρταρόω tartaroō; from **Τάρταρος Tartaros**) Much confusion and misunderstanding has been caused through some Bible translations like the King James Version, which renders all of our original language words as hell: Sheol, Hades, Gehenna, and Tartarus. If we correctly understand Gehenna and Hades, we will discover a truth that we never knew before. Gehenna is pictorial of a place where the dead go, who receive total destruction, with no hope of a resurrection, as Gehenna was an incinerator. On the other hand, Hades is the grave, where there is the hope of a future resurrection. Tartarus was not a place per see but rather a condition. God had stripped the angel/demons of certain powers, leaving them in a weakened condition, because they had forsaken their dwelling place in heaven and had sexual relations with the women before the flood producing the Nephilim. One of the powers the demons lost was the power to materialize as humans.

Genesis 2:17 Updated American Standard Version

[17] but from the tree of the knowledge of good and evil you shall not eat, for in the day that you eat from it you shall surely die."

What is the punishment for sin here? What is the punishment for rebellion here? Was there some footnote that added eternal torment? Why would God hold back eternal torment from Adam? Was it just/right to not inform Adam of eternal torment? Was the serpent [Satan] right, saying God was withholding knowledge from Adam and Eve? Or, maybe ... it was exactly as God said. "you eat from it you shall surely die."

Ezekiel 18:4 Updated American Standard Version

[4] Behold, all souls are mine; the soul of the father as well as the soul of the son is mine: the soul who sins shall die.

Romans 6:23 Updated American Standard Version

[23] For the wages of sin is death[137]

In his review in **Andover Newton**[138] Quarterly Robert M. McCoy reported in 1963, "The translation of the New Testament is evidence of the

---

[137] WHAT WILL HAPPEN If YOU DIE?: Should You Be Afraid of Death or of People Who Have Died? By Edward D. Andrews ISBN-13: 978-1945757839
(https://www.amazon.com/dp/1945757833)

[138] Andover Newton Theological School (ANTS) was a graduate school and seminary in Newton, Massachusetts. Affiliated with the American Baptist Churches USA and the United Church of Christ, it was an official open and affirming seminary, meaning that it was open to

presence in the movement of scholars qualified to deal intelligently with the many problems of Biblical translation. One could question why the translators have not stayed closer to the original meaning, as do most translators. ... In not a few instances the New World Translation contains passages which must be considered as 'theological translations.' This fact is particularly evident in those passages which express or imply the deity of Jesus Christ."[139]

In 1963, theologian **Anthony A. Hoekema**[140] wrote: "Their New World Translation of the Bible is by no means an objective rendering of the sacred text into modern English but is a biased translation in which many of the peculiar teachings of the Watchtower Society are smuggled into the text of the Bible itself."[141] A little exaggeration (using "many") going on here again and a bias on his part for not stating that all translation committees are guilty of theological bias in their translations.

In 1967, **Robert H. Countess** wrote "that NWT has certain praiseworthy features —for example, an apparatus criticus— everyone must admit", but he disagrees with the fact that John 1:1 is translated as "a god", and says "is most unfortunate for several reason."[142] In 1982, in his critical analysis The Jehovah's Witness' New Testament he wrote that the NWT "must be viewed as a radically biased piece of work."[143] Remember 31,102 verses, and a mere 100 verses that may or may not be guilty of some theological bias. This does not quite fit "radically biased" and again another critic that does not mention all translations evidence theological bias.

---

students of same-sex attraction or transgender orientation and generally advocated for tolerance of it in church and society.In November 2015, the school announced that it would sell its campus and become part of Yale Divinity School in New Haven, Connecticut, a process it completed in July 2017.

[139] McCoy, Robert (January 1963). "Jehovah's Witnesses and Their New Testament". Andover Newton Quarterly. 3 (3): 15–31. MacLean, Gilmour (September 1966). "The Use and Abuse of the Book of Revelation". Andover Newton Quarterly. 7 (1): 25–26. The New World translation was made by a committee whose membership has never been revealed-a committee that possessed an unusual competence in Greek ... It is clear that doctrinal considerations influenced many turns of phrase, but the work is no crack-pot or pseudo-historical fraud.* ... *See Robert M. McCoy 'Jehovah's Witnesses and Their New Testament', Andover Newton Quarterly, Jan., 1963, Vol. 3, No. 3, pp. 15–31

[140] Anthony Andrew Hoekema (1913, in Drachten – 17 October 1988) was a Calvinist minister and theologian who served as professor of Systematic theology at Calvin Theological Seminary, Grand Rapids, for twenty-one years.

[141] Anthony A. Hoekema, The Four Major Cults, Christian Science, Jehovah's Witnesses, Mormonism, Seventh-day Adventism, William B. Eerdmans, 1963, ISBN 0802831176, pp. 208–209

[142] Countess 1967, pp. 160.

[143] Countess 1967, pp. 160.

Julius R. Mantey, co-author of A Manual Grammar of the Greek New Testament and A Hellenistic Greek Reader, described the NWT's rendering of John 1:1 as "a shocking mistranslation" and "Obsolete and incorrect." He also stated that the NWT "changed the readings in scores of passages to state what Jehovah's Witnesses believe and teach. That is a distortion not a translation."[144] And so it goes, more embellishment without even trying to be objective like some of the others.

Theologian **William Barclay**[145] concluded that "the deliberate distortion of truth by this sect is seen in the New Testament translation. ... It is abundantly clear that a sect which can translate the New Testament like that is intellectually dishonest."[146] Based on Barclay's comments then all Bible translations are all "intellectually dishonest" because all have some theological bias.

George D. Chryssides[147] states that the unfavorable criticisms by Rowley, Mantey and Barclay "were extremely vague," but that Metzger "mentioned a few specific passages which he believed were wrongly translated."[148]

Theologian **John Ankerberg**[149] accused the New World Translation's translators of renderings that conform "to their own preconceived and unbiblical theology." John Weldon and Ankerberg cite several examples wherein they consider the NWT to support theological views overriding appropriate translation.[150]

---

[144] Julius Robert Mantey, Depth Exploration in the New Testament, Vantage Press, 1980, ISBN 0533045355, pp. 136–137

[145] William Barclay (born 5 December 1907 in Wick, Scotland; died 24 January 1978 in Glasgow, Scotland) was a Scottish author, radio and television presenter, Church of Scotland minister, and Professor of Divinity and Biblical Criticism at the University of Glasgow. He wrote a popular set of Bible commentaries on the New Testament that sold 1.5 million copies.

[146] R. Rhodes, The Challenge of the Cults and New Religions, The Essential Guide to Their History, Their Doctrine, and Our Response, Zondervan, 2001, p. 94

[147] George D. Chryssides (born 1945) is a British academic and researcher on new religious movements and cults, has taught at several British universities, becoming head of Religious studies at the University of Wolverhampton in 2001. He is currently honorary research fellow in contemporary religion at York St John University and the University of Birmingham.Chryssides is the author of several books and articles, with a particular interest in the academic study of new religious movements, on which he has published extensively.

[148] Chryssides 2019, pp. 232.

[149] John Ankerberg (born December 10, 1945) is an American Christian television host, author, and speaker. He is an ordained Baptist minister and has authored or coauthored more than 150 books and study guides.

[150] Ankerberg, John and John Weldon, 2003, The New World Translation of the Jehovah's Witnesses, accessible online Archived October 29, 2012, at the Wayback Machine

The New Catholic Encyclopedia states, "[Jehovah's Witnesses] are allowed no other books than the Bible and the society's own publications, which includes its own translation of the Bible with an impressive critical apparatus. The work is excellent except when scientific knowledge comes into conflict with the accepted doctrines of the movement. In their so-called New World Translation, the term Kyrios is rendered Jehovah instead of Lord everywhere in the New Testament (237 times) except at Philippians 2.11, where St. Paul refers the word to Christ."[151] Wow, this is just an outright lie. You have Jehovah's Witnesses that are actually Bible scholars, like Fleming and Furuli mentioned above, who teach Biblical Hebrew in universities. They and dozens more like them have extensive libraries. Many of these are elders in the Kingdom Halls and are in good standing.

In 2004, historian **Jason BeDuhn**[152] examined New Testament passages that he believed "bias is most likely to interfere with translation"[153] from nine of "the Bibles most widely in use in the English-speaking world."[154] For each passage, he compared the Greek text with the renderings of each English translation and looked for biased attempts to change the meaning. BeDuhn states that the New World Translation was "not bias free,"[155] adding that whilst the general public and various biblical scholars might assume that the differences in the New World Translation are the result of religious bias, he considered it to be "the most accurate of the translations compared,"[156] and a "remarkably good translation."[157] He also states that "most of the differences are due to the greater accuracy of the NW as a literal, conservative translation."[158] Despite his positive review, BeDuhn said the introduction of the name "Jehovah" into the New Testament 237 times was

---

[151] Catholic University of America staff (2003). "Jehovah's Witnesses". In Berard L. Marthaler (ed.). The New Catholic Encyclopedia. Vol. 7: Hol-Jub (2 ed.). Detroit: Thompson/Gale. p. 751.

[152] Jason David BeDuhn (born 1963) is a historian of religion and culture, currently Professor of Religious Studies at Northern Arizona University.

[153] BeDuhn 2003, pp. 165.

[154] BeDuhn 2003, pp. viii. Jason D. BeDuhn, Truth in Translation: Accuracy and Bias in English Translations of the New Testament, 2004, pp. 163, 165, 169, 175, 176. BeDuhn compared the King James, the (New) Revised Standard, the New International, the New American Bible, the New American Standard Bible, the Amplified Bible, the Living Bible, Today's English and the NWT versions in Matthew 28:9, Philippians 2:6, Colossians 1:15–20, Titus 2:13, Hebrews 1:8, John 8:58, John 1:1.

[155] BeDuhn 2003, pp. 165.

[156] BeDuhn 2003, pp. 163.

[157] BeDuhn 2003, pp. 165.

[158] BeDuhn 2003, pp. 165.

"not accurate translation by the most basic principle of accuracy,"[159] and that it "violate[s] accuracy in favor of denominationally preferred expressions for God."[160] In his rebuttal, **Thomas Howe** strongly criticizes BeDuhn's positive review of the New World Translation, stating that BeDuhn's main goal is to deny the deity of Christ.[161] Just as I criticized exaggeration of the others, I will do so here. While BeDuhn is correct on some things, he does overstate his case because he only considered a handful of verses. That is not really enough to offer any real insights.

Kingdom Interlinear Translation of the Greek Scriptures

Thomas Winter considered the Kingdom Interlinear Translation of the Greek Scriptures to be a "highly useful aid toward the mastery of koine (and classical) Greek," adding that the translation "is thoroughly up-to-date and consistently accurate."[162]

Controversial Passages

Much criticism of the New World Translation involves the rendering of certain texts in the New Testament considered to be biased in favor of specific Witness practices and doctrines.[163] These include the use of "torture stake" instead of "cross" as the instrument of Jesus' crucifixion;[164] the use of

---

[159] BeDuhn 2003, pp. 169.

[160] BeDuhn 2003, pp. 170. Jason D. BeDuhn, Truth in Translation: Accuracy and Bias in English Translations of the New Testament, 2004, pp. 163, 165, 169, 175, 176. BeDuhn compared the King James, the (New) Revised Standard, the New International, the New American Bible, the New American Standard Bible, the Amplified Bible, the Living Bible, Today's English and the NWT versions in Matthew 28:9, Philippians 2:6, Colossians 1:15–20, Titus 2:13, Hebrews 1:8, John 8:58, John 1:1.

[161] Thomas A Howe, Bias in New Testament Translations?, 2010, p. 326 (back cover), "In this critical evaluation, BeDuhn's arguments are challenged and his conclusions called into question."—See also Thomas A. Howe, The Deity of Christ in Modern Translations, 2015

[162] Winter, Thomas (April 1974). "Review of New World Bible Translation Committee's The Kingdom Interlinear Translation of the Greek Scriptures". Faculty Publications, Classics and Religious Studies Department: 376. Retrieved October 30, 2018. "I think it is a legitimate and highly useful aid toward the mastery of koine (and classical) Greek. After examining a copy, I equipped several interested second-year Greek students with it as an auxiliary text. ... a motivated student could probably learn koine Greek from this source alone. ... translation by the anonymous committee is thoroughly up to date and consistently accurate."

[163] Penton, M. J. (1997), Apocalypse Delayed (2nd ed.), University of Toronto Press, pp. 174–176. Robert M. Bowman Jr, Understanding Jehovah's Witnesses, (Grand Rapids MI: Baker Book House, 1992) Samuel Haas, Journal of Biblical Literature, Vol. 74, No. 4, (Dec. 1955), p. 283, "This work indicates a great deal of effort and thought as well as considerable scholarship, it is to be regretted that religious bias was allowed to colour many passages." Ankerberg, John and John Weldon, 2003, The New World Translation of the Jehovah's Witnesses, accessible online Archived October 29, 2012, at the Wayback Machine

[164] Paul 2003, pp. 85. Penton, M. J. (1997), Apocalypse Delayed (2nd ed.), University of Toronto Press, pp. 174–176.

the indefinite article ("a") in its rendering of John 1:1 to give "the Word was a god;"[165] the term "public declaration"[166] at Romans 10:10, which may reinforce the imperative to engage in public preaching;[167] the term "taking in knowledge" rather than "know" at John 17:3 to suggest that salvation is dependent on ongoing study;[168] and the placement of the comma in Luke 23:43, which affects the timing of the fulfillment of Jesus' promise to the thief at Calvary.[169]

Russia Ban

The New World Translation was banned in Russia in 2017,[170] after the prosecution used quotes from Wikipedia to argue that the translation is extremist and not a true Bible.[171] This decision was questioned by international observers, and even by **Alexander Dvorkin**[172] who had previously asked for Jehovah's Witnesses' organization to be banned.[173]

FINAL ANALYSIS: What the renowned scholars above basically said was that the NWT is a pretty good translation, a literal translation, except in the case of a few verses, mostly, they chose so-called Trinity verses, out of 31,102 verses. So, all in all, the translator's greatest sin is the denial of the deity of Christ and trying to depersonalize the Holy Spirit into the active force of God.[174]

---

[165] Paul 2003, pp. 85. Penton, M. J. (1997), Apocalypse Delayed (2nd ed.), University of Toronto Press, pp. 174–176. C.H. Dodd: "The reason why [the Word was a god] is unacceptable is that it runs counter to the current of Johannine thought, and indeed of Christian thought as a whole." Technical Papers for The Bible Translator, Vol 28, No. 1, January 1977

[166] Penton, M. J. (1997), Apocalypse Delayed (2nd ed.), University of Toronto Press, pp. 174–176

[167] Penton, M. J. (1997), Apocalypse Delayed (2nd ed.), University of Toronto Press, pp. 174–176

[168] Penton, M. J. (1997), Apocalypse Delayed (2nd ed.), University of Toronto Press, pp. 174–176.

[169] Botting, Heather; Gary Botting (1984), The Orwellian World of Jehovah's Witnesses, University of Toronto Press, pp. 98–101, ISBN 0-8020-6545-7

[170] https://www.rferl.org/a/russia-jehovahs-witnesses-bible-translation-banned/28684384.html

[171] https://web.archive.org/web/20181212082258/https://www.jw-russia.org/pages/17081610-203.html the reference to Wikipedia is at time 14:45

[172] Alexander Leonidovich Dvorkin (Russian: Александр Леонидович Дворкин; born 20 August 1955 in Moscow) is a Russian anti-cult activist. From 1999 to 2012 he was professor and head of the department of the study of new religious movements (cults) at Saint Tikhon's Orthodox University.

[173] http://pravoslavie.ru/105915.html

[174] **Attribution**: This chapter incorporates text from the public domain: Wikipedia, the free encyclopedia, and Edward D. Andrews has added his insights.

CHAPTER 3 Principles of Bible Translation and the New World Translation

REVIEW: Let us begin by laying a foundation of how the NWT has felt for over 130 years. They have long felt that the literal translation philosophy was giving the reader the Word of God in English. Here are some quotes from their literature over time. Their code is w = Watchtower followed by the year, then month and day, and then the page number. Before moving on let me remind the readers that this author is the chief translator of the Updated American Standard Version (UASV),[175] which is to be released late 2021. You can read what is available now here: https://www.uasvbible.org/ It will be the most literal translation since the 2020NASB has dropped back into some interpretive translation philosophy. The reason for telling you again is that this author feels that the JWs made a mistake in moving from a literal translation to an interpretive translation.

The primary purpose of the UASV is to give the Bible readers what God said by way of his human authors, not what a translator thinks God meant in its place.—Truth Matters!

The primary goal of the UASV is to be accurate and faithful to the original text. The meaning of a word is the responsibility of the interpreter (i.e., reader), not the translator.—Translating Truth!

Now, let's see how the JWs used to value those same principles, setting aside their propensity of theological bias in a handful of Bible verses.

*** w50 9/15 p. 317 par. 13 New World Translation of the Christian Greek Scriptures ***

A literal translation has been striven for as far as the modern English idiom has made this possible without awkwardness.

REVIEW: This is the best translation philosophy. But in 2013 that philosophy was abandoned.

*** w61 5/15 p. 320 Questions From Readers ***

This rendering of the New World Translation is therefore both literal and explicit, in keeping with its being a literal translation.

*** w66 7/15 p. 424 par. 2 The Long-suffering of God an Eternal Blessing to Mankind ***

---

[175] https://www.uasvbible.org/

Long-suffering is endurance of ill-treatment without irritation or retaliation. It means possessing a spirit that is tolerant of those whose conduct or speech exasperates and provokes to anger or indignation. The literal meaning of the Greek word of which "long-suffering" is the translation is "long-tempered," the opposite of our familiar expression "short-tempered." In three Hebrew Scripture passages (Ex. 34:6; Num. 14:18; Ps. 86:15) the New World Translation substitutes "slow to anger," a more literal rendering of the Hebrew phrase "length of face or nostrils, where anger flares up," for the Authorized Version's "long-suffering." In many passages, however, such as at Nehemiah 9:17; Psalm 103:8; 145:8; Jeremiah 15:15; Joel 2:13; Jonah 4:2 and Nahum 1:3, the two translations are interchangeable. The two expressions "long-suffering" and "slow to anger" are, therefore, seen to be synonymous or of the same meaning.

*** w81 12/15 p. 11 Your Bible—How It Was Produced ***

Since the 1961 edition contained no footnotes, a number of footnote readings from the earlier editions were put in the main text to conform more closely to the literal meaning of the original languages.

*** w97 10/15 p. 12 Part Three—How the Bible Came to Us ***

The meaning must not be bent to conform to a particular doctrinal understanding. Second, consistency should be maintained, the translation holding to one rendering for each major word as far as the context reasonably permits. Such an approach helps readers to see how Bible writers used specific words. Third, the translation should be as literal as possible without obscuring the meaning. Literalness gives the reader closer access to the flavor of the original languages and the associated thought processes. And fourth, it should be easy for the common people to read and understand. The rather literal style of the English New World Translation facilitates translating it into other languages.

*** w08 5/1 p. 21 How Can You Choose a Good Bible Translation? ***

Because the context can affect the way a word is translated, the New World Translation uses nearly 16,000 English expressions to translate some 5,500 Biblical Greek terms, and it uses over 27,000 English expressions to translate about 8,500 Hebrew terms. [ftn. It is noteworthy that some English Bible translations use a greater variety of equivalents than the New World Translation and thus are less consistent.] Why this variety in the way words are translated? The translation committee judged that to render the best sense of these words according to the context was more important than to produce a strictly literal translation. Even so, the New World Translation is as consistent as possible in rendering Hebrew and Greek words into the target language.

Is such a translation available? Millions of readers of this journal favor using the New World Translation. Why? Because they agree with the approach taken by its translation committee, as stated in the foreword to the first English edition: "We offer no paraphrase of the Scriptures. Our endeavor all through has been to give as literal a translation as possible, where modern English idiom allows and where a literal rendition does not for any clumsiness hide the thought."

REVIEW: Now, to be fair and balance, they have also spoken about excessive or extreme literal renderings, which is actually a bad thing and should be relegated to footnotes.

*** *w61 1/1 pp. 29-30 Was There a Resurrection?* ***

A reasonable solution to this problem is given by the rendering of the verses in question in the New World Translation of the Christian Greek Scriptures. While a literal translation, it puts clarity of thought ahead of literalness. It reads: "And the memorial tombs were opened and many bodies of the holy ones that had fallen asleep were thrown up, (and persons, coming out from among the memorial tombs after his being raised up, entered into the holy city,) and they became visible to many people."

REVIEW: Yes, the translator does want to put clarity ahead of literalness but this better be very extreme cases. A literal rendering that is very hard to understand will pause the reader, slow him down so that he is forced to dig deeper into the Word of God. He merely must drop his eyes t the footnote below and taking in what the author meant by the words that he used. Now, let's consider the misrepresentation of an interlinear as being a literal translation, which it is not. It is a Bible study tool, nothing more. When those who view it as a literal Bible translation, they misconstrue what a literal translation is, and the reader may then choose to move from the Word of God in English to interpretive translations.

*** *w98 2/1 p. 32 "It Is the Best Interlinear New Testament Available"* ***

The Kingdom Interlinear Translation of the Greek Scriptures is published by Jehovah's Witnesses to help lovers of God's Word get acquainted with the original Greek text of the Bible. It contains The New Testament in the Original Greek on the left-hand side of the page (compiled by B. F. Westcott and F. J. A. Hort). A literal word-for-word English translation is found under the lines of Greek text. In the narrow right-hand column is the New World Translation of the Holy Scriptures, which allows you to compare the interlinear translation with a modern English translation of the Bible.

REVIEW: This is very misleading on several fronts. This has been the Witnesses philosophy for 125 years that the literal translation gets you closest to what God says. Moreover, this statement is deceiving just like those of the dynamic equivalent translations do. They are using word-for-word and interlinear right next to each other, which makes it seem as though they are the same. They are not. An interlinear is not even, strictly speaking, a translation. It is the original language with the lexical definitions beneath the original language words. There is absolutely no consideration of the grammar and syntax of the English under the original language words. Note below the interlinear is first, with a literal English translation that follows. Notice that the English translation brings the Hebrew or Greek over into correct English Grammar and Syntax.

This belief or misrepresentation of an interlinear as being a literal translation will truly misinform the churchgoer. However, the Jehovah's Witnesses are not alone in this. The modern-day movement in Christianity is trying to move Christians from literal translations written on an 10th-12th grade level (ASV1901, RSV1952, NASB1995, ESV2001, UASV2021) to interpretive translations written on a 6th-8th grade level (CEV1995 NLT2015, GNT1992, NIV2011).

δικαιοσύνη	δὲ	θεοῦ	διὰ πίστεως
righteousness	but	of God	through faith

Ἰησοῦ	Χριστοῦ
of Jesus	of Christ

εἰς	πάντας	τοὺς	πιστεύοντας.
into	all	the	believing

οὐ	γάρ	ἐστιν	διαστολή
not	for	there is	distinction

Image 3 Taken from Bill Mounce's article Literal Translations and Paraphrases

ΠΡΟΣ ΡΩΜΑΙΟΥΣ 3:22 1881 Westcott-Hort New Testament (WHNU)

righteousness but
22 δικαιοσυνη δὲ

of God through faith of Jesus Christ, into all the (ones) believing, not
θεοῦ διὰ πίστεως Ἰησοῦ Χριστοῦ, εἰς πάντας τοὺς πιστεύοντας, οὐ

for there is distinction.
γάρ ἐστιν διαστολή.

Romans 3:22 Updated American Standard Version (UASV)

[22] even the righteousness of God through faith in Jesus Christ for all those who believe; for there is no distinction;

Bill Mounce[176]

Without being simplistic, I have learned that translation is not translating words; it is translating meaning. To put it another way, translation is the process by which we reproduce the meaning of the text; translation does not replicate the form of the text.

Edward Andrews Response

What Mounce is really saying here is that he believes that the translator should interpret the meaning of the text and this is what is to be given to the Bible reader as a translation. Words carry the meaning of a text, so words are to be translated. When you interpret a verse, you want to express what the author meant by the words that he used. Mounce will want you to believe that it is either-or. However, it is not as you will see.

Bill Mounce

To explain this, I need to talk about what I have learned about translation theory in general, and it will take four more posts to complete the topic. Most people say there are two basic approaches to translation.

1. **Formal equivalence** says that the purpose of translation is to adhere as closely as possible to the grammatical structures of the original language, altering the translation only when necessary to convey meaning. "Word-for-word" describes this approach.

2. **The functional (dynamic)** view of translation uses the words (along with other things like grammar and context) to discover the original meaning — the "authorial intent" — and then conveys the same meaning in the target language. ["Interpretive" describes this approach]

Translations do not fit neatly into one of these approaches or the other; they fit along a continuum with significant overlap. For example, the same translation can be formal in one verse and functional in the next. However, most people think in terms of these two basic approaches.

---

[176] William D. Mounce is a scholar of New Testament Greek. William Mounce is the son of noted scholar Robert H. Mounce. He lives as a writer in Washougal, Washington. He is the President of BiblicalTraining, a non-profit organization offering educational resources for discipleship in the local church.

Edward Andrews

This is true to a degree. In dynamic equivalent (interpretive) translations though there is a tendency to go to the extreme. They want to interpret far more than is required. One basic thought to share at this point is, what if the interpretation of the translator is wrong, as some dynamic equivalent disagrees on interpretations because their translations interpret differently? Interpretation is the responsibility of the reader.

Mounce was the chief translator for the English Standard Version (ESV), by Crossway Bibles, a publishing ministry of Good News Publishers. Crossway has published several books to focus on the importance of literal translation over the dynamic equivalents. The 2006 (Translating Truth: The Case for Essentially Literal Bible Translation), the 2002 The Word of God in English by Leland Ryken, and the 2009 Understanding English Bible Translation: The Case for an Essentially Literal Approach by Leland Ryken. All three of these books are very beneficial, a must-read. However, notice that the ESV is not a literal translation, it is called an essentially literal translation. The question is, so is it essentially the Word of God? And if an almost literal translation is essentially the word of God, what does that make the dynamic equivalent translations? (NIV, TEV, GNT, CEV, etc.)

Bill Mounce

I have come to see that this is not accurate; there are at least five categories of translation theory. I will talk about the first two of them in this post.

Literal

Although I have already expressed my dislike of this term, I will use it here to make a point. If someone wants a "literal" translation, using the term "literal" in its improper sense, there is only one example of a "literal translation": the interlinear.

Edward Andrews

No, this is not true. Mounce is trying to redefine translations by calling a Bible study tool (interlinear) a translation like J. Scott Duvall and J. Danial Hays in their 2012 Grasping God's Word: A Hands-On Approach to Reading, Interpreting, and Applying the Bible

There has become a pattern for those who favor a dynamic equivalent translation, to use an interlinear Bible, which is not a translation, and refers to it as a word for word translation, because they know that this phrase is tied to translations like the KJV, ASV, RSV, ESV, and NASB. Below is an example from Duvall and Hays in the third edition of Grasping God's Word (GGW).

Grasping God's Word by J. Scott Duvall and Daniel J. Hays is a great book, so please take what is said with a grain of salt. However, what is quoted below is very misleading, and shows the length one will go to, to biasedly express their preference in translation philosophy. Within the table below are the egregious words from GGW.

Approaches to Translating God's Word

The process of translating is more complicated than it appears. Some people think that all you have to do when making a translation is to define each word and string together all the individual word meanings. This assumes that the source language (in this case, Greek or Hebrew) and the receptor language (such as English) are exactly alike. If life could only be so easy! In fact, no two languages are exactly alike. For example, look at a verse chosen at random—from the story of Jesus healing a demon-possessed boy (Matt. 17:18). The word-for-word English rendition is written below a transliteration of the Greek:

And he admonished him the Jesus and went out
18 καὶ   ἐπετίμησεν   αὐτῷ ὁ   ,   καὶ ἐξῆλθεν
from him the demon; and was healed the boy from the
ἀπ᾽ αὐτοῦ τὸ δαιμόνιον· καὶ ἐθεραπεύθη ὁ παῖς ἀπὸ τῆς
hour that.
ὥρας ἐκείνης.

Should we conclude that the English line is the most accurate translation of Matthew 17:18 because it attempts a literal rendering of the verse, keeping also the word order? Is a translation better if it tries to match each word in the source language with a corresponding word in a receptor language? Could you even read an entire Bible "translated" in this way? - Duvall, J. Scott; Hays, J. Daniel (2012-05-01). *Grasping God's Word: A Hands-On Approach to Reading, Interpreting, and Applying the Bible* (Kindle Locations 494-507). Zondervan. Kindle Edition.

Because these authors, like Bill Mounce, favor the dynamic equivalent translation philosophy, they misrepresent the literal translation philosophy here, to the extent of being disingenuous. They give you, the reader, an interlinear (study tool) rendering of Matthew 17:18, and then refer or infer that it is a literal translation, which by association would include the ASV, RSV, NASB, ESV, and the UASV. Again, an interlinear is not a Bible translation; it is a Bible study tool for persons who do not read Hebrew or

Greek. What is placed under the Greek is the lexical rendering, while not considering grammar and syntax, i.e., they are the words in isolation. Now, to demonstrate that J. Scott Duvall and Daniel J. Hays are being sly at best, let us look at the literal translations, to see if they read anything like the interlinear that Duvall and Hays used; or rather, do the literal translations consider grammar and syntax when they bring the Greek over into their English translation.

ASV	NASB1995	UASV
18 And Jesus rebuked him; and the demon went out of him: and the boy was cured from that hour.	18 And Jesus rebuked him, and the demon came out of him, and the boy was cured at once.	18 And Jesus rebuked him, and the demon came out of him and the boy was healed from that hour.
RSV	**ESV**	**CSB**
18 And Jesus rebuked him, and the demon came out of him, and the boy was cured instantly.	18 And Jesus rebuked the demon, and it came out of him, and the boy was healed instantly.	18 Then Jesus rebuked the demon, and it came out of him, and from that moment the boy was healed.

1984 NWT	2013 NWT
18 Then Jesus rebuked it, and the demon came out of him; and the boy was cured from that hour.	18 Then Jesus rebuked the demon, and it came out of him, and the boy was cured from that hour.

As can be clearly seen from the above four literal translations (ASV, NASB, UASV, and the RSV) and the essentially literal ESV and the optimally literal CSB, they are nothing like the interlinear that Duvall and Hays tried to pawn off on us as a word-for-word translation, i.e., a literal translation.

Bill Mounce

An interlinear will list the Greek words in Greek word order, and under each Greek word there will be a gloss for its meaning. See Romans 3:22 in the graphic above.

Edward Andrews

Here it is again for your convenience

68

righteousness   but

22   δικαιοσύνη   δὲ

of God through   faith   of Jesus   Christ.   into   , all   the   (ones) , believing,   not

θεοῦ διὰ πίστεως Ἰησοῦ Χριστοῦ, εἰς πάντας τοὺς πιστεύοντας, οὐ

for   there is   distinction.

γὰρ ἐστιν διαστολή.

Bill Mounce

Is it understandable? Barely. Is it translation? No. As much as I would like the word "literal" to go away, I doubt it will. Will people start to use the word accurately? I hope so. But please, do not believe the marketing hype: there is no such thing as a "literal" translation. The very idea is linguistic nonsense.

Edward Andrews

Again, an interlinear is not a Bible translation; it is a Bible study tool for persons who do not read Hebrew or Greek. What is placed under the Greek is the lexical rendering, while not considering grammar and syntax, i.e., they are the words in isolation. Now, to demonstrate that Mounce is moving the translation goal post like J. Scott Duvall and Daniel J. Hays let us look at the literal translations, to see if they read anything like the interlinear that Mounce used; or rather, do the literal translations consider grammar and syntax when they bring the Greek over into their English translation.

ASV	NASB1995	UASV
[22] even the righteousness of God through faith in Jesus Christ unto all them that believe; for there is no distinction;	[22] even *the* righteousness of God through faith in Jesus Christ for all those who believe; for there is no distinction;	[22] even the righteousness of God through faith in Jesus Christ for all those who believe; for there is no distinction;
RSV	**ESV**	**CSB**
[22] the righteousness of God through faith in Jesus Christ for all who believe. For there is no distinction;	[22] the righteousness of God through faith in Jesus Christ for all who believe. For there is no distinction:	[22] The righteousness of God is through faith in Jesus Christ to all who believe, since there is no distinction.

1984 NWT	2013 NWT
[22] yes, God's righteousness through the faith in Jesus Christ, for all those having faith. For there is no distinction.	[22] yes, God's righteousness through the faith in Jesus Christ, for all those having faith. For there is no distinction.

As can be clearly seen from the above four literal translations (ASV, NASB, UASV, and the RSV) and the essentially literal ESV and the optimally literal CSB, they are nothing like the interlinear that Mounce is trying to pawn off on us as a word-for-word literal translation, i.e., a literal translation.

Bible Study Tool

Interlinear Bible Study Tool: WH, UBS, NA, etc.

Literal Translations

- **Literal Bible Translations**: KJV, YLT, ASV, RSV, NASB, UASV
- **Semi-Literal Translations**: ESV, CSB

Interpretive Dynamic Equivalent Translations

- **Hyper Interpretive Dynamic Equivalent Translations**: CEV, GNB, TEV, ERV, SEB, NIRV
- **Interpretive Dynamic Equivalent Translations**: NLT, ICB, ISV, GW
- **Moderate Interpretive Dynamic Equivalent Translations**: NIV, NRSV, NET, NABRE

It would seem that the Bible scholars who favor the interpretive dynamic equivalent translations are making a joint effort to redefine the spectrum of Bible translations, which will aid their cause of trying to move publishers away from producing literal Bible translations. We have gone from the conservative historical-grammatical interpretation (objective) to the liberal-moderate historical-critical method of interpretation (subjective), from the conservative goal in textual studies of getting back to the original words to the liberal-moderate getting back to the earliest text possible, and from conservative literal translation to the liberal-moderate interpretive translations.

REVIEW: What the Witnesses and those of the dynamic equivalent camp appear to be doing is trying to prejudice readers against the literal translation philosophy. Because, if a reader thought the interlinear rendering is what is meant by word-for-word (which has long been a phrase applicable to literal translations), it would make them seem nonsensical. Let us continue with the NWT's Appendix.

- No two languages are exactly alike in grammar, vocabulary, and sentence structure. A professor of Hebrew, S. R. Driver, wrote that languages "differ not only in grammar and roots, but also . . . in the

70

manner in which ideas are built up into a sentence." Different languages require quite different thought patterns. "Consequently," continues Professor Driver, "the forms taken by the sentence in different languages are not the same."

In his letter to the Ephesians, the apostle Paul used an expression that is literally translated "in the (dice) cube of the men." (Ephesians 4:14, *The Kingdom Interlinear Translation of the Greek Scriptures*) This expression refers to the practice of cheating others when using dice. In most languages, however, a literal rendering of this allusion makes little sense. Translating this expression as "the trickery of men" is a clearer way to convey the meaning.

When writing to the Romans, Paul used a Greek expression that literally means "to the spirit boiling." (Romans 12:11, *Kingdom Interlinear*) Does this wording make sense in your language? The expression actually means to be "aglow with the spirit."

REVIEW: This quote of Driver is found in the 2009 Watchtower, under the article, "How can You Choose a Good Bible Translation?" It is specifically under the heading, "Are Word-for-Word Translations Best?" Notice how they mislead as I quote the article in a box below.

REVIEW: First, they are using interlinear and literal interchangeably, as though they were the same, as they did with the word-for-word in the above. They are not the same, as we have clearly demonstrated. We will demonstrate it again here. We will quote the verse they speak of with three literal translations.

Ephesians 4:14	Ephesians 4:14	Ephesians 4:14
English Standard Version (ESV)	New American Standard Bible (NASB)	Updated American Standard Version (UASV)
¹⁴ so that we may no longer be children, tossed to and fro by the waves and carried about by every wind of doctrine, by human **cunning**, by craftiness in deceitful schemes.	¹⁴ As a result, we are no longer to be children, tossed here and there by waves and carried about by every wind of doctrine, by the **trickery** of men, by craftiness in deceitful scheming;	¹⁴ So that we may no longer be children, tossed to and fro by the waves and carried about by every wind of teaching, by the trickery of men, by **craftiness** with regard to the scheming of deceit;

71

REVIEW: The Greek word *kybeia* has the literal sense of trickery (dice playing). It is "any type of misrepresentation intended to take advantage of a person in some way." Do any of these literal translations use "(dice) cube," which is what found in the Kingdom Interlinear? No, they actually use terms that are found in other interlinears, and lexicons, "cunning," "trickery," "craftiness," or "sleight." All of these are straight from the lexicon, to use any of them is what literal translations do, and it is known as lexical interpretation. What happens with dynamic equivalent translations is, they take it a step further, and they may use a phrase like 'intentionally deceiving.' Thus, the Witnesses like those of the dynamic equivalent are being intentionally deceiving by using word-for-word (known for literal translations), literal, and interlinear interchangeably. We will do one more from the above, Romans 12:11.

Romans 12:11	Romans 12:11	Romans 12:11
English Standard Version (ESV)	New American Standard Bible (NASB)	Updated American Standard Version (UASV)
[11] Do not be slothful in zeal, **be fervent in spirit**, serve the Lord.	[11] not lagging behind in diligence, **fervent in spirit**, serving the Lord;	[11] Do not be slothful in zeal,[177] be **fervent in spirit**, serving the Lord;

REVIEW: Again, we have three literal translations, do any of them say literally "to the spirit boiling"? No. All three have fervent for the Greek word *zeontes*. The literal sense of *zeontes* is "to be inflamed (boil)." Like many words, it can be used figuratively of "emotions, anger, love, eagerness to do good or evil, **to be stirred up emotionally,** *be enthusiastic/excited/on fire.*"[178] It can be used in the sense of "fervent in spirit" (burning zeal) like Apollos was as a new Christian (Ac 18:25), or when Paul admonishes the Roman Christians to be "fervent in spirit." (Rom 12:11) While it is true that to a degree "fervent in spirit" is an interpretation of the literal "boil"; otherwise, it would read, "not lagging behind in diligence, **to the spirit boiling**, serving the Lord." It should be still said that the range of meaning of the word is "boil (primary meaning), enthusiastic, fervent, excited, on fire, zealous." It literally means to be inflamed, boil, to be or become emotionally inflamed. Therefore, the literal translations above are still treating it literally, as to be dynamic equivalent, would be to render it "spiritual glow" (Moffatt), "heart

---

[177] Or *diligent*

[178] William Arndt, Frederick W. Danker, and Walter Bauer, *A Greek-English Lexicon of the New Testament and Other Early Christian Literature* (Chicago: University of Chicago Press, 2000), 426.

72

full of devotion" (TEV/GNB), "eagerly follow" (CEV), or "a heart full of love" (NLV). Do you see what the dynamic equivalents have done; they decided to interpret what was meant by "fervent in spirit" or rather a "boiling spirit."

https://www.youtube.com/watch?v=alZ-6kzuUmU

REVIEW: Now, getting back to the NWT, and its position that no two languages are alike, this is absolutely true, and no one would argue otherwise. However, this does not give a translator or a committee to go beyond lexical interpretation, into a commentary mode. However, this is not to say that the primary literal meaning of a word can always be used in ever context either. Literal translations attempt to keep the same corresponding English word or phrase as long as it is possible, but they respect that the context might require another of those words in the range of meaning.

The Bible was originally written in ancient Hebrew, Aramaic, and Greek. Today it is available in whole or in part in about 2,600 languages. The vast majority of people who read the Bible do not understand the original languages and therefore must rely on a translation. What principles should guide how the Bible is translated, and how did these govern the rendering of the *New World Translation of the Holy Scriptures?*

Some might conclude that a strict, word-for-word, interlinear-style translation would enable the reader to get closest to what was expressed in the original languages. However, that is not always the case. Consider a few of the reasons:

- No modern language exactly mirrors the vocabulary and grammar of Biblical Hebrew, Aramaic, and Greek, so a word-for-word translation of the Bible could be unclear or at times could even convey the wrong meaning.

- The meaning of a word or an expression may vary depending on the context in which it is used.

A translator may be able to mirror the literal rendering of the original language in some passages, but this must be done very carefully.

Here are some examples of how word-for-word translation can be misunderstood:

- The Scriptures use the expressions "sleep" and "fall asleep" to refer both to physical sleep and to the sleep of death. (Matthew 28:13; Acts 7:60) When these expressions are used in contexts that refer to death, Bible translators can use such wording as "fall asleep in death," which helps the modern reader avoid confusion. – 1 Corinthians 7:39; 1 Thessalonians 4:13; 2 Peter 3:4.

- The apostle Paul used an expression found in Ephesians 4:14 that can be literally translated "in the playing of dice of men." This ancient idiom alludes to the practice of cheating others when using dice. In most languages, a literal rendering of this allusion makes little sense. Translating this expression as "the trickery of men" is a clearer way to convey the meaning.

- At Romans 12:11, a Greek expression is used that literally means "to the spirit boiling." This wording does not convey the intended meaning in English, so it is rendered "aglow with the spirit" in this translation.

- During his famous Sermon on the Mount, Jesus used an expression that is often translated "Blessed are the poor in spirit." (Matthew 5:3, *King James*

ΟΙΠΤωΧΟΙ ΤωΠΝΕΥΜΑΤΙ

MATTHEW 5:3

Literal English: "the poor in spirit"

Idea: "those conscious of their spiritual need"

- *Version*) But in many languages, a literal rendering of this expression is obscure. In some cases, a strictly literal translation could imply that "the poor in spirit" are mentally unbalanced or lacking in vitality and determination. However, Jesus was here teaching people that their happiness depended, not on satisfying their physical needs, but on recognizing their need for God's guidance. (Luke 6:20) Thus, such renderings as "those conscious of their spiritual need" or "those who know their need for God" convey more accurately the meaning of the original expression. – Matthew 5:3; *The New Testament in Modern English*.

REVIEW: While there is no problem with taking a literal sense of a word, and going to what it means in the context, this does not always mean that one is off in the weeds of dynamic equivalence, i.e., interpretive translation. The literal sense of the Greek word *ptochos* is one who has little money or possessing little of something. In this case, one is "poor in spirit" or "possessing little in spirit." It is true that most Christians and even pastors have misunderstood this literal wording, and they have tried to explain how a person can be both happy or blessed while being "poor in spirit," or "possessing little in spirit," or even "spiritual poverty." You see, the happy one is, the one who becomes aware of his "possessing little in spirit," or "spiritual poverty." In other words, he recognizes that salvation is beyond himself, and he needs another, namely Jesus Christ. This thought of knowingly being low on something, but having God is something that Jesus Jewish listeners would have been well aware of, as the concept is found throughout the Old Testament. (Ps 40:17; 69:29–30, 33–34; Isa. 57:15; 61:1; 66:2, 5) Thus, the modern day read carries the obligation of not reading the Bible like it is some novel, but slowing down, pondering and meditating, and yes, even researching when at first glance, the verse is not easily understood.

יָד The Hebrew word *yadh* is usually rendered "hand," but depending on the context, this word may be rendered "authority," "generosity," "power," and many other ways

- In many contexts, the Hebrew word translated "jealousy" corresponds to the common meaning of the English word, namely, to feel anger over the apparent unfaithfulness of a close associate or to envy others for their possessions. (Proverbs 6:34; Isaiah 11:13) However, the same Hebrew word also has a positive connotation. For example, it may be used of the "zeal," or protective ardor, that Jehovah shows for his servants or of his "requiring exclusive devotion." (Exodus 34:14;_2 Kings 19:31; Ezekiel 5:13;_Zechariah 8:2) It may also be used of the "zeal" that his faithful servants have for God and his worship or of their 'tolerating no rivalry' toward him. – Psalm 69:9; 119:139; Numbers 25:11.

- The Hebrew expression that usually refers to the human hand has a wide variety of meanings. Depending on the context, this word may be rendered "authority," "generosity," or "power." (2 Samuel 8:3;1 Kings 10:13; Proverbs 18:21) In fact, this particular word is translated over 40 different ways in the English edition of the *New World Translation of the Holy Scriptures.*

REVIEW: The English word "hand" has over 20 different meanings, and will be determined by the context as well. This does not mean that you are not translating literal, because you do not use the primary meaning of the word, hand, the part of the human arm below the wrist. Any of the ranges within the lexicon are literal renderings. Let us take Proverbs 18:21 as example.

Proverbs 18:21	Proverbs 18:21	Proverbs 18:21
English Standard Version (ESV)	New American Standard Bible (NASB)	Updated American Standard Version (UASV)
[21] Death and life are in the **power** [yad, hand] of the tongue, and those who love it will eat its fruits.	[21] Death and life are in the **power** [yad, hand] of the tongue, And those who love it will eat its fruit.	[21] Death and life are in the **power** [yad, hand] of the tongue, and those who love it will eat its fruits.

[If you doubt the above are literal renderings, her are three dynamic equivalents, i.e., interpretive translations.]

Proverbs 18:21	Proverbs 18:21	Proverbs 18:21
Contemporary English Version (CEV)	Good News Translation (GNT)	New Century Version (NCV)
[21] Words can bring death or life! Talk too much, and you will eat everything you say.	[21] What you say can preserve life or destroy it; so you must accept the consequences of your words.	[21] What you say can mean life or death. Those who speak with care will be rewarded.

REVIEW: I do not believe I even need to argue the case of which are literal, and which are not. Below we resume with the Appendices.

In view of these factors, Bible translation involves more than simply rendering an original-language word with the same term each time it occurs. A translator must use good judgment in order to select words in the target language that best represent the ideas of the original-language text. In addition, there is a need to structure the sentences in a way that conforms to the rules of grammar of the target language, making the text easy to read.

REVIEW: Let me put the above in easy to read language, which is, we are going to a dynamic (interpretive) translation, which gives all of the responsibility to the translator, not the reader. In other words, they are more concerned with the reader's side of the equation, than get at the Word of God in corresponding English. What they are saying is, when the translator deems something too difficult to understand, they will interpret that literal meaning for you, and give you the interpretation. The problem with this is what if the interpretation is wrong.

REVIEW: An example would be the ancient Hebrews would have used the kidney to symbolize the deepest recesses of the inner person, while the modern-day person would use the heart similarly. J. N. Oswalt wrote, "When used figuratively, the term refers to the innermost aspects of personality."[179] An example of this would be Psalm 16:7. The top row of translations below is the three most literal, with the second row being somewhat literal. However, you see that none says, "During the nights my **kidneys** have corrected me." That is the way the 1984 NWT rendered it, with the 2013 revision saying, "During the night, my **innermost thoughts** correct me." However, they do the extra mile offering an alternative reading, plus the literal reading in a footnote: "Or 'my deepest emotions.' Lit., 'my kidneys.'" You will notice that the main text and 2013 footnote renderings cover two different thoughts, the same split from our translations below, "innermost thoughts" (mind) or "deepest emotions" (heart). The LEB goes all the way through to the dynamic equivalent level, with its "innermost being," and the HCSB even further down the interpretive rabbit hole.

REVIEW: We are not saying that it is wrong to substitute new body part that carries the same meaning as the other of old, in exchange for the modern-day reader (heart or mind), but it is going too far into the interpretive well with "conscience," "innermost being," "innermost thoughts," or "deepest emotions." You see "innermost being," "innermost thoughts," or "deepest emotions." are descriptive of what the kidneys stood for to the ancient Israelites, which is stepping over into the interpretive realms, but the HCSB is completely interpretive with its "conscience" rendering, because it is telling us what the "innermost being," "innermost thoughts," or "deepest emotions" are. You will see that this is the case with the dynamic equivalent translation, the Today's English Version AKA the Good News Bible, "I will praise the Lord, who advises me. My **conscience** warns me at night."

---

[179] *Theological Wordbook of the Old Testament,* edited by R. Laird Harris, 1980, Vol. 1, p. 440

Psalm 16:7	Psalm 16:7	Psalm 16:7
English Standard Version (ESV)	New American Standard Bible (NASB)	Updated American Standard Version (UASV)
[7] I bless the Lord who gives me counsel; into the night also my **heart** instructs me.	[7] I will bless the Lord who has counseled me; indeed, my **mind** instructs me in the night.	[7] I bless Jehovah who has given me counsel; Indeed, my **kidneys** instructs me in the night.

Psalm 16:7	Psalm 16:7	Psalm 16:7
Lexham English Bible (LEB)	Holman Christian Standard Bible (HCSB)	New Revised Standard Version (NRSV)
[7] I will bless Yahweh who advises me; yes, *at* night my *innermost being* instructs me.	[7] I will praise the Lord wo counsels me— even at night my **conscience** instructs me.	[7] I bless the Lord who gives me counsel; in the night also my **heart** instructs me.

REVIEW: Let it be noted that it is the reader's responsibility to study the historical setting of Bible times, the Bible backgrounds, who would then discover what the Israelites meant by their use of "kidney." How though can he do that, if we remove what the original author said, and replace it with what he meant by what he said? Now, we return to the New World Translation appendices.

At the same time, extremes in rewording the text must be avoided. A translator who liberally paraphrases the Bible according to how he interprets the overall idea could distort the meaning of the text. How so? The translator may erroneously insert his opinion of what the original text means or may omit important details contained in the original text. So while paraphrases of the Bible may be easy to read, their very freeness at times may prevent the reader from getting the true message of the text.

REVIEW: This is true, but it is not just true of the paraphrase, but also of the dynamic equivalents (CEV, NLT, TEV, etc.), but to a lesser degree.

Doctrinal bias can easily color a translator's work. For example, Matthew 7:13 says: "Spacious is the road leading off into destruction." Some translators, perhaps affected by doctrinal bias, have used the term "hell" rather than what the Greek term really means, namely, "destruction."

REVIW: Doctrinal or theological bias is very real, and it affects all of us, no one is exempt from it.[180] In order to be fair, all translators come to the translation job with the greatest of intentions of setting aside doctrinal bias at the door. The NWT is correct about the paraphrase, though. Whether you believe that our punishment is eternal torment in hellfire, or eternal destruction, i.e., death; you need the verses to be rendered correctly, so as to get at the correct understanding of a doctrine. Below are three literal translations, followed by one paraphrase, take notice of the difference. You will notice that the literal ESV, NASB, and the ASV all have "destruction," while the paraphrase The Living Bible has "hell."

Matthew 7:13 English Standard Version (ESV)	**Matthew 7:13** New American Standard Bible (NASB)	**Matthew 7:13** American Standard Version (ASV)
13 "Enter by the narrow gate. For the gate is wide and the way is easy that leads to **destruction,** and those who enter by it are many.	13 "Enter through the narrow gate; for the gate is wide and the way is broad that leads to **destruction,** and there are many who enter through it.	13 Enter ye in by the narrow gate: for wide is the gate, and broad is the way, that leads to **destruction,** and many are they that enter in thereby.

Matthew 7:13 Living Bible (TLB)

13 "Heaven can be entered only through the narrow gate! The highway to **hell** is broad, and its gate is wide enough for all the multitudes who choose its easy way.

---

[180] Christian Publishing House has several blogs on this very issue that touches on the doctrine of hellfire,

Hellfire – Eternal Torment?
https://christianpublishinghouse.co/2016/10/15/hellfire-eternal-torment/
What Did Jesus Teach About Hell?
https://christianpublishinghouse.co/2016/10/15/what-did-jesus-teach-about-hell/
Is Hellfire Part of Divine Justice?
https://christianpublishinghouse.co/2016/10/15/hellfire-part-of-divine-justice/
Is the Hellfire Doctrine Truly Just?
https://christianpublishinghouse.co/2016/10/15/is-the-hellfire-doctrine-truly-just/

[We now return to the NWT.]

A Bible translator must also consider that the Bible was written using the common, everyday language of average people, such as farmers, shepherds, and fishermen. (Nehemiah 8:8, 12; Acts 4:13) Therefore, a good translation of the Bible makes the message it contains understandable to sincere people, regardless of their background. Clear, common, readily understood expressions are preferred over terms that are rarely used by the average person.

REVIEW: While it is true that the intended audience would have better understood what was written to them than we could ever hope to, this does not mean the text was easy to understand. The apostle Peter had this to say about the apostle Paul's letters, "as he [Paul] does in all his letters when he speaks in them of these matters. There are some things in them that are **hard to understand** ..." We have books on Bible backgrounds, custom and culture, as it is the reader's responsibility to get back into the world of the time. It is then his responsibility to ascertain what the author meant by the words that he used, as should have been understood by his readers, and are there any implications for him. Again, how does a reader know to investigate what the original author said, if the translator has removed what the author said, and has replaced it with what he meant by what he said? We return to the NWT.

https://www.youtube.com/watch?v=IAaE9fSk2Uk

Quite a number of Bible translators have taken the unjustifiable liberty of omitting God's name, Jehovah, from modern translations even though that name is found in ancient Bible manuscripts. (See Appendix A4.) Many translations replace the name with a title, such as "Lord," and some even obscure the fact that God has a name. For example, in some translations, Jesus' prayer recorded at John 17:26 reads: "I made you known to them," and at John 17:6, "I have revealed you to those whom you gave me." However, a faithful rendering of Jesus' prayer reads: "I have made *your name* known to them," and "I have made *your name* manifest to the men whom you gave me."

As stated in the foreword to the original English edition of the *New World Translation:* "We offer no paraphrase of the Scriptures. Our endeavor all through has been to give as literal a translation as possible, where the modern English idiom allows and where a literal rendition does not for any clumsiness hide the thought." Thus, the New World Bible Translation Committee has endeavored to strike a balance between using words and phrasing that mirror the original and, at the same time, avoiding wording that reads awkwardly or hides the intended thought. As a result, the Bible can be read with ease and the reader can have full confidence that its inspired message has been transmitted faithfully.—1 Thessalonians 2:13.

REVIEW: There is no argument here on that matter. We would wholeheartedly agree. Please read, "The Divine Name: Does it Really Matter?"

http://christianpublishinghouse.co/2016/11/01/is-the-fathers-personal-name-important/

CHAPTER 4 Features of the 2013 New World Translation Revision

The *New World Translation of the Christian Greek Scriptures* was released in English in 1950, and the complete *New World Translation of the Holy Scriptures* was published in 1961. Since then, tens of millions of readers in well over 100 languages have benefited from this accurate yet readable rendering of the Holy Scriptures from the original languages.

REVIEW: There is little doubt that most would disagree with this statement, some vehemently so. However just as there is assuredly theological bias in the NWT of 1984 and the 2013 revision, it exists in other translations too. Let me tell you a story about the release of the **New** King James Version. The translators came to a well-respected evangelical university and released the new translation to an audience of university instructors. Once the speaker was finished, he asked if there were any questions, and the professor from the New Testament department shot his hand up in the air. He asked the translation committee, 'why did you keep the interpolation at 1 John 5:7, 'the Father, the Word, and the Holy Spirit; and these three are one.' We all know this was added in and is not part of the original." The speaker said, 'we wanted to remove it, but the publishers wanted to retain it, because they did not think it would sell as well.' Below are three examples of how 1 John 5:7 should read, followed by the NKJV,

1 John 5:7	1 John 5:7	1 John 5:7
English Standard Version (ESV)	New American Standard Bible (NASB)	Holman Christian Standard Bible (HCSB)
[7] For there are three that testify:	[7] For there are three that testify:	[7] For there are three that testify:

1 John 5:7 New King James Version (NKJV)

[7] For there are three that bear witness in heaven: the Father, the Word, and the Holy Spirit; and these three are one.

[If you need another example, we can turn to John 8:58 in the,]

John 8:58 Good News Translation (GNT)

[58] "I am telling you the truth," Jesus replied. "Before Abraham was born, 'I Am'."

REVIEW: Notice that the "I Am" is capitalized, when there is absolutely no reason for doing so, other than theological bias. It is the translation committees attempt to turn the "I am" into a title, for the sake of Exodus 3:14.

Over the past half century, however, languages have changed. The current New World Bible Translation Committee recognized the need to respond to those changes in order to touch the heart of today's reader. For this reason, a number of style and vocabulary changes have been made in this revision, with the following objectives in mind:

REVIEW: While it is true that languages have changed, but more than that is true as well. The shift of going from the literal translation philosophy to the dynamic equivalent interpretive translation had changed too. I personally believe that this had a major impact on their decision to come out with a revision. Moreover, I believe too that the skills of their translation committee have improved over the years, and they saw the need to revise as well.

- **Use of modern, understandable language.** For example, the expression "long-suffering" can be misunderstood to mean "someone who suffers for a long time." However, the intended idea is that of deliberate restraint, which is better expressed by the term "patience." (Galatians 5:22) The now obsolete meaning of "dumb" was replaced with "speechless." (Matthew 9:32, 33) The term "harlot" was changed to "prostitute." (Genesis 38:15) In this revision, "fornication" is usually rendered as "sexual immorality"; "loose conduct" as "brazen conduct"; and "revelries" as "wild parties." (Galatians 5:19-21) The expression "time indefinite" was replaced with such terms as "forever," "lasting," "everlasting," or "long ago," to convey the intended meaning in each context.— Genesis 3:22; Exodus 31:16; Psalm 90:2; Ecclesiastes 1:4; Micah 5:2.

- The term "seed" in ancient Hebrew and Greek could refer to plant seed as well as to human offspring, or descendants, or to semen. Because it is no longer common in English to use the term "seed" when referring to humans, it was replaced with expressions that convey the intended idea according to the context. (Genesis 1:11; 22:17;48:4; Matthew 22:24; John 8:37) In most cases, the term "offspring" is now used when referring to the Edenic promise, found at Genesis 3:15.

- The English verb "impale" was used in previous versions of this Bible in connection with the execution of Jesus. While this term could refer to the way that Jesus was nailed to the torture stake, it is more often used in reference to the ancient method of execution by running a sharp stake through the body and fixing the victim on it. Since Jesus was not impaled *with* the torture stake, this revision uses such expressions as "executed on a stake" and "nailed to the stake" with regard to the manner in which Jesus was fastened to the torture stake.—Matthew 20:19; 27:31, 35.

- **Biblical expressions clarified.** Some terms used in previous editions of the English *New World Translation* often needed to be explained in order to be properly understood. For example, the Hebrew term "Sheol" and the Greek term "Hades" are used in the Bible to refer to the common grave of mankind. Those terms are unknown to many, and "Hades" has a dual meaning as a result of its usage in Greek mythology. Therefore, both terms were replaced with what was meant by the Bible writers, "the Grave." The terms "Sheol" and "Hades" are now given in footnotes. — Psalm 16:10; Acts 2:27.

- In past editions, the Hebrew word *ne'phesh* and the Greek word *psy·khe'* were consistently rendered "soul." In view of the many misconceptions regarding the meaning of the word "soul," this approach helped the reader to see how the inspired Bible writers used these original-language terms. Depending on the context, those words may refer (1) to a person, (2) to the life of a person, (3) to living creatures, (4) to the desires and appetite of a person or, in some cases, (5) even to dead individuals. However, since such use of the word "soul" is not common in English, the decision was made to render these original-language words according to their intended meaning, usually with a footnote that reads "Or 'soul.'" (See, for example, Genesis 1:20; 2:7; Leviticus 19:28; Psalm 3:2; Proverbs 16:26; Matthew 6:25.) However, in some poetic or well-known contexts, the word "soul" was retained in the main text, along with a footnote referring to the Glossary or showing another possible rendering. — Deuteronomy 6:5; Psalm 131:2; Proverbs 2:10; Matthew 22:37.

- Similarly, the word "kidney" was retained when it refers to the literal organ. However, when it is used figuratively in such verses as Psalm 7:9 and 26:2 and Revelation 2:23, the intended idea of "deepest emotions" or "innermost thoughts" is conveyed in the main text, and the literal idea is given in a footnote.

- Like its Hebrew and Greek equivalents, the English expression "heart" has both a literal and a figurative meaning, so it was usually retained in the main text. However, in a few contexts where the sense was not clear, a more explicit rendering was used. For example, in the book of Proverbs, "in want of heart" now reads "lacking good sense," and the literal idea is given in a footnote. Other expressions, for instance, "fat," "flesh," and "horn," were handled similarly, according to the context. (Genesis 45:18; Ecclesiastes 5:6; Job 16:15) Some of these expressions are discussed in the "Glossary of Bible Terms."

- **Enhanced readability.** In previous editions of the English *New World Translation,* auxiliary expressions were used to indicate whether the Hebrew verb is in the imperfect or the perfect state. For example, the continuous action often expressed by imperfect verbs was indicated by means of the expressions "proceeded to," "went on to," "came to be," and so forth. The emphasis often conveyed by the Hebrew perfect verb was denoted by the added expressions "certainly," "must," "actually," and similar ones. As a result, these terms were used thousands of times in the text. In this revision, auxiliary terms were retained in certain contexts by using such expressions as "kept," "keep on," and "used to" when there was a valid reason to express continuous action. (Genesis 3:9; 34:1; Proverbs 2:4) However, they were omitted to enhance readability when the auxiliary expressions were not critical for conveying the original meaning.

- **Conveying the correct idea of words involving gender.** Hebrew and Greek nouns indicate male or female gender, and in Greek, also neuter. At times, though, reflecting the gender of the original-language term may obscure the intended meaning. In both Hebrew and Greek, plural nouns are generally masculine, not only when referring exclusively to males but also when referring to both males and females. For example, though the expression "the sons of Israel" may refer to the 12 sons of Jacob, it more often refers to the entire nation of Israel, both men and women. (Genesis 46:5; Exodus 35:29) So in the revision, this phrase was often rendered "Israelites" to show that it refers to the entire nation. Similarly, the expression "fatherless boy" was rendered "fatherless child" or "orphan" to show that it may refer to a boy or a girl. On the other hand, since the Bible uses the male gender in reference to God and to his Son, as well as to various angels and demons, there is no basis for using genderless terms as is done in some modern translations.

REVIEW: I pause at this point because; this is now the common practice to placate the liberal-progressive world that we live in, nothing more.

God had his Word penned in certain times, places, and cultures. Who are we to bow to the liberal-progressive world, and alter that Word for the sake of not causing offense, to a people, who could care less about the Bible? If you want to have a better understanding of this issue, please read, "Gender-Inclusive Language in Bible Translation."

https://wp.me/p6EZsO-zi

REVIEW: If you want an in-depth analysis of this, you can read, The TNIV and the Gender-Neutral Bible Controversy by Wayne Grudem and Vern Poythress (Jan 1, 2005)

- **Omission of indicators for second person plural.** Past editions also indicated whether the pronouns "you" and "your" and second person verbs were singular or plural by using small capital letters to show plurality. This feature was not retained in this revision, but readers may consult earlier editions of this translation for this information.

- All adjustments in the Bible text were made prayerfully, carefully, and with deep respect for the fine work of the original New World Bible Translation Committee.

CHAPTER 5 Other Features of this 2013 New World Translation Revision

"I have appointed you as a light of nations."—ACTS 13:47.

This Bible edition contains a limited number of footnotes. The footnotes generally fall into the following categories:

- **"Or"** Alternative ways the text could be rendered from Hebrew, Aramaic, or Greek that would give the same overall idea.—Genesis 1:2, footnote on "active force"; Joshua 1:8, "undertone."

- **"Or possibly"** Alternative ways the text could be rendered that would convey a valid yet different overall idea.—Genesis 21:6, "laugh with me"; Zechariah 14:21, "Canaanite."

- **"Lit."** A word-for-word translation from the Hebrew, Aramaic, or Greek or the basic meaning of an original-language expression.—Genesis 30:22, "pregnant"; Exodus 32:9, "obstinate."

- **Meaning and background information** Meaning of names (Genesis 3:17, "Adam"; Exodus 15:23, "Marah"); details about weights and measures (Genesis 6:15, "cubits"); the antecedent of a pronoun (Genesis 38:5, "He"); helpful information in the Appendix and the Glossary.—Genesis 37:35, "Grave"; Matthew 5:22, "Gehenna."

- The front section, entitled "An Introduction to God's Word," contains an outline of basic teachings found in the Bible. Immediately following the Bible text is the "Table of the Books of the Bible," the "Bible Words Index," and the "Glossary of Bible Terms." The Glossary helps the reader understand selected expressions according to their Bible-specific usage. Appendix A contains the following sections: "Principles of Bible Translation," "Features of This Revision," "How the Bible Came to Us," "The Divine Name in the Hebrew Scriptures," "The Divine Name in the Christian Greek Scriptures," "Chart: Prophets and Kings of Judah and of Israel," and "Main Events of Jesus' Earthly Life." Appendix B contains maps, charts, and other information useful to diligent Bible students.

- In the main text of the Bible, each book features an outline of its chapter contents, along with the related verses, giving the reader an overview of the entire book. The center column of each page contains the most relevant marginal references from previous editions, pointing to related Bible verses.

REVIEW: In the final analysis, the New World translation has chosen to abandon the literal translation of God's Word. This will not concern most evangelical Christians, but it should. While you will certainly disagree with the doctrine of the Jehovah's Witnesses, they have been the most effective evangelists, in the last 125 years. It is they, who are stealing your members. That is not even my point.

REVIEW: The main argument of those that support dynamic equivalents is that they are more effective in the evangelism field, and new ones cannot grasp the literal translations. This is a weak excuse for the fact that, almost no churches go out into the community to evangelize. Therefore, how could they know? The Witness defy that point because they have been outpacing everyone else for 125 years, using a literal translation all along. The problem with the Christian denominations is that they do not prepare their church members to evangelize their communities; so of course, they are ineffective in using a literal translation. They are ineffective in using any translation.

REVIEW: There is little doubt that the 2013 revision of the New World Translation is easier to read, but is it more accurate, does it say what God's Word said, or what the committee interprets that Word to mean? Setting aside the handful of theologically biased verses, if we had to give you a sense of where the 2013 NWT lands on the translation spectrum it is between the interpretive translation the NIV and the essentially literal translation ESV. As you might have guessed, the qualifier "essentially" being added to the literal means that the ESV is not actually a literal translation.

CHAPTER 6 Examining Whether the Divine Name Really Matters

"Jehovah" (Heb., יהוה, YHWH), God's personal name, initially occurs in Genesis 2:4. The ultimate disgrace that modern translators render to the heavenly Father of the Holy Scriptures is the elimination or the disguising of his personal name. In fact, His name occurs in the Hebrew text 6,828 times as יהוה (JHVH), usually referred to as the Tetragrammaton (i.e., "having four letters"). By retaining the name "Jehovah," the UASV has remained faithful to the original-language texts and have not followed in the footsteps of those who would of substituting titles such as "Lord," "the Lord," "Adonai" or "God" for the personal name of the Father, the Tetragrammaton.

To Whom Should We Pray

For this modern world of interfaith,[181] involving persons of different religious faiths, who hold the position that they can bring about peace and unity in a divided world by their joining, believing that all religions are acceptable, regardless of their differences. Therefore, for these modernist ones believe that all prayers go to the same place regardless of whether one prays to Jehovah of Israel and Christians, or Allah of the Muslims, or Krishna of the Hindus, or Akal Purakh of the Sikhs, and so on. Is interfaith reasonable as far as the Bible is concerned?

Yes, for true Christians, the Bible, particularly a good literal translation is their guidebook. The Bible tells us of an all-powerful Creator, whose name is Jehovah (Psa. 83:18, KJV), who created other powerful spirit persons (Cherubs, Seraphs, angels), long before the creation of the universes, which includes earth, and finally the creation of man and woman. It tells us of a rebellion in the Garden of Eden, where Adam sinned against his Creator believing a rebel angel, who said that Adam and Eve could walk on their own and did not really need their Creator. The Bible tells us that they were expelled from the Garden of Eden and the tree of life before having children. Sin and death entered the world that day and Adam, Even and their offspring started to get ill, grow old and die. It also became common for those people in many thousands of generations thereafter to direct to their prayers to carved images, to false gods, like the Babylonian Marduk and Tammuz, the Assyrian Asshur, the Egyptian Osiris, his consort Isis, and their son Horus. In addition, there were the Canaanite gods El and Baal, the Medo-Persian god Zoroaster, the Grecian god Zeus, who was the sky and thunder god, who

---

[181] According to the World Christian Encyclopedia, there are some "10,000 distinct religions worldwide."

ruled as king of the gods of Mount Olympus. The Roman triad of Jupiter (the king of the gods of the sky and light), Juno (the queen of the gods and wife of Jupiter, who presided over matters concerning to women), and Minerva, the goddess of wisdom and patron of arts, trade, and the art of war, who was born fully armed from the head of Jupiter. However, the one true God of the Bible, Jehovah, regularly warned,

Psalm 115:4-6 Updated American Standard Version (UASV)

⁴ Their idols are silver and gold,
the work of the hands of man.
⁵ They have mouths, but cannot speak;
eyes, but cannot see.
⁶ They have ears, but cannot hear;
noses, but cannot smell.

The Bible is filled with prayers, with God by way of his authors talking about the importance of prayers, and sadly the fact that many prayers are often directed to false gods or some carved image. Many times over, the Scriptures warn against such practices. In many ways, the Bible tells us of the foolish ones who misdirected their prayers to a god who was unable to hear them because he or she was made of stone, wood, or some other carved object. Many may recall the true prophet Elijah challenged four hundred and fifty prophets of Baal on Mount Carmel, asking them to pray to their god, to bring fire to a sacrificial bull atop a wooden altar, thereafter, Elijah would pray to Jehovah, the God of Israel. In this test, they would discover who the true God was. The Baal prophets accepted the challenge, praying from morning until noon, so much so, they worked themselves up even with loud outcries.

Then, at noon Elijah mocked them, saying, "Cry aloud, for he is a god. Either he is musing, or he is relieving himself, or he is on a journey, or perhaps he is asleep and must be awakened." So, they cried with a loud voice and cut themselves according to their custom with swords and lances until the blood gushed out on them. Noon was past, and they prophesied in a frenzy until the time the evening grain offering is presented, but there was no voice and no one answering; no one was paying attention.

Then Elijah said to all the people, "Come near to me." And all the people came near to him. And he repaired the altar of Jehovah that had been thrown down. Elijah took twelve stones, according to the number of the tribes of the sons of Jacob, to whom the word of Jehovah came, saying, "Israel shall be your name," and with the stones he built an altar in the name of the Lord. And he made a trench about the altar, as great as would contain two seahs of seed. And he put the wood in order and cut the bull in pieces

90

and laid it on the wood. And he said, "Fill four jars with water and pour it on the burnt offering and on the wood." And he said, "Do it a second time." And they did it a second time. And he said, "Do it a third time." And they did it a third time. And the water ran around the altar and filled the trench also with water.

Then Elijah said to all the people, "Come near to me." And all the people came near to him. And he repaired the altar of Jehovah that had been thrown down. Elijah took twelve stones, according to the number of the tribes of the sons of Jacob, to whom the word of Jehovah came, saying, "Israel shall be your name," and with the stones he built an altar in the name of the Lord. And he made a trench about the altar, as great as would contain two seahs of seed. And he put the wood in order and cut the bull in pieces and laid it on the wood. And he said, "Fill four jars with water and pour it on the burnt offering and on the wood." And he said, "Do it a second time." And they did it a second time. And he said, "Do it a third time." And they did it a third time. And the water ran around the altar and filled the trench also with water.

And at the time of the offering of the oblation, Elijah the prophet came near and said, "O Jehovah, God of Abraham, Isaac, and Israel, let it be known this day that you are God in Israel, and that I am your servant, and that I have done all these things at your word. Answer me, O Jehovah, answer me, that this people may know that you, O Jehovah, are God, and that you have turned their hearts back." Then the fire of the Jehovah fell and consumed the burnt offering and the wood and the stones and the dust, and licked up the water that was in the trench. When all the people saw it, they fell on their faces; and they said, "Jehovah, he is God; Jehovah, he is God." (1 Kings 18:20-39)

Baal, which means "owner" or "master," was the god of the Canaanites, "lord of Canaanite religion and seen in the thunderstorms, Baal was worshiped as the god who provided fertility. He proved a great temptation for Israel. 'Baal' occurs in the OT as a noun meaning 'lord, owner, possessor, or husband,' as a proper noun referring to the supreme god of the Canaanites, and often as the name of a man. The noun comes from a verb that means to marry or rule over. The verb form occurs in the Hebrew text 29 times, whereas the noun occurs 166 times. The noun appears in a number of compound forms which are proper names for locations where Canaanite deities were worshiped, such as Baal-peor (Num. 25:5; Deut. 4:3; Ps. 106:28; Hos. 9:10), Baal-hermon (Judg. 3:3; 1 Chron. 5:23), and Baal-gad (Josh. 11:17;

12:7; 13:5).[182] On the other hand, sadly, modern publishers sadly removed Jehovah, the personal name of the Father from the Bible.

Actually, the Father's personal name occurs in the Hebrew text 6,828 times as יהוה (YHWH or JHVH), generally referred to as the Tetragrammaton, which literally means, "having four letters." By removing the personal name of the Father, Jehovah, modern translators have violated God's Word where it says to not add nor take away, and they have failed to be faithful to the original. Rather, these modern translations have followed the practice of substituting titles such as "Lord," "the Lord," "Adonai" or "God" for the divine name. Before we take a brief moment to look into this allegation, let us go back 1,900 years when there was the practice of substituting titles (e.g., Lord) for the Father's personal name that developed among the Jews and was applied in later copies of the Greek Septuagint, the Latin Vulgate, and many other translations.

Now, let us take a moment to look at when the Father's personal name was restored to God's Word. William Tyndale first restored the Father's personal name, Jehovah, to the English Bible. In 1530, he published a translation of the first five books of the Bible into English. He included Jehovah's name once, in Ex 6:3. In a note in this edition, Tyndale wrote, "Iehovah is God's name ... Moreover, as oft as thou seist LORD in great letters (except there be any error in the printing) it is in Hebrew Iehovah." Following in the footsteps of Tyndale, other translators of the time began to use the Father's name in a few places out of the 6,828 times that it occurs in the Hebrew Old Testament. Rathet, they chose to write "LORD" or "GOD" in most places where the personal name of the Father occurs in Hebrew. This is true of the 1611 King James Version as well, where Jehovah's name occurs only four times, namely, in Ex 6:3; Ps 83:18; Isa 12:2; 26:4.

Most translations use all capital letters to make the title 'LORD.' Exceptions are the American Standard Version, which uses 'Jehovah,' over 5,000 times, while the Amplified Bible uses 'Lord,' and The Jerusalem Bible, the Lexham English Bible, and the Holman Christian standard Bible uses 'Yahweh.'

How Some Translators Feel about the Personal Name of God

American Standard Version of 1901: "[The translators] were brought to the unanimous conviction that a Jewish superstition, which regarded the Divine Name as too sacred to be uttered, ought no longer to dominate in the English or any other version of the Old Testament. ... This Memorial Name, explained in Ex. iii. 14, 15, and emphasized as such over and over in the

---

[182] James Newell, "Ball," ed. Chad Brand et al., *Holman Illustrated Bible Dictionary* (Nashville, TN: Holman Bible Publishers, 2003), 152.

original text of the Old Testament, designates God as the personal God, as the covenant God, the God of revelation, the Deliverer, the Friend of his people. … This personal name, with its wealth of sacred associations, is now restored to the place in the sacred text to which it has an unquestionable claim."

Steven T. Byington, translator of The Bible in Living English, explains why he uses God's name: "The spelling and the pronunciation are not highly important. What is highly important is to keep it clear that this is a personal name. There are several texts that cannot be properly understood if we translate this name by a common noun like 'Lord,' or, much worse, by a substantivized adjective [for example, the Eternal]."

Holman Christian Standard Bible of 2003: However, the HCSB OT uses Yahweh, the personal name of God in Hebrew, when a biblical text emphasizes Yahweh as a name: "His name is Yahweh" (Ps 68:4). Yahweh is also used in places of His self-identification as in "I am Yahweh" (Is 42:8). Yahweh is used more often in the HCSB than in most Bible translations because the word Lord in English is a title of God and does not accurately convey to modern readers the emphasis on God's personal name in the original Hebrew.

How Does the Father Feel About His Own Personal Name?

Isaiah 42:8 American Standard Version (ASV)

[8] I am Jehovah, that is my name; and my glory will I not give to another, neither my praise unto graven images.

Malachi 3:16 American Standard Version (ASV)

[16] Then they that feared Jehovah spake one with another; and Jehovah hearkened, and heard, and a book of remembrance was written before him, for them that feared Jehovah, and that thought upon his name.

Micah 4:5 American Standard Version (ASV)

[5] For all the peoples walk everyone in the name of his god; and we will walk in the name of Jehovah our God for ever and ever.

Proverbs 18:10 American Standard Version (ASV)

[10] The name of Jehovah is a strong tower; The righteous runs into it, and is safe.

Joel 2:32 American Standard Version (ASV)

[32] And it shall come to pass, that whosoever shall call on the name of Jehovah shall be delivered; for in mount Zion and in Jerusalem there shall be

those that escape, as Jehovah hath said, and among the remnant those whom Jehovah doth call.

Why Do Most Translations Leave the Divine Name of the Father Out?

The Bible: An American Translation of 1935: "In this translation we have followed the orthodox Jewish tradition and substituted 'the Lord' for the name 'Yahweh' and the phrase 'the Lord God' for the phrase 'the Lord Yahweh.' In all cases where 'Lord' or 'God' represents an original 'Yahweh' small capitals are employed."

AUTHOR RESPONSE: The question that quickly comes to mind is, 'did Jesus not say something about Jewish tradition and God's Word?' Yes, at Mark 7:13, he said to the Jewish religious leaders that they were, "making void the word of God by your tradition that you have handed down." Therefore, the following question that begs to be answered is, 'why on earth would we follow Jewish tradition of removing God's personal name, if Jesus condemned them for just such type of activity?' The other question that we might ask is, 'who is the one person who would like to see God's personal name removed from the Bible? Satan? Does a personal name not signify a personal relationship? Are we not seeking a personal relationship with God? Did God not personally give us his personal name?

Revised Standard Version of 1952: "For two reasons the Committee has returned to the more familiar usage of the King James Version [that is, omitting the name of God]:(1) the word 'Jehovah' does not accurately represent any form of the Name ever used in Hebrew; and (2) the use of any proper name for the one and only God, as though there were other gods from whom he had to be distinguished, was discontinued in Judaism before the Christian era and is entirely inappropriate for the universal faith of the Christian Church."

AUTHOR RESPONSE: Let us take issue with number (1) first. That would be those translator's personal opinion about the correct pronunciation, as there are many other world-renowned Hebrew scholars who would argue otherwise, such as Dr. Gleason L. Archer. Even if that were not so, we know that Jesus does not accurately represent the original form of his name. Who is the brave soul who would suggest that we remove the name of God's Son, Jesus, for the title of "Christ"? As for point number (2), this just is not the case; there are millions of other gods (albeit false) that are worshiped. Even the Apostle Paul said,

1 Corinthians 8:5 Lexham English Bible (LEB)

5 For even if after all there are so-called gods, whether in heaven or on earth, just as there are many gods and many lords

Of course, these other gods are false, and there is only one true God, Jehovah God. The use of God's personal name sets him off from these others.

English Standard Version of 2001: Scholars call this the "Tetragrammaton," a Greek term referring to the four Hebrew letters YHWH. The exact pronunciation of YHWH is uncertain, because the Jewish people considered the personal name of God to be so holy that it should never be spoken aloud [Jewish tradition]. Instead of reading the word YHWH, they would normally read the Hebrew word 'adonay ("Lord"), and the ancient translations into Greek, Syriac, and Aramaic also followed this practice. When the vowels of the word 'adonay are placed with the consonants of YHWH, this results in the familiar word Jehovah that was used in some earlier English Bible translations. As is common among English translations today, the ESV usually renders the personal name of God (YHWH) with the word Lord (printed in small capitals).

AUTHOR RESPONSE: The irony is the fact that the ESV removes the personal name of the only one true God, while they retain the personal names of the false gods. If God gave us his personal name, and had it inspired to be penned 6,828 times in the Hebrew Old Testament, who has the authority to remove that personal name and replace it with an impersonal title? What text gives anyone that authority?

Why have we bought out so much time for this issue of the divine name?

Joel 2:32 American Standard Version (ASV)

32 And it shall come to pass, that whosoever shall call on the name of Jehovah shall be delivered; for in mount Zion and in Jerusalem there shall be those that escape, as Jehovah has said, and among the remnant those whom Jehovah does call.

This verse is quoted two times in the New Testament, by two apostles, Peter and Paul:

Acts 2:21 Lexham English Bible (LEB)

21 And it will be that everyone who calls upon the name of the Lord will be saved.'[a]

Romans 10:13 Lexham English Bible (LEB)

13 For "everyone who calls upon the name of the Lord will be saved."[a]

More is Needed than Just Being Aware of the Divine Name

Jehovah chose his own name, one rich in meaning. "Jehovah" literally means "He Causes to Become." The divine name certainly was not new. The divine name was known and used clear back in the beginning with Adam and Eve. The Patriarchs also knew and used the divine name, as well as received promises from Jehovah. However, keeping in mind the meaning of God's name, "He Causes to Become," the patriarchs did not know Jehovah in an experiential way, as the one that would cause the promises to be fulfilled. (Genesis 12:1, 2; 15:7, 13-16; 26:24; 28:10-15.) They knew the promises, but Moses was about to experience the results. No matter what was to get in the way of Moses and the Israelites, no matter the difficulties they faced, Jehovah was going to become whatever they needed, to deliver them from slavery and into the Promised Land.

Exodus 34:5-6 American Standard Version (ASV)

5 And Jehovah descended in the cloud, and stood with him there, and proclaimed the name of Jehovah. 6 And Jehovah passed by before him, and proclaimed, Jehovah, Jehovah, a God merciful and gracious, slow to anger, and abundant in loving-kindness and truth.

Deuteronomy 32:3-5 American Standard Version (ASV)

3 For I will proclaim the name of Jehovah: Ascribe ye greatness unto our God. 4 The Rock, his work is perfect; for all his ways are justice: A God of faithfulness and without iniquity, just and right is he. 5 They have dealt corruptly with him, they are not his children, it is their blemish; they are a perverse and crooked generation.

Leviticus 22:32 American Standard Version (ASV)

32 And ye shall not profane my holy name; but I will be hallowed among the children of Israel: I am Jehovah who sanctified you,

Psalm 8:1 American Standard Version (ASV)

1 O Jehovah, our Lord, How excellent is thy name in all the earth, Who hast set thy glory upon the heavens!

Psalm 148:13 American Standard Version (ASV)

¹³ Let them praise the name of Jehovah; For his name alone is exalted; His glory is above the earth and the heavens.

Exodus 3:15 American Standard Version (ASV)

¹⁵ And God said moreover unto Moses, Thus shalt thou say unto the children of Israel, Jehovah, the God of your fathers, the God of Abraham, the God of Isaac, and the God of Jacob, hath sent me unto you: this is my name forever, and this is my memorial unto all generations.

Malachi 1:11 American Standard Version (ASV)

¹¹ For from the rising of the sun even unto the going down of the same my name shall be great among the Gentiles; and in every place incense shall be offered unto my name, and a pure offering: for my name shall be great among the Gentiles, says Jehovah of armies.

Exodus 9:16 American Standard Version (ASV)

¹⁶ but in very deed for this cause have I made you to stand, to show you my power, and that my name may be declared throughout all the earth.

Ezekiel 36:23 American Standard Version (ASV)

²³ And I will sanctify my great name, which hath been profaned among the nations, which you have profaned in the midst of them; and the nations shall know that I am Jehovah, says the Lord Jehovah, when I shall be sanctified in you before their eyes.

And may we be determined to stand firm for what was revealed to us in Scripture, not cowering to fainted hearted scholarship, who would rather please man than the Creator of heaven and earth. Let us say as the prophet Micah boldly said many centuries ago,

Micah 4:5 American Standard Version (ASV)

⁵ For all the peoples walk
    each in the name of its god,
but we will walk in the name of Jehovah our God
    forever and ever.

The greatest indignity of modern translators is their rendering of the Father's personal name as a title "LORD" or "GOD," removing or the concealing of his special personal name. Before moving on, let us say that Yahweh is not an appropriate rendering of the Father's personal name. First, the Father's personal name, the Tetragrammaton (יהוה), has three syllables (Je·ho·vah) not two syllables (Yah·weh). Second, many Hebrew kings and others used by God personally in Bible times used part of the Father's personal name in their name, like **Jeho**ash, **Jeho**ram, **Jeho**iakim, **Jeho**iachin, **Jeho**ram, **Jeho**hanan, **Jeho**nadab, **Jeho**ahaz, and even the wife of High Priest **Jeho**iada; daughter of King **Jeho**ram of Judah, **Jeho**sheba, among many more. We notice that the beginning of the Father's personal name is used in every one of these cases. Does anyone find it a bit troubling that the Bibles (JB, LEB, HCSB), which choose to use the so-called scholarly "Yahweh" rendering still spell the above names with Jeho? Why do these same translations not spell **Jeho**ash "**Yah**ash"? We will look at how the Holman Christian Standard Bible (and the HCSB revision, the 2017 Christian Stanard Bible) and the Lexham English Bible render the Father's personal name and then how they render **Jeho**sheba, **Jeho**ram, and **Jeho**ash.

The Father's Personal Name

NOTE: The 2017 Christian Standard Bible is simply an updated version of the 2009 Holman Christian Standard Bible. Note that the updated HCSB, the CSB has removed God's personal name.

Isaiah 42:8 Holman Christian Standard Bible (HCSB)

⁸ I am **Yahweh**, that is My name;
I will not give My glory to another
or My praise to idols.

Isaiah 42:8 Lexham English Bible (LEB)	**Isaiah** 42:8 Christian Standard Bible (CSB)
⁸ I *am* **Yahweh**; that *is* my name, and I do not give my glory to another, nor my praise to the idols.	⁸ I am the **LORD**. That is my name, and I will not give my glory to another or my praise to idols.

The Father's Personal Name Used In Bible Person's Names, Especially Kings

2 Kings 11:2 Christian Standard Bible (CSB)

² **Jeho**sheba, who was King **Jeho**ram's daughter and Ahaziah's sister, secretly rescued Joash son of Ahaziah from among the king's sons who were being killed and put him and the one who nursed him in a bedroom. So he was hidden from Athaliah and was not killed.

2 Kings 11:2 Holman Christian Standard Bible (HCSB)	2 Kings 11:2 Lexham English Bible (LEB)
² **Jeho**sheba, who was King **Jehor**am's daughter and Ahaziah's sister, secretly rescued Joash [**Jeho**ash] son of Ahaziah from the king's sons who were being killed and put him and the one who nursed him in a bedroom. So he was hidden from Athaliah and was not killed.	² But **Jeho**sheba the daughter of King **Jo**ram [**Jeho**ram] and sister of Ahaziah took **Jeho**ash the son of Ahaziah, and she stole him from among the sons of the king who were being put to death, *putting* him and his nurse in the inner bedroom. So they hid him from the presence of Athaliah, and he was not killed.

Remember, it was the Jewish Pharisees, who rejected Jesus and were told by him: "So for the sake of your tradition you have made void the word of God." (Matthew 15:6; Mark 7:13) One of their traditions was not to pronounce the personal name of the Father. Thus, is it not a bit foolish for modern translators to follow in the footsteps of the very men, who were condemned and rejected by Jesus? Substituting the personal name of the Father for a title truly weakens the Word of God.

It even further boggles the mind that they do the same thing with how Jesus (Gr. Iēsous) name. They say the Hebrew is Yeshua, when, in fact it is Joshua shortened form of Jehoshua, meaning "Jehovah Is Salvation." Dr. Brown writes, "The original Hebrew-Aramaic name of Jesus is yeshuʻa, which is short for yehōshuʻa (Joshua), just as Mike is short for Michael. The name yeshuʻa occurs 27 times in the Hebrew Scriptures, primarily referring to the high priest after the Babylonian exile, called both yehōshuʻa (see, e.g., Zechariah 3:3) and, more frequently, yeshuʻa (see, e.g., Ezra 3:2)."[183] Really, the name Yeshua occurs in the verses he cited? Well, let us look at the translations that use the Father's personal name in their translation, namely, the Holman Christian Standard Bible (HCSB) (and the HCSB revision, the 2017 Christian Standard Bible) and the Lexham English Bible (LEB)

Zechariah 3:3 Christian Standard Bible (CSB)

³ Now **Joshua** was dressed with filthy clothes as he stood before the angel.

---

[183] What is the original Hebrew name for Jesus? And is it true .., https://askdrbrown.org/library/what-original-hebrew-name-jesus-and-it-true-name-(accessed October 26, 2016).

Ezra 3:2 Christian Standard Bible (CSB)

2 **Jeshua** son of Jozadak and his brothers the priests along with Zerubbabel son of Shealtiel and his brothers began to build the altar of Israel's God in order to offer burnt offerings on it, as it is written in the law of Moses, the man of God.

Zechariah 3:3 Holman Christian Standard Bible (HCSB)	**Zechariah 3:3** Lexham English Bible (LEB)
3 Now **Joshua** was dressed with filthy clothes as he stood before the Angel.	3 And **Joshua** was clothed in filthy garments and was standing *before* the angel.
Ezra 3:2 Holman Christian Standard Bible (HCSB)	**Ezra 3:2** Lexham English Bible (LEB)
2 **Jeshua** son of Jozadak and his brothers the priests along with Zerubbabel son of Shealtiel and his brothers began to build the altar of Israel's God in order to offer burnt offerings on it, as it is written in the law of Moses, the man of God.	2 And **Jeshua** son of Jehozadak and his brothers the priests stood up, and Zerubbabel the son of Shealtiel and his brothers built the altar of the God of Israel, in order to offer burnt offerings on it, as it is written in the law of Moses, the man of God.

Clearly, Jehovah, the personal name of the Father, is a unique and special name, applying to only one person, the Almighty Father of the Hebrew Old Testament, and only one person would want the removal of the personal name of the Father, namely, Satan. Why? Most certainly, almost every Christian who has read Acts 2:21 and Romans 10:13 below has thought that the reference to "the Lord," was to Jesus Christ, the Son of the Father; when, in fact, it is a reference to the Father.

Joel 2:32 American Standard Version (ASV)

32 And it shall come to pass, that **whosoever shall call on the name of Jehovah shall be delivered**; for in mount Zion and in Jerusalem there shall be those that escape, as Jehovah has said, and among the remnant those whom Jehovah does call.

This verse is quoted two times in the New Testament, by two apostles, Peter and Paul:

Acts 2:21 Lexham English Bible (LEB)

21 And it will be that everyone who calls upon the name of the Lord will be saved.'[a]

[a]Footnotes: Acts 2:21 A quotation from Joel 2:28–32

Romans 10:13 Lexham English Bible (LEB)

13 For "everyone who calls upon the name of the Lord will be saved."[a]

[a]Footnotes: Romans 10:13 A quotation from Joel 2:32

Dr. John McRay in his book *Archaeology and the New Testament* writes,

This whole issue becomes even more intriguing when we consider the possibility that the New Testament autographs, written almost entirely by Jewish Christians (the possible exception being Luke-Acts), may have preserved the Jewish custom and retained the divine name in Aramaic script in quotations from the Old Testament. Thus, they may have followed the lead of some Jewish authors who used one script for the divine name when they quoted Scripture and another when they themselves referred to God. Similarly, it was customary at Qumran to use the Tetragram freely when one was either copying or introducing Scripture quotations into a commentary, but to use El ("God") in original material written for a commentary.[184]

Having references to Yahweh clearly indicated would be of enormous help, for any verses that refer to "the Lord" are unclear as to whether Christ or God (Yahweh) is meant. For example, Peter's quotation (in Acts 2:34) of David, "The Lord said to my Lord," is unclear until the Hebrew original (Ps. 110:1) is read: "Yahweh says to my Adonai." Such verses that quote the Old Testament would be clearer if YHWH (the Tetragram) were used in the New Testament.

Another case in point is Romans 10:16, which quotes Isaiah 53:1, "Lord, who has believed our report?" "Lord" would seem to refer to Christ, for "the word of Christ" is a reading which appears in the most recent New Testament texts of verse 17, even though many of the ancient witnesses have "the word of God."[185] Actually, the word Lord does not appear in the Hebrew text of Isaiah 53:1, although it does appear in the Greek text, which Paul quotes, as κυριε. Since this word became a surrogate in Christian copies of the Septuagint for YHWH, it is natural to assume that κυριε in the Septuagint of Isaiah 53:1 refers to YHWH. It undoubtedly

[184] Howard ("Tetragram and the New Testament," 66-67) presents two illustrations: 1 QpHab 10:6-7 (equals Hab. 2:13) and 1 QpHab 11: 10 (equals Hab. 2:16).

[185] See the discussion in Bruce M. Metzger, A Textual Commentary on the Greek New Testament (New York: United Bible Societies, 1971), 525.

slipped into the Septuagint from an early Hebrew lemma (in commentaries, the setting forth of a text prior to its discussion) which led to the inference that the YHWH mentioned in the second part of Isaiah 53:1 is the person being addressed in the first part of that verse. Since this verse is Scripture rather than commentary, Jewish scribal practice would have dictated the use of "Yahweh" rather than "Adonai." The verse would then have read, "Yahweh, who has believed our report?"[186] This is the way Paul would have understood the Septuagint. Contrary to current textual criticism, then, the reading in Romans 10:17 should probably be "the word of God" rather than "the word of Christ." Rudolf Bultmann's argument that "the unmodified expression 'the Lord' is unthinkable (nicht denkbar)" in Jewish usage (and thus unthinkable in Isa. 53:1a)[187] is now rebutted by several Palestinian Aramaic texts which have the word Mare or Marya ("Lord") as a title for God. Thus, pre-Christian Jews did refer to God in an absolute sense as "the Lord."[188]

Again, how does the Father feel about his own personal name? We return to the one verse that says it all.

Isaiah 42:8 American Standard Version (ASV)

⁸ I am Jehovah, that is my name; and my glory will I not give to another, neither my praise unto graven images.

Returning to Elijah, we ask did the prayers of the Baal prophets go to the same place as Elijah. Baal worship corrupted people with ritual prostitution and even offering up human life in their sacrifices. In contrast, the worship of the Father elevated the Israelite people to superior moral and ethical values, never even considering such degrading practices. Just think, if we were in a bad way and were writing a letter to one of our closest and dearest friend, would we use their personal name (Dear Janice), or would we use an impersonal title (Dear Miss). Surely not! Who is the Father of humankind? Isaiah the prophet answers but who has the accurate rendering?

1901 ASV	Isa 63:16 For thou art our Father, though Abraham knoweth us not, and Israel doth not acknowledge us: **thou, O Jehovah,**	2016 UASV	Isa 63:16 For you are our Father, though Abraham does not know us, and Israel does not recognize us; **you, O Jehovah, are**

---

[186] Other examples are discussed by Howard, "Tetragram and the New Testament," 76-83

[187] Rudolph Bultmann, Theology of the New Testament, 2 vols. (London: SCM, 1952), 1.51 equals Theologie des Neuen Testaments (Tübingen: Mohr, 1948), 52.

[188] Joseph A. Fitzmyer, "The Aramaic Language and the Study of the New Testament," JBL 99 (1980): 13.

McRay, John (2008-02-01). Archaeology and the New Testament (Kindle Locations 5515-5582). Baker Academic. Kindle Edition.

art our **Father**; our Redeemer from everlasting is thy name.	**our Father**, our Redeemer from of old is your name.
2013 LEB | Isa 63:16 For you are our father, although Abraham does not know us, and Israel does not acknowledge us. You, **Yahweh** are our father, Our Redeemer from of old is your name.	**2009 HCSB | Isa 63:16** Yet You are our Father, even though Abraham does not know us and Israel doesn't recognize us. You, **Yahweh**, are our Father; from ancient times, Your name is our Redeemer.
2001 ESV | Isa 63:16 For you are our Father, though Abraham does not know us, and Israel does not acknowledge us; **you, O <u>LORD</u>, are our Father**, our Redeemer from of old is your name.	**1995 NASB | Isa 63:16** For You are our Father, though Abraham does not know us And Israel does not recognize us. **You, O <u>LORD</u>, are our Father**, Our Redeemer from of old is Your name.

DEBUNKING THE MYTH OF THE SACRED NAMERS

- – Debunking the Myths of Sacred Namers-Part I
- https://wp.me/p6EZsO-5SC
- – Debunking the Myths of Sacred Namers-Part II
- https://wp.me/p6EZsO-5SD
- – Debunking the Myths of Sacred Namers-Part III
- https://wp.me/p6EZsO-5SE
- – Debunking the Myths of Sacred Namers-Part IV
- https://wp.me/p6EZsO-5SF

CHAPTER 7 Examining Sheol and Hades (Grave)

What Really Is Hades?

When the word "hell" is mentioned, many people have different images that come to mind. However, for most Christians the general consensus is the same. For them, "hell" is a place of eternal torment, i.e., a place of punishment for sinners. These have heard this their entire lives, so anyone that would say otherwise is dismissed as a heretic worse case scenario or not a true conservative Christian best case scenario. Let us offer a few biblical reasons within this short introduction chapter as to why the reader should consider the other side of the story, i.e., eternal destruction as opposed to eternal torment. Later chapters will dig deeper, making the case for eternal destruction. Thus, this introduction should, at least, offer the motivation for reading the rest of the book.

FIRST, let us start with Paul, who as we know was known as Saul before becoming the apostle Paul. Nevertheless, the objective way of believing certain Bible doctrines as being the truth is as follows. The biblical view of the doctrine _____ is _____, and it is the truth, unless, enough evidence comes along to say otherwise. If we grow in knowledge and understanding, our conclusions based on previous knowledge may need to be revised. For increased knowledge can require adjustments in one's thinking. We must remember the Apostle Paul studied under the renowned Pharisee Gamaliel, who was the grandson of Hillel, the Elder (110 B.C.E.[189] – 10 C.E.), the founder of one of the two schools within Judaism. Paul describes himself as "circumcised on the eighth day, of the people of Israel, of the tribe of Benjamin, a Hebrew of Hebrews; as to the law, a Pharisee; as to zeal, a persecutor of the church; as to righteousness under the law, blameless." (Phil 3:5-6) He also states, "But whatever gain I had, I counted as loss for the sake of Christ. Indeed, I count everything as loss because of the surpassing worth of knowing Christ Jesus my Lord. For his sake I have suffered the loss of all things and count them as rubbish, in order that I may gain Christ" (Phil. 3:7-8) Thus, we know that the Israelites were God's chosen people and the only way to God for some 1,500 years. However, Jesus brought a new way, Christianity. Saul/Paul was slow to accept this because he could not see Jesus Christ as the long-awaited Messiah. Nevertheless, after

---

[189] B.C.E. years ran down toward zero, although the Romans had no zero, and C.E. years ran up from zero. (100, 10, 3, 2, 1 ◄B.C.E. | C.E.► 1, 2, 3, 10, and 100)

Jesus visited Paul on the road to Damascus and Ananias, a Christian disciple of Damascus, visited Paul, he saw the Old Testament Scriptures pointing to the Messiah accurately, he was able to humble himself and accept a different belief, i.e., Christianity was the truth and the way.

To believe without enough support, to believe in the face of contrary evidence is irrational. Therefore, we must humbly examine the facts behind what we believe, to establish the truth continually. Just as the apostle Paul exhorted the Christians at Corinth to "examine yourselves, to see whether you are in the faith. Test yourselves" (2 Cor. 13:5), we could say the very same thing about our beliefs. We could say, 'examine our beliefs, to see whether they are the truth, test our beliefs.' Now, this is not to suggest that our beliefs are to be ever changing, but that they should be able to stand up to scrutiny when they are challenged by something we have heard or read. However, this refinement of our beliefs should not be confused with allowing unfounded, damaging doubts to grow in our hearts and minds, doubts that can destroy our confidently established beliefs and our relationship with our heavenly Father. **Unfounded doubt** is defined as something that is not supported by any evidence or a minuscule amount of evidence, to cause uncertainty of belief or opinion that often interferes with our decision-making skills.

SECOND, we need to dig deeper into biblical truths, not as a sign of unfounded doubt but to make sure what we believe is so. If we believe that we can survive off the basic Bible knowledge that we acquired in the beginning and the simple snacks we receive at each Christian meeting, we are sadly mistaken because our spiritual health will deteriorate. It would be similar to our believing that we could maintain our physical health by simply eating here and there.

Acts 17:10-11 Updated American Standard Version (UASV)

Paul and Silas in Berea

[10] The brothers immediately sent Paul and Silas away by night to Berea, and when they arrived, they went into the synagogue of the Jews. [11] Now these were more noble-minded than those in Thessalonica, for they received the word with great eagerness, examining the Scriptures daily to see whether these things were so.

Note that they **(1)** "received the word with all eagerness," and then went about **(2)** "examining the Scriptures daily to see if these things were so." If the apostle Paul was to be examined to see if what he said was so, surely uninspired commentators must be examined as well.

1 Timothy 1:13 Updated American Standard Version (UASV)

13 although formerly I [Saul/Paul] was a blasphemer, and a persecutor, and a violent man. But I was shown mercy because I had acted unknowingly with a lack of trust,

Romans 10:2-3 Updated American Standard Version (UASV)

2 For I [Saul/Paul] bear them witness that they [the Jews] have a zeal for God, but not according to accurate knowledge.[190] 3 For, being ignorant of the righteousness of God, and seeking to establish their own, they did not submit to God's righteousness.

What has been demonstrated here thus far? Just because one is very active in their Christian denomination or church, this activity does not guarantee that they are receiving God's approval or that they are doctrinally correct. See Jesus words below for those who believed that they were in an approved relationship. It takes real heart and character to accept that one may be on the wrong path when it comes to long held biblical beliefs. It takes an act of humility to accept that we may need to make an adjustment in our view of a certain doctrine.

Matthew 7:21-23 Updated American Standard Version (UASV)

21 "Not everyone who says to me, 'Lord, Lord,' will enter the kingdom of heaven, but the one who does the will of my Father who is in heaven. 22 On that day many will say to me, 'Lord, Lord, did we not prophesy in your name, and cast out demons in your name, and do many mighty works in your name?' 23 And then I will declare to them, 'I never knew you; depart from me, you who practice lawlessness.'

It was Saul/Paul's zeal and his conscience that was pricked to defend what he thought was the truth, and yet he clearly admitted that his was over-zealous, that his zeal was misdirected, because of ignorance. This should cause us to pause and reflect. The presence of false teachers in the Christian congregation from the first century onward means that one cannot just accept naively that they are getting the truth. It would be foolish to assume such.

1 Thessalonians 5:21 Updated American Standard Version (UASV)

21 But examine everything carefully; hold fast to that which is good;

---

[190] *Epignosis* is a strengthened or intensified form of *gnosis* (*epi*, meaning "additional"), meaning, "true," "real," "full," "complete" or "accurate," depending upon the context. Paul and Peter alone use *epignosis*.

The Greek word *dokimazete* rendered simply as "test" in the English Standard Version or the Holman Christian Standard Bible denotes a careful examination of "everything." If one is to make a careful examination of everything, it will require that they are not just passively going along, but rather, one should be buying out the time, to have an accurate understanding of God's Word, by doing an in-depth study of what they believe to be true.

Certainly, if what Paul had to say about the Scriptures was under examination, no one else is above having their beliefs examined. The Jews of Berea did not just accept what Paul was saying about the death and resurrection of Jesus, as being so. Moreover, Paul commended them for their due diligence. (See 17:3) This was no brief or superficial examination of the Scriptures either; they met daily to examine the Scriptures. For the above reasons, it is only through living by faith and accurate knowledge that we can receive God's favor.

Examine Everything Carefully

When we are considering what the punishment is for sin, Scripture is the final authority. However, we do not want to delve off into inappropriate proof-texting, which is the practice of using isolated Scripture quotations, out of context, from the Bible to establish a particular doctrinal position. Note that proof texting in and of itself is not wrong. It is only wrong if we do it out of context, which causes us to end up with what we believe the text is saying rather than what the authors meant by their own words.

Romans 5:12 Updated American Standard Version (UASV)

12 Therefore, just as through one man sin entered into the world, and death through sin, and so death spread to all men, because all sinned,

In the above text, Paul addresses sin and its effect. In the same book, he goes on to write, "For the wages of sin is death, but the free gift[191] of God is eternal life in Christ Jesus our Lord." (Rom. 6:23, UASV) Paul under inspiration tells us that the punishment for sin is death, which leads to the questions, how are we to understand the word "hell" in the face of this revelation? What is hell? What do the Hebrew and Greek words behind the English rendering "hell" (Sheol, Hades, Gehenna, and Tartarus) really mean? After the death of a person, does life of some kind, in some form continue? After determining what hell is, we must then decide who goes there. Moreover, does the Bible offer any hope for those in hell? All of this and far more will be addressed throughout this publication.

---

191 Lit *gracious gift*; Gr *kharisma*

Is Hades a Place of Eternal Torment?

Hundreds of millions of both Catholic and Protest Christians have long held that hell is a place of eternal torment for the damned. According to the Encarta Encyclopedia, "Hell, in theology, any place or state of punishment and privation for human souls after death. More strictly, the term is applied to the place or state of eternal punishment of the damned, whether angels or human beings. The doctrine of the existence of hell is derived from the principle of the necessity for the vindication of divine justice, combined with the human experience that evildoers do not always appear to be punished adequately in their lifetime. Belief in a hell was widespread in antiquity and is found in most religions of the world today."

However, it would seem that hellfire and brimstone have lost their spark. The same encyclopedia goes on to say, "In modern times the belief in physical punishment after death and the endless duration of this punishment has been rejected by many. The question about the nature of the punishment of hell is equally controversial. Opinions range from holding the pains of hell to be no more than the remorse of conscience to the traditional belief that the "pain of loss" (the consciousness of having forfeited the vision of God and the happiness of heaven) is combined with the "pain of sense" (actual physical torment).[192]

Probably the most famous hellfire and brimstone preacher was Jonathan Edwards (1703-1758), used to put the fear of God into the hearts and minds of the 18th-century Colonial Americans with detail, explicit, lifelike, word pictures of hell

"Sinners in the Hands of an Angry God" Known for his fiery sermons, clergyman Jonathan Edwards helped start the Great Awakening, an American religious revival of the 1740s.

> The God that holds you over the pit of hell, much as one holds a spider, or some loathsome insect over the fire, abhors you, and is dreadfully provoked: his wrath towards you burns like fire; he looks upon you as worthy of nothing else, but to be cast into the fire; he is of purer eyes than to bear to have you in his sight; you are ten thousand times more abominable in his eyes, than the most hateful venomous serpent is in ours. You have offended him infinitely more than ever a stubborn rebel did his prince; and yet it is nothing but his hand that holds you from falling into the fire every moment.

---

[192] Microsoft ® Encarta ® 2006. © 1993-2005 Microsoft Corporation. All rights reserved.

O sinner! Consider the fearful danger you are in: it is a great furnace of wrath, a wide and bottomless pit, full of the fire of wrath, that you are held over in the hand of that God, whose wrath is provoked and incensed as much against you, as against many of the damned in hell. You hang by a slender thread, with the flames of divine wrath flashing about it, and ready every moment to singe it, and burn it asunder;[193]

Like Edwards, many other Catholic and Protestant preachers, say that God has this eternal place in the offing for the wicked. However, what does the Bible really teach?

Hell

Without being bogged down in doctrinal issues, let us just deal with the facts. "Hell" is the English translation for the Hebrew word Sheol and the Greek word Hades. Therefore, we need not ask, what Hell is. However, what did the word mean when it was first placed in English translations? Webster's Eleventh New International Dictionary, under "Hell" says: [Middle English, from Old English; akin to Old English helan to conceal, Old High German helan, Latin celare, Greek kalyptein] before 12th century"[194] The word "hell" meant to 'cover' over or 'conceal,' so it would have meant a place 'covered' or 'concealed,' such as a grave.

Sheol

Webster's Dictionary, "[Hebrew Shĕ'ōl] 1597: the abode of the dead in early Hebrew thought"[195] Collier's Encyclopedia (1986, Vol. 12, p. 28) says: "Since Sheol in Old Testament times referred simply to the abode of the dead and suggested no moral distinctions, the word 'hell,' as understood today, is not a happy translation." Some translations choose to use a transliteration, Sheol, as opposed to the English hell, AT, RSV, ESV, LEB, HCSB, and NASB.

---

[193] Edwards, Jonathan (2010-05-20). Sinners In The Hands Of An Angry God (Kindle Locations 151-152). Old Land Mark Publishing. Kindle Edition.

[194] Frederick C. Mish, "Preface," *Merriam-Webster's Collegiate Dictionary*. (Springfield, MA: Merriam-Webster, Inc., 2003). hell

[195] Frederick C. Mish, "Preface," *Merriam-Webster's Collegiate Dictionary*. (Springfield, MA: Merriam-Webster, Inc., 2003). sheol

Hades

Everyone knows that Hades was "the underground abode of the dead in Greek mythology."[196] However, as far as early Christianity, the Greek translation of the Old Testament, the Septuagint, uses the word Hades 73 times, employing it 60 times to translate the Hebrew word Sheol. Luke at Acts 2:27 write, "For you will not abandon my soul to Hades, or let your Holy One see corruption." Luke was quoting Psalm 16:10, which reads, "For you will not abandon my soul to Sheol, or let your holy one see corruption." Notice that Luke used Hades in place of Sheol. Therefore, Hades is the Greek equivalent of Sheol, as far as Christians and the Greek New Testament is concerned. In other words, Hades is also the abode of the dead in early Christian thought. Some translations choose to use a transliteration, Hades, as opposed to the English hell, ASV, AT, RSV, ESV, LEB, HCSB, and NASB.

Gehenna

Gehenna Hebrew Ge' Hinnom, literally, valley of Hinnom appears 12 times in the Greek New Testament books, and many translators render it by the word "hell." Most translations have chosen poorly not to use a transliteration, Gehenna or Geenna, as opposed to the English hell, ASV, AT, RSV, ESV, LEB, HCSB, and NASB. There is little doubt that the New Testament writers and Jesus used "Gehenna" to speak of the place of final punishment. What was Gehenna?

According to the Holman Illustrated Bible Dictionary (p. 632), Gehenna or the Valley of Hinnom was "the valley south of Jerusalem now called the Wadi er-Rababi (Josh. 15:8; 18:16; 2 Chron. 33:6; Jer. 32:35) became the place of child sacrifice to foreign gods. The Jews later used the valley for the dumping of refuse, the dead bodies of animals, and executed criminals."[197] We would disagree with the other comments by the Holman Illustrated Dictionary, "The continuing fires in the valley (to consume the refuse and dead bodies) apparently led the people to transfer the name to the place where the wicked dead suffer." This just is not the case.

In the Old Testament, the Israelites did burn sons in the fires as part of a sacrifice to false gods, but not for the purpose of punishment, or torture. By the time of the New Testament period, hundreds of years later, the only thing thrown in Gehenna was trash and the dead bodies of executed

---

[196] Frederick C. Mish, "Preface," *Merriam-Webster's Collegiate Dictionary.* (Springfield, MA: Merriam-Webster, Inc., 2003). hades

[197] Chad Brand et al., eds., "Gehenna," *Holman Illustrated Bible Dictionary* (Nashville, TN: Holman Bible Publishers, 2003), 632.

criminals. For what purpose were these thrown into Gehenna? It was used as an incinerator, a furnace for destroying things by burning them. Notice that any bodies thrown in Gehenna during the New Testament period were already dead. Thus, if anything, these people saw Gehenna as a place where they destroyed their trash and the bodies of dead criminals. Thus, if Jesus used this to illustrate the place of the wicked, it would have represented destruction as the punishment.

How Are We to Understand the "Fire"?

Mark 9:43-48 Updated American Standard Version (UASV)

[43] "If ever your hand makes you stumble, cut it off. It is better for you to enter into life maimed than to go off with two hands into Gehenna,[198] the unquenchable **fire**, [44] ———[199] [45] And if your foot causes you to sin, cut it off. It is better for you to enter life lame than with two feet to be thrown into Gehenna.[200] [46] ———[201] [47] And if your eye makes you stumble, throw it out, it is better for you to enter the kingdom of God with one eye, than, having two eyes, to be cast into Gehenna,[202] [48] where their worm does not die and the fire is not quenched.

Matthew 13:42 Updated American Standard Version (UASV))

[42] and will throw them into the furnace of fire; in that place there will be weeping and gnashing of teeth.

Here is why we should use the transliteration as opposed to the English "hell." Jesus did not use the word "Hades" in the above texts, the equivalent of Sheol, but rather Gehenna. Jesus used comparisons in his teaching, using things that his listeners could relate. As we learned in the above Gehenna was a garbage dump that was used as an incinerator, to destroy whatever was thrown in, and only the bodies of criminals were thrown in after they were already dead. In other words, the fire was used as a symbol, not of torment,

---

[198] **Gehenna:** *geenna* (Gehenna) occurs 12 times and is the Greek name for the valley of Hinnom, southwest of Jerusalem (Jer. 7:31), where the horrendous worship of Moloch took place, and it was prophetically said that where dead bodies would be thrown. (Jer. 7:32; 19:6) It was an incinerator where trash and dead bodies were destroyed, not a place to be burned alive or tormented. Jesus and his disciples used Gehenna to symbolize eternal destruction, annihilation, or the "second death," an eternal punishment of death.

[199] WH NU ℵ B C L W ΔΨ 0274 f¹ 28 565 itᵏ syrˢ cop omit; A D Θ f¹³ Maj, "where their worm does not die and the fire is not quenched." This verse is identical to verse 48 and is missing from the earliest and best manuscripts, as well as several text types. It is an interpolation.

[200] IBID, Gehenna

[201] WH NU ℵ B C L W ΔΨ 0274 f¹ 28 565 itᵏ syrˢ cop omit; A D Θ f¹³ Maj, "where their worm does not die and the fire is not quenched." This verse is identical to verse 48 and is missing from the earliest and best manuscripts, as well as several text types. It is an interpolation.

[202] IBID Gehenna

but rather of being destroyed, complete destruction, namely annihilation by fire.

What did Jesus mean by "there will be weeping and gnashing of teeth"? We can look at what he said about those, who believed they were on the right path,

Matthew 7:21-23 Updated American Standard Version (UASV)

21 "Not everyone who says to me, 'Lord, Lord,' will enter the kingdom of heaven, but the one who does the will of my Father who is in heaven. 22 On that day many will say to me, 'Lord, Lord, did we not prophesy in your name, and cast out demons in your name, and do many mighty works in your name?' 23 And then I will declare to them, 'I never knew you; depart from me, you who practice lawlessness.'

In other words, those who will be weeping and gnashing of teeth" are those who believed they had the truth, but did not. Can we imagine giving our whole life to what we think to be the correct path, only to get to the edge and discover, we are on the wrong path because we chose to do our will, not the will of the Father? Now then, what about what John penned in the book of Revelation?

Revelation 21:8 Updated American Standard Version (UASV)

8 But as for the cowards and unbelievers, and the detestable, as for murderers, and the sexually immoral[203] persons and sorcerers and idolaters and all liars, their portion will be in the lake that burns with fire and sulphur, which is the second death."

John speaks of a "lake that burns with fire and sulfur," where the wicked are thrown. It would seem that if hellfire were the truth, this would be the place. However, we are simply told by John; this is "the second death." Moreover, he had told his readers earlier,

Revelation 20:13-14 Updated American Standard Version (UASV)

13 And the sea gave up the dead which were in it, and death and Hades[204] gave up the dead which were in them; and they were judged, every one of

---

[203] **Sexual Immorality:** (Heb. *zanah*; Gr. *porneia*) A general term for immoral sexual acts of any kind: such as adultery, prostitution, sexual relations between people not married to each other, homosexuality, and bestiality. – Num. 25:1; Deut. 22:21; Matt. 5:32; 1 Cor. 5:1.

[204] Hades is the standard transliteration into English of the corresponding Greek word haides, which occurs ten times in the UASV. (Matt. 11:23; 16:18; Lu 10:15; 16:23; Ac 2:27, 31; Rev. 1:18; 6:8; 20:13, 14.) It has the underlying meaning of 'a place of the dead, where they are conscious of nothing, awaiting a resurrection, for both the righteous and the unrighteous.' (John 5:28-29; Acts 24:15) It corresponds to "Sheol" in the OT. It does not involve torment and punishment.

them according to their deeds. ¹⁴ Then death and Hades²⁰⁵ were thrown into the lake of fire. This is the **second death**, the lake of fire.

Notice that death, which is what we inherited from our first parents Adam and Eve, as well as Hades (gravedom), is going to be "thrown into the lake of fire." Is not death and Hades abstract, are they able to be tormented and suffer forever. No. However, the fire does picture their eternal destruction, which will take place once they 'give up the dead who were in them.' Note that Paul clearly said, "The last enemy to be destroyed is death." – 1 Corinthians 15:26.

The fire and burning within Scripture are simply representing annihilation or eternal destruction. Therefore, there is no eternal torment in Sheol (gravedom), Hades (the equivalent of Sheol) hell (English translation), Gehenna (symbol of destruction), or the lake of fire (symbol of destruction). What about the parable of the sheep (righteous) and the goats (wicked), which has the goats, or the wicked going away into eternal punishment?

Matthew 25:46 Updated American Standard Version (UASV)

⁴⁶ And these will go away into eternal **punishment** [*Kolasin*],²⁰⁶ but the righteous into eternal life."

Kolasin "akin to *kolazoo*"²⁰⁷ "This means 'to cut short,' 'to lop,' 'to trim,' and figuratively a. 'to impede,' 'restrain,' and b. 'to punish,' and in the passive 'to suffer loss.'²⁰⁸ The first part of the sentence is only in harmony with the second part of the sentence, if the eternal punishment is eternal death. The wicked receive eternal death and the righteous eternal life. We might at that Matthews Gospel was primarily for the Jewish Christians, and under the Mosaic Law, God would punish those who violated the law, saying they "shall be cut off [penalty of death] from Israel." (Ex 12:15; Lev 20:2-3) We need further to consider,

2 Thessalonians 1:8-9 Updated American Standard Version (UASV)

⁸ in flaming fire, inflicting vengeance on those who do not know God and on those who do not obey the gospel of our Lord Jesus. ⁹ These ones

---

²⁰⁵ Hades is the standard transliteration into English of the corresponding Greek word haides, which occurs ten times in the UASV. (Matt. 11:23; 16:18; Lu 10:15; 16:23; Ac 2:27, 31; Rev. 1:18; 6:8; 20:13, 14.) It has the underlying meaning of 'a place of the dead, where they are conscious of nothing, awaiting a resurrection, for both the righteous and the unrighteous.' (John 5:28-29; Acts 24:15) It corresponds to "Sheol" in the OT. It does not involve torment and punishment.

²⁰⁶ That is eternal cutting off, from life. Lit., "lopping off; pruning."

²⁰⁷ W. E. Vine, Merrill F. Unger, and William White Jr., Vine's Complete Expository Dictionary of Old and New Testament Words (Nashville, TN: T. Nelson, 1996), 498.

²⁰⁸ Gerhard Kittel, Gerhard Friedrich, and Geoffrey William Bromiley, Theological Dictionary of the New Testament (Grand Rapids, MI: W.B. Eerdmans, 1985), 451.

will pay the penalty of **eternal destruction**, from before the Lord[209] and from the glory of his strength,

Notice that Paul says too that the punishment for the wicked is "eternal destruction." Many times, in talking with those that support the position of eternal torment in some hellfire, they will add a word to Matthew 25:46 in their paraphrase of the verse, 'eternal conscious punishment.' However, Jesus does not tell us what the eternal punishment is, just that it is a punishment, and it is eternal. Therefore, those who support eternal conscious fiery torment will read the verse to mean just that, while those, who hold the position of eternal destruction, will take Matthew 25:46 to mean that. Considering that Jesus does not define what the eternal punishment is, this verse is not a proof text for either side of the argument. Does Jesus' parable, The Rich Man, and Lazarus, not support the hellfire doctrine? (Luke 16:19-31)

Interpreting Parables

Jesus gave us some 40 parables or illustrations, filling them with symbols and images that represented a message he was trying to share. Now, we get to this one, and we want to take it literally? Robert H. Stein writes,

> Similarly, the parable of the rich man and Lazarus (Luke 16:19–31) is to be interpreted as a parable, and thus according to the rules governing the interpretation of parables. It is not to be interpreted as a historical account. (Luke reveals this by the introduction "A certain man …" which is used in the Gospel to introduce parables [cf. Luke 10:30; 14:16; 15:11; 16:1; 19:12]. This is clearer in the Greek text than in most translations, but it is fairly obvious in the NASB.)[210]

In discussing interpretation rules, stein goes on to say,

> In a similar way, there are different "game" rules involved in the interpretation of the different kinds of biblical literature. The author has played his "game," has sought to convey his meaning, under the rules covering the particular literary form he used. Unless we know those rules, we will almost certainly misinterpret his meaning. If we interpret a parable (Luke 16:19–31) as if it were narrative, or if we interpret poetry (Judg. 5) as if it were narrative, we will err. Similarly, if we interpret a narrative such as the resurrection of Jesus (Matt. 28:1–10) as a parable, we will also err (1 Cor. 15:12–19).[211]

---

[209] Lit *from before the face of the Lord*

[210] Robert H. Stein, A Basic Guide to Interpreting the Bible: Playing by the Rules (Grand Rapids, MI: Baker Books, 1994), 30.

[211] IBID., 76.

Step One in Understanding Parables

Read the context of the parable. You need to find out the setting of the parable, looking for the conditions and the circumstances. Why was the parable told? What prompted its being told?

Step Two in Understanding Parables

Consider the cultural backgrounds, such as the laws and customs of the setting, as well as the idioms that were spoken of earlier.

Step Three in Understanding Parables

This is a two-point step. The first point is to look to the author of the parable for the upcoming meaning of the parable. An interpreter of a parable by Jesus would see what he meant in the context it was spoken, and then consider his teaching as a whole. The second point is, do not assign subjective meanings to the elements of a parable. Generally, a parable teaches one basic point.

Stage One: Discovering the Main Characters

In any given parable, it is highly important to find the main 2–3 characters.

Stage Two: Looking to the End

As is true with any kind of story, the end of the story carries the weight of importance. This is no different with parables. The ending is where the answers lie.

Stage Three: Who Carries the Conversation

Which character carries the conversation?

Stage Four: Who Gets the Most Press

Generally, whoever gets the most coverage in a story is the primary character, followed by the secondary person that must exist to facilitate the story and its main point.

The setting of the parable of The rich man and Lazarus (Lu 16:19-31) is Jesus speaking, with the Pharisees listening in, who were well known as one who hungered for riches. What was Jesus teaching by this parable?

It had nothing to do with punishment for sin. It had to do with two different groups of people, the rich man (Jewish religious leaders) and the beggar Lazarus (poor Jewish people), as there was about to be a drastic change in their privileged and lowly positions. The Rich man, the Jewish religious leaders, opposed Jesus and the Good News of the Kingdom that he brought because he was busy sharing it with the common Jewish people. This, in fact, tormented the Jewish religious leaders to no end, to the point of their seeking to kill him. (Luke 20:19, 20, 46, 47) Conversely, the beggar

115

Lazarus represents, the poor, common Jewish people, who were looked upon with disdain, like beggars by the Jewish religious leaders, were being given the privilege position of becoming disciples of Jesus, and the first to enter into the kingdom. – 1 Cor. 1:26-29.

What is the meaning of the "tormented with fire and sulfur" in Revelation 14:9-11?

Revelation 14:9-11 Updated American Standard Version (UASV)

9 And another angel, a third, followed them, saying with a loud voice, "If anyone worships the beast and its image and receives a mark on his forehead or on his hand, 10 he also will drink of the wine of the wrath of God, which is mixed in full strength in the cup of his anger; and he will be **tormented with fire and burning sulphur** in the presence of the holy angels and in the presence of the Lamb. 11 And the smoke of their torment goes up forever and ever, and they have no rest, day or night, these worshipers of the beast and its image, and whoever receives the mark of its name."

In the above text, those who worshipping the symbolic "beast and its image," they will be "tormented with fire and sulfur." The context here is not what happens after these one's deaths, but rather what happens to them while they are alive. What is it that torments these ones while they are alive? It is the proclamations of Christians that worshipers of the "beast and its image" will experience, to such a level that it is referred to as "tormented with fire and sulfur." Looking at the context of 14:11, it is not the torment that lasts forever; it is 'the smoke of their torment that goes up forever and ever.' What is smoke is a signal of their symbolic burning that will rise forever because the lesson learned will never be forgotten. Is there yet another example of this in Scripture? Yes.

The Judgment of Edom

Isaiah 34:9-12 Updated American Standard Version (UASV)

9 And her[212] streams shall be changed to pitch,
and her soil into sulfur;
her land shall become burning pitch.
10 Night and day it will not be quenched;
its smoke shall go up forever.
From generation to generation it will lie waste;
none will pass through it forever and ever.
11 But the pelican and the porcupine[213] will possess it,

---

212 I.e. Edom's
213 The animals rendered *pelican* and *porcupine* are uncertain

the owl and the raven will dwell in it.
He will stretch the line of confusion over it,
  and the plumb line of emptiness.
¹² Its nobles, there is no one there to call it a kingdom,
  and all its princes will be nothing.

Was Edom thrown into some literal hellfire to burn forever? No. The Edomite nation, an enemy of God's people, was removed, which is described in the above in poetic terms, highly symbolic language. It was as though fire and sulfur consumed Edom. If we were to go to the geographical location of ancient Edom, would we see smoke still rising? No. The smoke was and still is today, a signal of a lesson learned from the destruction that Edom faced. This smoke-filled lesson will rise forever, in that the lesson learned will live on forever through the Word of God. After Jesus destroys the last enemy death, is it believed that the Bible will no longer be needed? The Bible is a book that will stand forever, as a signal of what humanity already experienced. Let us take this one step further as we look at our next text that is often drawn on to support hellfire doctrine.

Revelation 20:10 Updated American Standard Version (UASV)

¹⁰ And the devil who deceived them was thrown into the lake of fire and brimstone, where the beast and the false prophet are also; and they will be tormented (Greek, *basanos*) day and night forever and ever.

The Greek word used here for "torment," *basanizo*, primarily means "to test by rubbing on the touchstone" (basanos, "a touchstone"), then, "to question by applying torture."[214] The Bible is our case law (law established by previous verdicts), which will serve as a touchstone[215] (a standard by which something is judged) that humans were never designed to walk on their own, but to live under the sovereignty of their Creator. The issues raised by Satan will have been settled by humanities walking through thousands of years of an object lesson, for which the Bible is the case law, the touchstone, which will be around forever, as a reminder of the issues raised and settled.

The Moral Test

We know that man and woman were created in the image of God, and so when we hear of people who have tortured criminals, we call that inhumane. Would we expect that the One, whose image we are made in would see the eternal torment of sinners as humane? This would be

---

[214] W. E. Vine, Merrill F. Unger, and William White Jr., Vine's Complete Expository Dictionary of Old and New Testament Words (Nashville, TN: T. Nelson, 1996), 176.

[215] A touchstone is a hard black stone formerly used to test the purity of gold and silver according to the color of the streak left when the metal was rubbed against it.

incompatible with the very person of God. How are we to know how God views justice?

(Exodus 21:23-24) But if there is harm, then you shall pay life for life, eye for eye, tooth for tooth, hand for hand, foot for foot,

(Leviticus 24:20) fracture for fracture, eye for eye, tooth for tooth; whatever injury he has given a person shall be given to him.

(Deuteronomy 19:21) Your eye shall not pity. It shall be life for life, eye for eye, tooth for tooth, hand for hand, foot for foot.

(Judges 1:7) And Adoni-bezek said, "Seventy kings with their thumbs and their big toes cut off used to pick up scraps under my table. As I have done, so God has repaid me." And they brought him to Jerusalem, and he died there.

(Matthew 5:38-42) "You have heard that it was said, 'An eye for an eye and a tooth for a tooth.' But I say to you, Do not resist the one who is evil. But if anyone slaps you on the right cheek, turn to him the other also. And if anyone would sue you and take your tunic, let him have your cloak as well. And if anyone forces you to go one mile, go with him two miles. Give to the one who begs from you, and do not refuse the one who would borrow from you."

The above texts are but a few of how God views justice, and it is all too clear that he sees it as the punishment needs to be proportionate, to be the best response to crime. In other words, if an Israelite were to steal his neighbor's cow, he would have to replace it with the cow, and any financial loss he suffered, even some extra as punitive damages. However, would God expect that thief to have to work as a slave to his neighbor for the rest of his life, and his children and grand children's lives as well? Note that that punishment would be way out of proportion to the crime.

Now, let us look at the punishment that God gave Adam and Eve if they were to rebel sinfully, rejecting him and his sovereignty, by choosing to eat from the tree he had commanded them not to eat from.

Genesis 2:17 Updated American Standard Version (UASV)

[17] but from the tree of the knowledge of good and evil you shall not eat,[216] for in the day that you eat from it you shall surely die."[217]

Eat from the tree (i.e., reject God as sovereign) = death. The punishment for sin was death. Please go back and look at Genesis 2:17 in the

---

[216] Lit *eat from it*
[217] Lit *dying you* [singular] *shall die*. Heb *moth tamuth*; the first reference to death in the Scriptures

Bible, in several different translations. Do we notice some footnote from God that said, "And 4,000 years from now, when Jesus arrives, I am going to change the sentence from death to eternal torment in some literal lake of fire?"

Imagine we live in some small American town. We get our driver's licenses. Then, one day, we are pulled over for going 35-Miles Per Hour (MPH) in a 25 MPH zone. The police officer writes us a ticket and tells us to appear in court the following month, where the judge will fine us $50.00. We arrive at court the next month, and are in front of the magistrate, and he just found us guilty and sentences us not to a $50.00 fine, but to be taken outside of the courthouse and shot to death by a firing squad. Would anyone suggest that the punishment of a death sentence was proportionate to the crime of a speeding ticket? Would anyone find justice in the law enforcement officer saying the penalty was a mere $50.00 fine, and then the judge later raising the penalty to such an extreme level of capital punishment? God gave Adam the sentence of death, for committing the greatest sin of any human in history, as he had rejected God in perfection, and sentencing billions to death along with him. Would it then be justice, for God to raise the punishment bar to eternal torment in the Lake of Fire? Let us now look at imperfect humanity.

(Romans 3:23) for all have sinned and fall short of the glory of God,

(Romans 5:12) therefore, just as sin came into the world through one man, and death through sin, and so death spread to all men because all sinned

(Romans 6:7) For one who has died has been set free from sin.

(Romans 6:23) For the wages of sin is death, but the free gift of God is eternal life in Christ Jesus our Lord.

If Adam commits the greatest sin a human could commit, and he gets death, how is it justice that imperfect humans are supposedly getting eternal torment in a Lake of Fire?

There are five factors to imperfect humans being even less culpable (Guilty) than Adam was. **(1)** We are imperfect and live in an imperfect world, compounded by the fact that God's Word says we are mentally bent and lean toward doing bad. We read, "When the LORD saw that the wickedness of man on the earth was great and that the whole bent of his thinking was never anything but evil, the LORD regretted that he had ever made man on the earth." (Gen. 6:5, AT) **(2)** We have a wicked spirit creature, Satan the Devil, who is misleading the entire world of humankind. We read, "Be sober-minded; be watchful. Your adversary the devil prowls around like a roaring lion, seeking someone to devour." (1 Pet 5:8, ESV) **(3)** We live in a world that caters to the imperfect flesh. We read, "For all that is in the world, the desires of the flesh and the desires of the eyes and pride in possessions, is not

119

from the Father but is from the world. And the world is passing away along with its desires, but whoever does the will of God abides forever." (1 John 2:16-17) **(4)** We are unable to understand our inner person, which the Bible informs us is wicked: "The heart is deceitful above all things and desperately sick; who can understand it?" (Jer. 17:9) **(5)** In imperfection, man is unable of directing his own step. – Jeremiah 10:23.

Unlike Adam, we are imperfect from the start, and Adam received death for sin. Adam was perfect, with the natural desire to do good, he was mentally perfect, and he lived in a paradise, in direct communication with God. We are born mentally bent toward sin. We have Satan and demons after us. Our natural desire is toward bad. We have an imperfect, fallen world that surrounds us, which caters to our flesh desires. We have a heart (i.e., inner person) that is deceitful and desperately sick and are unable to walk on our own. Thus, who can make the case that it is right, and just that imperfect humans are to receive eternal torment in some literal Lake of Fire? If one who dies, is freed from sin, by having paid the wages of sin, which was paid for through death (Rom 6:23), not the ransom of Christ, why should he then be liable so at to have to suffer eternally in some fiery torment?

If humanity were punishing another human being with deliberate torture of fire, we would find this to be sickening and abhorrent. Our finding it so sickening and abhorrent is actually based on the conscience that God gave man, that same man, who was made in the image of God. This same God clearly stated that such an idea would never have even come into his mind.

Jeremiah 7:31 Updated American Standard Version (UASV)

[31] And they have built the high places of Topheth, which is in the Valley of the Son of Hinnom, to burn their sons and their daughters in the fire, which I did not command, **nor did it come into my heart.**[218]

The Just God

Genesis 1:27-28 Updated American Standard Version (UASV)

[27] So God created man in his own image,
in the image of God he created him;
male and female he created them.

[28] And God blessed them. And God said to them, "Be fruitful and multiply and fill the earth and subdue it, and have dominion over the fish of the sea and over the birds of the heavens and over every living thing that moves on the earth."

---

[218] I.e. *mind*

It was God's intention that his first couple, namely, Adam and Eve were to procreate, and cultivate the Garden of Eden until it covered the entire earth, filled with humans worshipping him. – Genesis 1:28

If the first couple had not rebelled, they and their offspring could have lived forever. – Genesis 2:15-17

One of the angels in heaven (who became Satan), abused his free will (James 1:14-15). He then willfully chose to rebel against God. Satan used a lowly serpent to contribute to Adam and Eve abusing their free will, and disobeying God, believing they did not need him, and could walk on their own. – Genesis 3:1-6; Job 1-2.

God removed the rebellious Adam and Eve from the Garden of Eden. (Gen. 3:23-24) The first human couple had children, but they all grew old and eventually died. (Gen. 3:19; Rom. 5:12), just as the animals died. – Ecclesiastes 3:18-20

Genesis 6:5 (AT) tells us just before the flood of Noah, that "the wickedness of man on earth was great, and the whole bent of his thinking was never anything but evil." After the flood, God said of man, "the bent of man's mind may be evil from his very youth." (Gen 8:21, AT) Jeremiah 10:23 tells us "that it is not in man who walks to direct his steps." Jeremiah 17:9 tells us that "The heart is deceitful above all things, and desperately sick; who can understand it?" Yes, the man was not designed to walk on his own. However, the man was also not designed with absolute free will, but free will under the sovereignty of his Creator. The imperfect man is mentally bent toward wickedness, fleshly desires, to which Satan has set up this world, so it caters to the fallen flesh of imperfect humans. The apostle John tells us, "For all that is in the world, the desires of the flesh and the desires of the eyes and pride of life, is not from the Father but is from the world." – 1 John 2:16.

Getting back to Genesis 1:27 that says, "God created man in his own image, in the image of God he created him; male and female he created them," which means that man is born with a moral nature, which creates within him a conscience that reflects God's moral values. (Rom 2:14-15) It acts as a moral law within all imperfect humans but even more so, those who have trained the conscience with God's Word. However, it has an opponent as fallen man also possesses the "law of sin," 'missing the mark of perfection,' the natural desire toward wickedness. Listen to the internal battle of the apostle Paul. –Romans 6:12; 7:22-23.

Romans 7:21-24 Updated American Standard Version (UASV)

[21] I find then the law in me that when I want to do right, that evil is present in me. [22] For I delight in the law of God according to the inner man, [23] but I see a different law in my members, warring against the law of

my mind and taking me captive in the law of sin which is in my members. 24 Wretched man that I am! Who will deliver me from this body of death?

However, there is hope,

Romans 7:25 Updated American Standard Version (UASV)

25 Thanks be to God through Jesus Christ our Lord! So then, I myself serve the law of God with my mind, but with my flesh, I serve the law of sin.

Yes, even imperfect man and woman have a conscience that reflects God's moral values. Therefore, when we hear of such things as ones being tortured, it is repugnant to us. Even if the person has committed some heinous crime, it is still sickening and abhorrent to the human mind, which reflects God's moral values on a small scale in our human imperfection. Therefore, we can only wonder how God, who has perfect moral values, would view the idea of torturing humans for an eternity, which is what the hellfire doctrine teaches.

Jeremiah 7:31 Updated American Standard Version (UASV)

31 And they have built the high places of Topheth, which is in the Valley of the Son of Hinnom, to burn their sons and their daughters in the fire, which I did not command, nor did it come into my heart.[219]

Imagine if we can, we have come home to find that our husband has inserted a pipe up the rectum of our 17-year-old daughter, with it coming out her mouth. He has her over a fire and is slowly cooking her alive. He has the fire set, so it will burn her very slowly, lasting days. He says that he is tired of her sinful actions, and she must pay for her rebellious spirit. How would our Christian conscience take that scene, would we simply set our purse down, and start helping him turn her on the thin rod on which she is impaled for roasting over the fire? Would we have no feeling as she screams out in agony? How do we place a loving and just God in such a light, when we only have a fraction of his moral values, and know that this scene would be so shocking and hurtful, it is unthinkable? Likely, as the reader started this paragraph, the language of even saying such things was so revolting that we have questioned why we even bought such a book. Keep in mind, it is our God given conscience that made us feel that way.

Regardless of this hypothetical daughter's sinful nature, and her rebellious spirit, a parent's heart would be torn in two. The disdain for the husband, the one who applied the torture, would be unbearable. The love of God is merciful and has the feeling of sympathy. A loving father may choose

---

[219] I.e. *mind*

122

to punish his child but never torture. In fact, the United States will not allow any form of capital punishment (i.e., death penalty) that includes any pain and suffering. This is true, even when they are executing people for the vilest crimes.

Nevertheless, much of Christianity teaches that God is a torturer, and his form of justice is to exceed the crime, because he is vindictive, as a human rejected his sovereignty, so he burns this one alive, in an eternal hellfire. If a child refused to follow the rules of the house, would we kick her out, or would we burn her slowly over a fiery pit in the backyard? Which is more just, to kick a person out of eternal life (annihilationism), or to torturously burn them alive for an eternity. Who would create a torture chamber, and see that as justice? Would this be one who is repeatedly described as the epitome of love, justice, mercy, kindness, and wisdom?

1 John 4:8 Updated American Standard Version (UASV)

[8] The one who does not love does not know God, because God is love.

Unreasonable Doctrine?

Does the above almighty being inflict eternal torture on a person, who has only sinned for 70 years? Does this sound like a person that deserves to be loved? Did not Adolf Hitler do the same thing to the Jews and Christians? Even if a human sinned every day of an 80-year lifetime grievously, would eternal fiery torment be a just punishment? Hardly! It would be unjust to God, who already told us how to view justice when he said an eye for an eye, a life for a life.

Deuteronomy 32:4 Updated American Standard Version (UASV)

[4] "The Rock, his work is perfect,
    for all his ways are just;
A God of faithfulness and without injustice,
    Righteous and upright is he.

What Does Deuteronomy 32:4 Mean?

God's justice, like every other aspect of his unparalleled personality, is perfect, not lacking in anything. Every time God expresses his justice, it is flawless, never too lenient and never too harsh.

Holman Old Testament Commentary

32:1-4. Although the words of Moses in his song were designed to testify against Israel's coming defections, the true subject of the song was the greatness of our God. Once convicted of their sin, Israel would be brought back to God not by the failure of their idols but by the supreme faithfulness and beauty of the Rock of Israel, a God who does no wrong.[220]

New American Commentary

32:3–4 There clearly is a subject shift in v. 3, where Moses appears as a character witness on the Lord's behalf. Also addressing the heavens and the earth, he extols the Lord's greatness, especially by the public proclamation of his name, that is, of his reputation (v. 3; cf. Exod 33:19; 34:5–6). The expected result was that all who heard should ascribe greatness ("praise") to God. Knowledge of God can lead to no other response than to acknowledge his might. Specific expressions of his power are his identification as "the Rock" (haṣṣûr; cf. vv. 15, 18, 30; Hab 1:12), the foundation and fortress (cf. Pss 31:3; 62:7; 71:3; 89:26; 95:1; Isa 30:29) whose works are upright (thus tāmîm, "having integrity") and whose ways are characterized by justice (mišpāṭ, "rectitude"; cf. Gen 18:25; Job 40:8; Pss 111:7; 119:149). In the context of self-defense these attributes speak most particularly to the Lord's own character. Thus he is also faithful in the sense that he is dependable ('ĕmûnâ; cf. Pss 88:11; 89:2–3, 6, 9; Isa 25:1; Hos 2:19), devoid of any hint of injustice ('ên 'āwel), a God who is righteous and just in all he does (v. 4b). These descriptions are especially apropos in a legal setting in which the reputation of the Lord may be under attack as he himself proceeds to level charges of impropriety against his covenant partner Israel.[221]

The main thoughts here, which apply to our discussion is, "God does no wrong," a God "devoid of any hint of injustice ('ên 'āwel), a God, who is righteous and just in all he does (v. 4b)."

Tsadaq, "to be righteous, be in the right, be justified, be just." This verb, which occurs fewer than 40 times in biblical Hebrew, is derived from the noun *tsedeq*. The basic meaning of *tsadaq* is "to be righteous." It is a legal term which involves the whole process of justice. God "is righteous" in all of His relations …"[222]

Now, let us look at the Son of God, and his perception of retribution.

---

[220] Anders, Max; McIntosh, Doug, *Deuteronomy*, Holman Old Testament Commentary (Nashville: Broadman & Holman Publishers, 2002), 359-360.

[221] Eugene H. Merrill, *Deuteronomy*, vol. 4, The New American Commentary (Nashville: Broadman & Holman Publishers, 1994), 410.

[222] W. E. Vine, Merrill F. Unger, and William White Jr., *Vine's Complete Expository Dictionary of Old and New Testament Words* (Nashville, TN: T. Nelson, 1996), 205.

Matthew 5:38-42 Updated American Standard Version (UASV)

[38] "You have heard that it was said, 'An eye for an eye, and a tooth for a tooth.'[223] [39] But I say to you, Do not resist the one who is wicked; but whoever slaps you on your right cheek, turn the other to him also. [40] If anyone wants to sue you and take your tunic,[224] let him have your cloak[225] also. [41] Whoever forces you to go one mile, go with him two. [42] Give to him who asks of you, and do not turn away from one that wants to borrow from you.

What Did Jesus Mean?

Holman New Testament Commentary

5:38–42. As many people do today, the scribes and Pharisees of Jesus' day must have taken the "eye for an eye" passages (Exod. 21:24; Lev. 24:19–20; Deut. 19:21) as justification for hurting others at least as badly as they had been hurt. The law was not given to exact revenge, but to legislate justice. Breaking the law has consequences, but personal vengeance has no place. These passages have often been wrongly taken as a minimum guideline for retaliation. What Jesus clarifies is that they were always intended as a maximum or a ceiling for retaliation, and that mercy was always an acceptable intention underlying these laws.

For the kingdom servant, legalistically "letting the punishment fit the crime" and insisting upon a "pound of flesh" falls short. We must actually consider blessing the repentant criminal. Mercy (withholding deserved punishment) and grace (giving undeserved gifts) are legitimate norms of conduct.

The **one mile** (5:41) refers to the practice of the Roman soldiers requiring civilians to carry their burden for one mile. By Roman law, the soldier could require no more than one mile of a single porter, but Jesus' kingdom servants (in representing the gracious spirit of their king) are to go beyond what is required of them.[226]

---

[223] A quotation from Ex. 21:24; Lev. 24:20

[224] Or *shirt*

[225] Or *coat*

[226] Stuart K. Weber, *Matthew*, vol. 1, Holman New Testament Commentary (Nashville, TN: Broadman & Holman Publishers, 2000), 69.

5:38–42 Jesus next alludes to Exod 21:24 and Deut. 19:21. Again, he formally abrogates an Old Testament command in order to intensify and internalize its application. This law originally prohibited the formal exaction of an overly severe punishment that did not fit a crime as well as informal, self-appointed vigilante action. Now Jesus teaches the principle that Christian kindness should transcend even straightforward tit-for-tat retribution. None of the commands of vv. 39–42 can easily be considered absolute; all must be read against the historical background of first-century Judaism. Nevertheless, in light of prevailing ethical thought Jesus contrasts radically with most others of his day in stressing the need to decisively break the natural chain of evil action and reaction that characterizes human relationships.

Antistēnai ("resist") in v. 39 was often used in a legal context (cf. Isa 50:8) and in light of v. 40 is probably to be taken that way here. Jesus' teaching then parallels 1 Cor 6:7 against not taking fellow believers to court, though it could be translated somewhat more broadly as "do not take revenge on someone who wrongs you" (GNB). We must nevertheless definitely resist evil in certain contexts (cf. Jas 4:7; 1 Pet 5:9). Striking a person on the right cheek suggests a backhanded slap from a typically right-handed aggressor and was a characteristic Jewish form of insult. Jesus tells us not to trade such insults even if it means receiving more. In no sense does v. 39 require Christians to subject themselves or others to physical danger or abuse, nor does it bear directly on the pacifism-just war debate. Verse 40 is clearly limited to a legal context. One must be willing to give as collateral an outer garment—more than what the law could require, which was merely an inner garment (cf. Exod 22:26–27). *Coat* and *shirt* reflect contemporary parallels to "cloak" and "tunic," though both of the latter looked more like long robes. Verse 41 continues the legal motif by referring to Roman conscription of private citizens to help carry military equipment for soldiers as they traveled.

Each of these commands requires Jesus' followers to act more generously than what the letter of the law demanded. "Going the extra mile" has rightly become a proverbial expression and captures the essence of all of Jesus' illustrations. Not only must disciples reject all behavior motivated only by a desire for retaliation, but they also must positively work for the good of those with whom they would otherwise be at odds. In v. 42 Jesus calls his followers to give to those who ask and not turn from those who would borrow. He presumes that the needs are genuine and commands us not to ignore them, but he does not specifically mandate how best we can help. As Augustine rightly noted, the text says "give to everyone that asks," not "give everything to him that asks" (*De Sermone Domine en Monte* 67). Compare Jesus' response to the request made of him in Luke 12:13–15. It is also crucial to note that "a willingness to forego one's personal rights, and to allow oneself to be insulted and imposed upon, is not incompatible with a firm stand for matters of principle and for the rights of others (cf. Paul's attitude in Acts 16:37; 22:25; 25:8–12)." Verses 39–42 thus comprise a "focal instance" of nonretaliation; specific, extreme commands attract our attention to a key ethical theme that must be variously applied as circumstances change.[227]

If the above are examples of how the Father and the Son see justice, retaliation, and retribution, it would clearly be injustice to torment someone in a pit of fire eternally, for a limited number of sins that was committed over a 70-80-year period.

There is only one person, who knows what happens after death, and it is God. He made it all too clear as to what happens to humans at death.

Ecclesiastes 3:19-20 Updated American Standard Version (UASV)

19 For the fate of the sons of men and the fate of beasts is the same. As one dies so dies the other; indeed, they all have the same breath and there is no advantage for man over beast, for all is vanity. **20** All go to the same place. All came from the dust and all return to the dust.

These verses have no mention of some eternal fiery torment. Humans simply return to the dust from which they came, no longer in existence, when they die. Some will receive a resurrection from the dead, other will simply remain dead forever.

If a person is to feel the torment of eternal hellfire, they have to be conscious. However, God inspired Solomon to write, "Yes, the living know they are going to die, but the dead know nothing. They have no further reward; they are completely forgotten." (Eccles 9:5) Based on this, it is impossible for those that have died, who "know nothing," to have knowledge of the anguishes of hellfire.

Dangerous Doctrine?

Some Christians would actually make the statement that 'the doctrine of hellfire is useful.' Why would they say that? They believe that it helps deter the Christian from sinning. Well, the same thing is believed about the death

---

[227] Craig Blomberg, *Matthew*, vol. 22, The New American Commentary (Nashville: Broadman & Holman Publishers, 1992), 113–114.

penalty for capital murder. Are not the United States prisons filled with death row inmates? In fact, the prison system is filled with all kinds of Christians, committing any number of different crimes. The truth is, the hellfire doctrine is actually harmful. If a person accepts that God tortures people for eternity, for sinning a mere 70-80 years, will they not view humans torturing humans as acceptable. Did not the Catholic Church torture Christians during the Inquisitions for simply disobeying the church? Yes, they burned them at the stake, stretched them on a rack,[228] until their bones broke, and beat them relentlessly.

If hellfire is so unreasonable logically, why do so many Christians, who claim to have the mind of Christ, accept such cruelty from their loving God? "Mind control (also known as brainwashing, coercive persuasion, thought control, or thought reform) is an indoctrination process that results in "an impairment of autonomy, an inability to think independently, and a disruption of beliefs and affiliations. In this context, brainwashing refers to the involuntary reeducation of basic beliefs and values"[229] The term has been applied to any tactic, psychological or otherwise, which can be seen as subverting an individual's sense of control over their own thinking, behavior, emotions or decision making."[230] Yes, these ones were raised in ultra-religious households, where they were taught the hellfire doctrine from childhood, up unto their adult years, so it is a deeply ingrain belief.

Keep in mind that after Adam sinned. Imperfect humans had and have had a natural inclination toward sin. It bears repeating again, Genesis 6:5 (AT) tells us just before the flood of Noah, that "the wickedness of man on earth was great, and the whole bent of his thinking was never anything but evil." After the flood, God said of man, "the bent of man's mind may be evil from his very youth." (Gen 8:21, AT) Jeremiah 10:23 tells us "that it is not in man who walks to direct his steps." Jeremiah 17:9 tells us that "The heart is

---

[228] The rack is a torture device consisting of a rectangular, usually wooden frame, slightly raised from the ground, with a roller at one or both ends. The victim's ankles are fastened to one roller and the wrists are chained to the other. As the interrogation progresses, a handle and ratchet attached to the top roller are used to very gradually stepwise increase the tension on the chains, inducing excruciating pain. By means of pulleys and levers this roller could be rotated on its own axis, thus straining the ropes until the sufferer's joints were dislocated and eventually separated. Additionally, if muscle fibers are stretched excessively, they lose their ability to contract, rendering them ineffective.

One gruesome aspect of being stretched too far on the rack is the loud popping noises made by snapping cartilage, ligaments or bones. One powerful method for putting pressure upon prisoners was to force them to watch someone else being subjected to the rack. Confining the prisoner on the rack enabled further tortures to be simultaneously applied, typically including burning the flanks with hot torches or candles or using pincers made with specially roughened grips to tear out the nails of the fingers and toes.-- http://en.wikipedia.org/wiki/Rack_(torture)

[229] Kowal, D. M. (2000). Brainwashing. In A. E. Kazdin (Ed.) , Encyclopedia of psychology, Vol. 1 (pp. 463-464). American Psychological Association.

[230] http://en.wikipedia.org/wiki/Brain_washing#cite_note-1

deceitful above all things, and desperately sick; who can understand it?" Yes, man naturally leans toward bad.

What is the Punishment for Sin?

If the hellfire doctrine does not exist, what is the punishment for sin? What is Adam's punishment for rejecting God, what is the rest of humanities punishment for rejecting the Gospel? What was Adam told would happen, if he sinned? He was told, "for in the day that you eat of it the tree of knowledge] you shall surely die." (Gen 2:17) What happened to Adam? God told him, "By the sweat of your face you shall eat bread, till you return to the ground, for out of it you were taken; for you are dust, and to dust you shall return." (Gen. 3:19) What did Paul say was the punishment for sin? "The wages of sin is death." (Rom. 6:23) Life was and is a gift from God. If we reject God, if we willfully, sin unrepentantly, the gift is taken away, and we die.

The same Christians who have been programmed to accept the contradiction of a loving God, who tortures humans forever, would actually ask, 'how is that just, because everyone dies?' It is true that we all die. Why? Paul tells us, "sin came into the world through one man [Adam], and death through sin, and so death spread to all men because all sinned." We are all sinners.

If we all are sinners, and we all die, what is the point in trying to live a Christlike life? Is it true justice, if the one who is attempting to live a virtuous life, should die, just as the wicked man dies? However, this is irrational thinking, and some things are being left out of the formula of justice. While both die, the righteous one will receive a resurrection, with the hope of eternal life. We see that Jesus 'gave his life as a ransom for many' (Matt. 20:28). We see that "all who are in the tombs will hear [the] voice [of Jesus] and come out, those who have done good to the resurrection of life, and those who have done evil to the resurrection of judgment." (John 5:28-29) We are told, "that there is going to be a resurrection, both of the righteous and the unrighteous." – Acts 24:15

Romans 5:18-21 Updated American Standard Version (UASV)

[18] So, then, as through one trespass there was condemnation to all men, so too through one act of righteousness there was justification of life to all men. [19] For as through the one man's disobedience the many were made sinners, so also through the obedience of the one the many will be made righteous. [20] The Law came in so that the transgression would increase; but where sin increased, grace abounded all the more, [21] so that, as sin reigned in

death, even so grace would reign through righteousness to eternal life through Jesus Christ our Lord.

Righteous Receive the Resurrection of Life

The wages of sin is death, and wages of willful unrepentant sin is eternal death (Heb. 6:4-6; 10:26-31), never being resurrected, as Paul said, "will suffer the punishment of eternal destruction." (2 Thess. 1:9) It is true that when we die, we no longer exist, except in the memory of God, as dead is dead. However, as we are seeing here, the righteous will receive a resurrection. Even those in the Old Testament had a hope for something better, as Job's words clearly demonstrate,

Job 14:13-15 Updated American Standard Version (UASV)

13 Oh that you would hide me in Sheol,
that you would conceal me until your wrath be past,
that you would appoint me a set time, and remember me!
14 If a man dies, will he live again?
All the days of my service I would wait,
till my relief should come.
15 You would call, and I would answer you;
you would long for the work of your hands.[231]

The righteous man Job believed that his remaining faithful to God, would result in God remember him after he had died, and one day, he would be resurrected. Jesus himself, speaking to a Jewish audience, confirmed the hope that the Israelites had been carrying for 2,000 years,

John 5:28-29 Updated American Standard Version (UASV)

28 Do not marvel at this, because an hour is coming when all who are in the memorial tombs will hear his voice 29 and come out, those who have done good things to a resurrection of life, and those who have practiced wicked things to the resurrection of judgment.

When Jesus returns, he will bring many angels, and wipe out the wicked. However, the righteous will not be destroyed, and the righteous prior to Jesus first coming back in the first century, will receive a resurrection. The unrighteous, which had never had the opportunity to know God, will also be resurrected for a chance to hear the Good News, and then, they will be judged on what they do during the millennial reign of Christ. Acts 24:15)

---

[231] This led him to consider the doctrine of resurrection and to wonder if it would be best for him to die and thus rest until the day when the dead rise (14:13–17). – David S. Dockery et al., *Holman Bible Handbook* (Nashville, TN: Holman Bible Publishers, 1992), 316.

Therefore, the punishment for sin is death, the punishment for those, who "keep on sinning deliberately after receiving the knowledge of the truth, there no longer remains a sacrifice for sins," i.e., eternal death. However, "there will be a resurrection of both the just and the unjust [i.e., those who never heard the Good News]." – Acts 24:15

Life on Earth under God's Kingdom

Isaiah 65:21-23 Updated American Standard Version (UASV)

21 They shall build houses and inhabit them;
   they shall plant vineyards and eat their fruit.
22 They shall not build and another inhabit;
   they shall not plant and another eat;
for like the days of a tree will the days of my people be,
   and the work of their hands my chosen ones will enjoy to the full.
23 They shall not labor in vain
   or bear children for calamity,
for they are the seed[232] made up of those blessed by Jehovah,,
   and their descendants with them.

On this, the Holman Old Testament Commentary says, "The injustices of life would disappear. Long life would be the rule for God's people, death at a hundred being like an infant's death that could only be explained as the death of a sinner. All of God's people would live to a ripe old age and enjoy the fruits of their life. The age of Messiah would clearly have dawned (cp. 11:6–9). No longer would people lose their property and crops to foreign invaders. Each of God's faithful people would enjoy the works of their hands. Labor would be rewarded in the field and in the birth place. Every newborn would escape the "horror of sudden disaster" (author's translation; NIV, misfortune). Curses would disappear. Every generation would be blessed by God."[233]

Revelation 21:3-4 Updated American Standard Version (UASV)

3 And I heard a loud voice from the throne, saying, "Behold, the tabernacle of God is among men, and he will dwell[234] among them, and they shall be his people,[235] and God himself will be among them,[236] 4 and he will wipe away every tear from their eyes, and death shall be no more, neither

---

[232] I.e., *offspring*
[233] Anders, Max; Butler, Trent (2002-04-01). Holman Old Testament Commentary - Isaiah (p. 374). B&H Publishing. Kindle Edition.
[234] Lit *he will tabernacle*
[235] Some mss *peoples*
[236] One early ms and be *their God*

shall there be mourning, nor crying, nor pain anymore, for the former things, have passed away."

"[God] will wipe away every tear from their eyes." (21:4) These are not tears of joy but rather tears that were the result of pain, suffering, old age, the loss of loved ones, and death. The Father will not only wipe away these tears of sorrow from our eyes but, he will remove them permanently forever, as he will have removed all that would ever lead to such tears, i.e., the removal of the *causes*.

"Death shall be no more." (21:4) Certainly, the enemy death has brought about more unwanted tears than anything else. After the thousand year reign of Christ, Satan will be released from the abyss for a while, succeeding to mislead many more. After that, those who have remained faithful will have the grip of death removed forever. The Father will remove the real cause of death; that is, the inherited sin from Adam. (Rom. 5:12) "The last enemy that will be abolished is death." (1 Cor. 15:26) Those who were faithful through the Great Tribulation, Armageddon, the Millennium, and the release of Satan for a little while will live for an eternity in a paradise earth, in human perfection, just as God had originally intended.

"Neither shall there be ... pain anymore." (21:4) The type of pain that is spoken of being removed here is the physical, mental, and emotional, which was brought on by the sin of Adam and the inherited imperfection that resulted after that. It will be no more.

This new life without tears, pain, mourning, crying, and death will certainly be a reality for those with a heavenly hope as they rule with Christ in heaven but also for those with an earthly hope, which is who is being spoken of here specifically. Notice that all of this was introduced with the words **"the tabernacle of God is among men."** (21:3) We know that men live here on earth. Moreover, the context is describing the renewed earth where **"death shall be no more."** This is referring the world where death had existed but will now be no more. Death has never existed in the spiritual heavens where the Father, the Son and the Holy Spirit, as well as the angels, live. However, for over six thousand years, death has existed here on the earth. Thus, the promises of Revelation 21:3-4 are meant specifically for those here on earth, which will be a restored or renewed earth.

The restored or renewed earth will be filled with people who fear God and sincerely love their neighbor. (Heb. 2:5; Lu 10:25-28.) The changes that take place as a result of God's heavenly Kingdom, namely, Jesus and his co-rulers, will be so weighty that the Bible speaks of "a new earth," i.e., a new faithful human society.

How is it that God "will dwell among them," that is among humankind after Armageddon? God would turn his attention to his people in the forthcoming renewed or restored earth, setting them free from sin and death. Then God will turn his attention to Satan the Devil, the god of this wicked world. The God of peace will abyss Satan for a thousand years, and then he will crush Satan by throwing him into the lake of fire. (2 Cor. 4:4; Rom. 16:20; Rev. 20:10, 14) After all of this, Jesus will hand the kingdom back over to the Father. (1 Cor. 15:28) After that, we do not know. However, we do know that more books will be opened during the millennium, where we will likely learn more.

The Divine Justice of Sheol and Hades

Genesis 1:27 tells us, "God created man in his own image, in the image of God he created him; male and female he created them." What does this verse mean? It means that man is born with a moral nature, which creates within him a conscience that reflects God's moral values. (Rom 2:14-15) It acts as a moral law within. Even in imperfection, we are born with a measure of that conscience, which can be developed toward good or bad. The Word of God develops a Christian conscience.

When we think of the pain and suffering in this world, it troubles our inner person to no end. When we hear of a young twelve-year-old girl, who is harassed to the point that she climbs a sixty-foot tower, to jump to her death, we can barely control our wrath. When we think of an older woman in her seventies, beat to death by a young punk, who steals her purse, we wish we could have five minutes alone with him. When we think of the starvation, the genocides by dictators, the natural disaster, and the like, we are emotionally sickened. Why are we emotionally sickened? Because were created in the image of God, and we possess his moral values.

Have we taken the time to ponder what we are claiming about the hellfire doctrine? We are saying that a person born,

(1) Imperfect

(2) With human weaknesses

(3) Who are mentally bent toward evil

(4) Who have a treacherous heart (inner person), and are unable to know it

(5) Who were born a sinner through no fault of their own

(6) Who have a natural (although contrary to what God intended) desire to do bad

(7) Who naturally lean toward evil

(8) Who have only sinned for 70-80-years

These ones will be tormented with fire for eternity. This is sickening and abhorrent. Some do not even want the United States government to torture known terrorists. They say that makes us like them, we should take the moral high ground. Yet, we are to accept that **eternal** torture inflicted by God is somehow acceptable. If a person kept breaking city laws like stealing, and he just would not change, could he be tortured. Could we strap him to a table and beat him hour after hour, day after day, week after week, year after year?

What happens is that we will eventually feel sorry for this person, especially if the punishment does not fit the crime. Would we give a person who stole some candy a hundred years in a maximum-security prison? What should we think of a person that has meted out such a punishment? Would any of us as a loving parent burn our child with a lighter, thinking that was just punishment. Of course we would not, but we expect far worse out of God. Is that not contrary to Scripture? Is that not contrary to our sense of justice, which in turn is contrary to the Creator, in whose image in which we were created? When we set aside our church tradition for a moment and truly ponder Scripture and reason, things become clearer.

Irrational Teaching

1 John 4:8 Updated American Standard Version (UASV)

[8] The one who does not love does not know God, because God is love.

Does this Scripture and the hundreds upon hundreds of other corresponding ones support God torturing someone, whose heart is treacherous, desires are toward evil, and natural leaning are toward sin, for a mere 80 years, forever. Bible scholars, pastors, and elders would have us think that this is divine justice. If this all is biblically true, this means that God planned or chose the world that would have a hellfire of torment, which would torture sinners for eternity. This does not sound like the God of the Bible, as far as this author is concerned. It would mean that God was responsible for torturing sinners for eternity.

God is the only person who knows what happens to us at death. He has revealed this to use through the Scriptures. God had warned Adam, if he ate of the tree of knowledge of good and bad, if you eat of it you will surely die. (Gen. 2:17) Wise King Solomon wrote,

Ecclesiastes 3:19-20 Updated American Standard Version (UASV)

[19] For the fate of the sons of men and the fate of beasts is the same. As one dies so dies the other; indeed, they all have the same breath and there is no advantage for man over beast, for all is vanity. [20] All go to the same place. All came from the dust and all return to the dust.

There is no mention of some eternal fiery torment. Think about this, God tells Adam, "of the tree of the knowledge of good and evil you shall not eat, for in the day that you eat of it you shall surely die." (Gen. 2:17) Why would God withhold the punishment of eternal torment from Adam and Eve? If hellfire were real, this would have been a very underhanded thing. Just think, he tells the people of the Old Testament that if you sin, "you shall surely die." Then, some 4,000 years later, he throws in, "oh, by the way, you will also burn in a fiery pit forever." Imagine that you broke a rule in school that you knew would get you detention. You arrive at detention after school, and the principal tells you, "Oh, by the way, we are going to beat you to death with a baseball bat."

Bad Bible Doctrine

The preaching of hellfire has been used as a scare tactic, which is a dreadful fear of God, not the biblical reverential fear of displeasing him. Psalm 111:10 says, "The fear of the Lord is the beginning of wisdom." We just saw God is love, why would it be prudent to fear him, and why would he want someone to fear him? Here is the answer from Norman L. Geisler,[237]

> **PROBLEM**: John affirms here that "perfect love casts out all fear." Yet we are told that the "fear of the Lord is the beginning of knowledge" (Prov. 1:7) and that we should "serve the Lord with fear" (Ps. 2:11). Indeed, Paul said, "knowing ... the terror Ifearl of the Lord, we persuade men" (2 Cor. 5:11).

> **SOLUTION**: Fear is being used in different senses. Fear in the good sense is a reverential trust in God. In the had sense it is a sense of recoiling torment in the face of God. While proper fear brings a healthy respect for God, unwholesome fear engenders an unhealthy sense that He is out to get us. Perfect love casts out this kind of "torment." When one properly understands that "God is love" (1 John 4:16), he can no longer fear Him in this unhealthy sense. For "he who fears has not been made perfect in love" (1 John 4:18). Nonetheless, at no time does proper love for God ever show disrespect for Him. Rather, it is perfectly compatible with a

---

[237] It should be noted that Dr. Norman L. Geisler does believe in the hellfire doctrine, and this author disagrees with him.

reverential awe for Him, which is what the Bible means by "fearing God" in the good sense (cf. 2 Cor. 7:1; 1 Peter 2:17).[238]

Again, religious leaders would be in denial to say that almost all scholars, pastors, and elders have not used hellfire, to scare people into becoming a disciple and keeping them. This is what the religious leaders do. When we go to the Bible belt part of the United States, do we find a lower crime or divorce rate? No, we do not. Another aspect to keep in mind, Christians that are fire and brimstone to the core, tend to be far more aggressive in their physical punishment of their children. Those who have a cruel God will tend to adopt that mindset with their children as well. The very heart and mind that God gave us are repelled by such a doctrine and the Bible itself says, when a person dies, "his breath departs, he returns to the earth; on that very day his plans perish." – Psalm 146:4.

What Is the Punishment for Sin?

Genesis 2:17 Updated American Standard Version (UASV)

[17] but from the tree of the knowledge of good and evil you shall not eat,[239] for in the day that you eat from it you shall surely die."[240]

Ezekiel 18:4 Updated American Standard Version (UASV)

[4] Look, all souls are mine; the soul of the father as well as the soul of the son is mine: the soul who sins will die.

Romans 6:23 Updated American Standard Version (UASV)

[23] For the wages of sin is death, but the free gift[241] of God is eternal life in Christ Jesus our Lord.

Romans 5:12 Updated American Standard Version (UASV)

[12] Therefore, just as sin came into the world through one man, and death through sin, and so death spread to all men because all sinned

The penalty of death can be avoided, if we walk with God until our death, or Jesus return, whichever comes first.

Romans 12:2 Updated American Standard Version (UASV)

---

[238] Thomas Howe; Norman L. Geisler. The Big Book of Bible Difficulties: Clear and Concise Answers from Genesis to Revelation (Kindle Locations 6287-6293). Kindle Edition.

[239] Lit *eat from it*

[240] Lit *dying you* [singular] *shall die.* Heb *moth tamuth*; the first reference to death in the Scriptures

[241] Lit *gracious gift*; Gr *kharisma*

[2] And do not be conformed to this world, but be transformed by the renewing of your mind, so that you may prove what the will of God is, that which is good and acceptable[242] and perfect.

Good for Doing Good

Job 14:13-15 Updated American Standard Version (UASV)

[13] Oh that you would hide me in Sheol,
that you would conceal me until your wrath be past,
that you would appoint me a set time, and remember me!
[14] If a man dies, will he live again?
All the days of my service I would wait,
till my relief should come.
[15] You would call, and I would answer you;
you would long for the work of your hands.

Yes, there is a resurrection hope,[243]

John 5:28-29 Updated American Standard Version (UASV)

[28] Do not marvel at this, because an hour is coming when all who are in the memorial tombs will hear his voice [29] and come out, those who have done good things to a resurrection of life, and those who have practiced wicked things to the resurrection of judgment.

The *College Press NIV Commentary* offers this thought, "In fact the time is coming when the dead will hear the voice of God and those who hear will live. Surely this implies a resurrection. Jesus expresses it stronger in verses 28f when he says that all in the graves will hear his voice, and they that hear will be raised to life. Two views of the resurrection jostle one another here: (1) as in the case of Lazarus (11:43) Jesus can summon the dead and give them physical life (2) the word of Jesus can give spiritual life to these who are dead in sin. Too much should not be made in the distinction of the two views because both are true and both are needed."[244]

---

[242] Or *well-pleasing*
[243] The Hope of a Resurrection – Where?
https://christianpublishinghouse.co/2016/10/15/the-hope-of-a-resurrection-where/
[244] Beauford H. Bryant and Mark S. Krause, *John*, The College Press NIV Commentary (Joplin, MO: College Press Pub. Co., 1998), Jn 5:28–29.

What Did Jesus Teach About Hades?

Mark 9:47-48 English Standard Version (ESV)	Mark 9:47-48 Good News Translation (GNT)
[47] And if your eye causes you to sin, tear it out. It is better for you to enter the kingdom of God with one eye than with two eyes to be thrown into hell, [48] 'where their worm does not die and the fire is not quenched.'	[47] And if your eye makes you lose your faith, take it out! It is better for you to enter the Kingdom of God with only one eye than to keep both eyes and be thrown into hell. [48] There 'the worms that eat them never die, and the fire that burns them is never put out.'

Mark 9:47-48 Updated American Standard Version (UASV)
[47] And if your eye makes you stumble, throw it out, it is better for you to enter the kingdom of God with one eye, than, having two eyes, to be cast into Gehenna,[245] [48] where their worm does not die and the fire is not quenched.

About one year later, Nisan 11th 33 C.E. on the Mount of Olives, Jesus spoke prophetically of a future time when he would say to the wicked,

Matthew 25:41, 46 English Standard Version (ESV)	Matthew 25:41, 46 New American Standard Bible (NASB)
[41] "Then he will say to those on his left, 'Depart from me, you cursed, into the eternal fire prepared for the devil and his angels. [46] And these will go away into eternal punishment, but the righteous into eternal life."	[41] "Then He will also say to those on His left, 'Depart from Me, accursed ones, into the eternal fire which has been prepared for the devil and his angels; [46] These will go away into eternal punishment, but the righteous into eternal life."

If we were to take Jesus' words in the above in isolation without looking at the Bible backgrounds or any of the original language words, it might seem like Jesus was teaching a hellfire doctrine of eternal torment. However, this would contradict other parts of Scripture that clearly teaches the punishment of eternal destruction." – 2 Thessalonians 1:9, ESV.

---

[245] *geenna* 12x pr. *the valley of Hinnom,* south of Jerusalem, once celebrated for the horrid worship of Moloch, and afterwards polluted with every species of filth, as well as the carcasses of animals, and dead bodies of malefactors; to consume which, in order to avert the pestilence which such a mass of corruption would occasion, constant fires were kept burning. – MCEDONTW

What did Jesus mean in the above text when he said people would be 'thrown into hell?' How are we to understand "the eternal fire" that Jesus warned us about, is it literal or symbolic? The original Greek word translated "hell" at Mark 9:47 is Geenna.

Gehenna Hebrew Ge' Hinnom, literally, valley of Hinnom appears 12 times in the Greek New Testament books, and many translators render it by the word "hell." Most translations have chosen poorly not to use a transliteration, Gehenna or Geenna, as opposed to the English hell, ASV, AT, RSV, ESV, LEB, HCSB, and NASB. There is little doubt that the New Testament writers and Jesus used "Gehenna" to speak of the place of final punishment. What was Gehenna?

According to the Holman Illustrated Bible Dictionary (p. 632), Gehenna or the Valley of Hinnom was "the valley south of Jerusalem now called the *Wadi er-Rababi* (Josh. 15:8; 18:16; 2 Chron. 33:6; Jer. 32:35) became the place of child sacrifice to foreign gods. The Jews later used the valley for the dumping of refuse, the dead bodies of animals, and executed criminals."[246] We would disagree with the other comments by the Holman Illustrated Dictionary, "The continuing fires in the valley (to consume the refuse and dead bodies) apparently led the people to transfer the name to the place where the wicked dead suffer." This just is not the case.

In the Old Testament, the Israelites did burn sons in the fires as part of a sacrifice to false gods, but not for the purpose of punishment or torture. By the time of the New Testament period, hundreds of years later, the only thing thrown in Gehenna was trash and the dead bodies of executed criminals. For what purpose were these thrown into Gehenna? It was used as an incinerator, a furnace for destroying things by burning them. Notice that any bodies thrown in Gehenna during the New Testament period were already dead. Thus, if anything, these people saw Gehenna as a place where they destroyed their trash and the bodies of dead criminals. Thus, if Jesus used this to illustrate as the place of the wicked, it would have represented destruction as the punishment.

The Valley of Slaughter

Jeremiah 7:30-34 Updated American Standard Version (UASV)

30 "For the sons of Judah have done evil in my sight, declares Jehovah. They have set their detestable things in the house that is called by my name, to defile it. 31 And they have built the high places of Topheth, which is in the

---

[246] Chad Brand, Charles Draper, et al., eds., "Gehenna," *Holman Illustrated Bible Dictionary* (Nashville, TN: Holman Bible Publishers, 2003), 631.

Valley of the Son of Hinnom, to burn their sons and their daughters in the fire, which I did not command, **nor did it come into my heart.**[247] 32 Therefore, behold, the days are coming, declares the Lord, when it will no more be called Topheth, or the Valley of the Son of Hinnom, but the Valley of Slaughter; for they will bury in Topheth, until there is no more place. 33 And the dead bodies of this people will be food for the birds of the air, and for the beasts of the earth, and none will frighten them away. 34 Then I will make to cease from the cities of Judah and from the streets of Jerusalem the voice of joy and the voice of gladness, the voice of the bridegroom and the voice of the bride; for the land will become a ruin.

This valley of Hinnom was on the outskirts of ancient Jerusalem. As we can see from the above text in Jeremiah, it was used for the practice of child sacrifice, a sickening and abhorrent practice that God condemned. God had said the idea of burning someone alive, 'did even come into his mind,' and he would execute such ones, not even torture these wicked ones. Therefore, God foretold that the Valley of Hinnom would become a place for the destruction of dead bodies, not to torture live victims.

Jesus reference to 'the worms that eat them never die, and the fire that burns them is never put out,' he was alluding to Isaiah 66:24. (See cross-reference NASB) Regarding "the corpses of the men Who have transgressed against [God]," Isaiah says that "their worm will not die And their fire will not be quenched." (NASB) Those listening to Jesus would have been very familiar with the book of Isaiah, knowing his reference was to the treatment of "the corpses of the men," who did not deserve to be buried.

Thus, it is all too clear that Jesus was using the Valley of Hinnom, or Gehenna, as a symbol of eternal destruction for those who would never receive a resurrection. He made this, even more, clear when he said, "fear [God] who is able to destroy both soul and body in hell [Gr Gehenna]." (Matt. 10:28, NASB) Therefore, Gehenna is a symbol of eternal death, not eternal torment in some eternal hellfire.

What about Jesus mention of "the eternal fire," is it literal or symbolic? (Matt 25:41) If we look at the whole verse, we can see that this eternal fire is "prepared for the devil and his angels." Is it possible for literal fire to burn spirit persons? Clearly, Jesus was using symbolism here, as we also consider the fact that the mention of "the sheep" and "the goats" mentioned in the same section of verses are not literal. The sheep and the goats are word pictures used to symbolize two groups of peoples. (Matt. 25:32-33) The

---

[247] I.e. *mind*

"eternal fire" that Jesus spoke of is used as a symbol for the burning up of the wicked in a figurative sense.

Well, some might ask, what about the wicked, who "will go away into eternal punishment"? First, eternal punishment does not automatically equate into eternal torment by eternal fire.

The basic meaning of the Greek word *kolasin* "akin to kolazoo,"[248] "means 'to cut short,' 'to lop,' 'to trim,' and figuratively a. 'to impede,' 'restrain,' and b. 'to punish,' and in the passive 'to suffer loss.'[249] The first part of the sentence is only in harmony with the second part of the sentence, if the eternal punishment is eternal death. The wicked receive eternal death and the righteous eternal life. We might at that Matthews Gospel was primarily for the Jewish Christians, and under the Mosaic Law, God would punish those who violated the law, saying they "shall be cut off [penalty of death] from Israel." (Ex 12:15; Lev 20:2-3) We need further to consider,

2 Thessalonians 1:8-9 Updated American Standard Version (UASV)

[8] in flaming fire, inflicting vengeance on those who do not know God and on those who do not obey the gospel of our Lord Jesus. [9] These ones will pay **the penalty of eternal destruction**, from before the Lord[250] and from the glory of his strength,

Notice that Paul says too that the punishment for the wicked is "eternal destruction." Many times, in talking with those that support the position of eternal torment in some hellfire, they will add a word to Matthew 25:46 in their paraphrase of the verse, 'conscious eternal punishment.' However, Jesus does not tell us what the eternal punishment is, just that it is a punishment and it is eternal. Therefore, those who support eternal conscious fiery torment will read the verse to mean just that, while those, who hold the position of eternal destruction, will take Matthew 25:46 to mean that. Considering that Jesus does not define what the eternal punishment is, this verse is not a proof text for either side of the argument.

Therefore, Jesus did not teach that God was going to torture the wicked in some eternal hellfire forever. Rather, Jesus said, "God so loved the world, that He gave His only begotten Son, that whoever believes in Him shall not perish, but have eternal life." (John 3:16, NASB) Implied in this verse is if we think we will receive eternal life, if we do not, we will not, which means we

---

[248] W. E. Vine, Merrill F. Unger, and William White Jr., Vine's Complete Expository Dictionary of Old and New Testament Words (Nashville, TN: T. Nelson, 1996), 498.

[249] Gerhard Kittel, Gerhard Friedrich, and Geoffrey William Bromiley, *Theological Dictionary of the New Testament* (Grand Rapids, MI: W.B. Eerdmans, 1985), 451.

[250] Lit *from before the face of the Lord*

will die. If Jesus meant that, the wicked received eternal life of another kind, suffering torment in a fiery hell, why not state so here. Rather, he says, if 'we do not believe, we will perish.' Let us look at verse 36, which informs us what the believer and the unbeliever will receive, "He who believes in the Son has eternal life; but he who does not obey the Son will not see life, but the wrath of God abides on him." If we refuse to accept Jesus, then we will not receive life. One has to be alive to receive eternal torment in some hellfire.

Short History of Hell as Eternal Torment

Greek Mythology (900 – 500 B.C.E.)

The *Encarta Encyclopedia* says, "**Hades**, in Greek mythology, god of the dead. He was the son of the Titans Cronus and Rhea and the brother of Zeus and Poseidon. When the three brothers divided up the universe after they had deposed their father, Cronus, Hades was awarded the underworld. There, with his queen, Persephone, whom he had abducted from the world above, he ruled the kingdom of the dead. Although he was a grim and pitiless god, unappeased by either prayer or sacrifice, he was not evil. In fact, he was known also as Pluto, lord of riches, because both crops and precious metals were believed to come from his kingdom below ground."

"The underworld itself was often called Hades. It was divided into two regions: Erebus, where the dead pass as soon as they die, and Tartarus, the deeper region, where the Titans had been imprisoned. It was a dim and unhappy place, inhabited by vague forms and shadows and guarded by Cerberus, the three-headed, dragon-tailed dog. Sinister rivers separated the underworld from the world above, and the aged boatman Charon ferried the souls of the dead across these waters. Somewhere in the darkness of the underworld Hades' palace was located. It was represented as a many-gated, dark and gloomy place, thronged with guests, and set in the midst of shadowy fields and an apparition-haunted landscape. In later legends the underworld is described as the place where the good are rewarded and the wicked punished."

"**Eurydice**, in Greek mythology, a beautiful nymph, and wife of Orpheus, the master musician. Shortly after their marriage Eurydice was bitten in the foot by a snake and died. Grief-stricken, Orpheus descended into the underworld to seek his wife. Accompanying his song with the strains of his lyre, he begged Hades, god of the dead, to relinquish Eurydice. His music so touched Hades that Orpheus was permitted to take his wife back with him on the condition that he would not turn around to look at her until they had reached the upper air. They had almost completed their ascent when Orpheus, overwhelmed by love and anxiety, looked back to see if Eurydice was following him. The promise broken, Eurydice vanished forever to the regions of the dead."

"**Tartarus**, in Greek mythology, the lowest region of the underworld. According to Hesiod and Virgil, Tartarus is as far below Hades as the earth is below the heavens and is closed in by iron gates. In some accounts Zeus, the father of the gods, after leading the gods to victory over the Titans, banished his father, Cronus, and the other Titans to Tartarus. The name Tartarus was later employed sometimes as a synonym for Hades, or the underworld in general, but more frequently for the place of damnation where the wicked were punished after death. Such legendary sinners as Ixion, king of the Lapiths, Sisyphus, king of Corinth, and Tantalus, a mortal son of Zeus, were placed in Tartarus."

Scandinavian Mythology (450 B.C.E. – 100 C.E.

The *Encarta Encyclopedia* says, "Many ancient mythological heroes, some of whom may have been derived from real persons, were believed to be descendants of the gods; among them were Sigurd the Dragon-slayer; Helgi Thrice-Born, Harald Wartooth, Hadding, Starkad, and the Valkyries. The Valkyries, a band of warrior-maidens that included Svava and Brunhild, served Odin as choosers of slain warriors, who were taken to reside in Valhalla. There the warriors would spend their days fighting and nights feasting until Ragnarok, the day of the final world battle, in which the old gods would perish and a new reign of peace and love would be instituted. Ordinary individuals were received after death by the goddess Hel in a cheerless underground world."

Zoroastrianism Mythology (650 - 330 B.C.E.

The *Encarta Encyclopedia* says, "**Zoroastrianism**, religion that arose from the teachings of the devotional poet Zoroaster, known as Zarathushtra to ancient Iranians, who is regarded as the faith's founding prophet. Scholars believe that Zoroaster lived sometime between 1750 and 1500 BC or 1400 and 1200 BC. The Zoroastrian scripture, called the Avesta, includes poems attributed to Zoroaster. The religion continues to be practiced today by Zoroastrian communities in India, Iran, the United States, Canada, and other countries."

"Zoroastrians believe that Ahura Mazda created humans as allies in the cosmic struggle against evil and that humanity will be resurrected and granted immortality once evil has been defeated. They further view the material world as a trap into which evil has been lured and in which evil will undergo defeat by divinities and humans working together. Zoroastrianism preaches that when someone dies his or her soul undergoes individual judgment based on actions while alive. If the soul's good deeds are greater than its evil deeds, it enters paradise. If the soul's evil deeds outweigh the good done while alive, it is cast into hell to await the day of universal judgment. In cases where a soul's good deeds equal its evil deeds, it is consigned to limbo."

"Close to the end of time a savior will resurrect the dead, Zoroastrianism claims. Ahura Mazda will descend to earth with the other good spirits. Each sinner, having already suffered in hell or limbo after death, will be purified. Thereafter, immortality will be granted to all humans. Ahura Mazda, the holy immortals, and other divine beings will annihilate the demons and force Angra Mainyu to scuttle back into hell, which will then be sealed."

"The Zoroastrian doctrine of heaven, hell, and limbo influenced other faiths. Islam absorbed not only the ideas of heaven, hell, and limbo, but also the scheme of individual judgment at a celestial bridge and the notion of final, universal judgment. Christianity further assimilated the Zoroastrian belief of the soul's afterlife and the appearance of a savior, resurrection, and eternal life at the end of the world. "[251]

Learning the Truth About Hell

Church leaders who teach that hell is is a place of some fiery torment where the wicked burn for eternity are supporting a gross distortion of God and his qualities. True enough, the Bible does say that God will destroy the wicked. (2 Thess. 1:6-9) Nevertheless, God's righteous indignation is not such, that it becomes unjust, out of balance with his other qualities.

God is not hateful, spiteful or bitter. He asks, "Do I have any pleasure in the death of the wicked?" (Eze. 18:23, NASB) Think it through, if God has no please in the death of the wick, how are we to believe he would find justice, joy, happiness, and delight in an eternity of horrific torture? God's outstanding quality is love. (1 John 4:8) He has even commanded us to love our enemies (Matt 5:44), i.e., be willing to share the gospel with them if their heart condition should change. This mindset seems completely out of place with the idea of eternal torment.

Being Released from Hell?

Much confusion and misunderstanding has been caused through some Bible translations like the King James Version, which renders all of our original language words as hell: *Sheol, Hades, Gehenna,* and *Tartarus.* If we have a correct understanding of Gehenna and Hades, we will discover a truth that we never knew before. *Gehenna* is pictorial of a place where the dead go, who receive total destruction, with no hope of a resurrection, as *Gehenna* was an

---

[251] Microsoft ® Encarta ® 2006. © 1993-2005 Microsoft Corporation. All rights reserved.

incinerator. *Hades*, on the other hand, is the grave, where there is the hope of a future resurrection.

After Jesus died and was resurrected, the apostle Peter stated the following about Jesus,

Acts 2:27 Updated American Standard Version (UASV)

[27] because you will not abandon my soul in Hades **[hell KJV]**, or let your Holy One see corruption.

Acts 2:31-32 Updated American Standard Version (UASV)

[31] he foresaw and spoke about the resurrection of the Christ, that he was not abandoned to Hades **[hell KJV]**, nor did his flesh see corruption. [32] This Jesus God raised up, and of that we all are witnesses.

Peter was quoting Psalm 16:10 in verse 31 of Acts 2, where he clearly stated Jesus was resurrected from hades,

Psalm 16:10 Updated American Standard Version (UASV)

[10] For you will not abandon my soul to Sheol **[hell KJV]**, or let your holy one see corruption.[252]

As we can see the transliteration of original language word, in Psalm is *Sheol* and in Acts, it is *Hades*, which is rendered by just one word in the King James Version. The King James Version renders *Sheol* as "hell," "the grave," and "the pit;" *Hades* is therein rendered both "hell" and "grave;" *Gehenna* is also translated "hell;" and *Tartarus* is rendered as "hell." When Jesus was in Hades for three days, he was not in some fiery place of torment. *Hades* [hell KJV] was the grave from which Jesus received a resurrection. Moreover, Jesus is not the only person who will receive a resurrection from Hades [hell KJV].

In connection with the resurrection, the Bible says, "Death and Hades **[hell KJV]** gave up the dead who were in them." (Rev. 20:13, 14, ESV) Here we see God emptying Hades, i.e., hell, which will mean that those who are worthy will be restored to life in a resurrection. (John 5:28-29; Acts 24:15) This is the great hope that should be in every Christian heart and mind, seeing those that we loved return from Hades [hell, KJV], namely, the grave! The God of infinite love will carry this out.

The Wicked Will Be No More

Psalm 37:10 Updated American Standard Version (UASV)

---

[252] Or, *the pit*

[10] Just a little while longer and the wicked one will be no more;
And you will look carefully for his place and he will not be there.

As we have seen through this publication, the punishment for those who reject Jesus Christ is total destruction rather than everlasting torment. This directly related to the soul [Heb. *nephesh*, Gr *psyche*] is the person ("man became a living soul," Gen 2:7, ASV), who has lost everlasting life, and the only way to have everlasting life restored is by way of our accepting the sovereignty of God. The doctrinal position of annihilationism is the complete destruction of the soul, i.e., the wicked person, which leaves the righteous with everlasting life.

Interpretation of Scripture

Those investigating the Scriptures must ask themselves, 'why would God use words like "destroy, destruction, perish, death" to mean something other than their plain meaning? This seems to fly in the face of the idea that the soul goes to some place of eternal torment, but rather are terminated by their destruction.

Psalm 1:6	... the way of the wicked will *perish*
Psalm 37:20	But the wicked will *perish*... the enemies of the Lord will be like the glory of the pastures, They vanish—like smoke they vanish away.
Psalm 92:7	evildoers flourish, ... are doomed to *destruction forever*
Matthew 10:28b	Rather fear him who can *destroy* both soul and body in hell.
John 3:16	... whoever believes in him should not perish (Gr destroyed) but have eternal life. ...
John 3:36	whoever does not obey the Son *shall not see life*, but the wrath of God remains on him.
Rom. 6:23	For the wages of sin is *death* ...,
Phil. 3:19	whose end is "destruction" ...

146

2 Thess. 1:9	These will pay the penalty of eternal *destruction* ...
Hebrews 10:39	But we are not of those who shrink back and are *destroyed*, but of those who have faith and preserve their souls.
James 4:12a	There is only one lawgiver and judge, he who is able to save and to *destroy*.
Rev. 20:14	This is the second death...

There is little doubt that the most difficult thing any human has to suffer through is death. However, for the wicked, who have rejected the sovereignty of God that is the extent of their pain and suffering, knowing that live is no more. The wages of sin is death, not eternal existence.

Hebrews 10:26-27 Updated American Standard Version (UASV)

26 For if we go on sinning deliberately after receiving the accurate knowledge[253] of the truth, there no longer remains a sacrifice for sins, 27 but a fearful expectation of judgment, and **a fury of fire that will consume the adversaries.**

The apostle Paul speaks of a figurative "fury of fire that will *consume* the adversaries." The *Greek-English Lexicon of the New Testament* says, "(a figurative extension of meaning of ἐσθίω 'to eat,' 23.1) to destroy, with the implication of doing away with all traces of an object – 'to destroy, to consume.'"[254]

2 Peter 3:7 Updated American Standard Version (UASV)

7 But by the same word the heavens and earth that now exist are stored up for fire, being kept until the day of judgment and **destruction of ungodly men.**

Peter tells us that the *ungodly will be destroyed.* The *Greek-English Lexicon of the New Testament* says, "to destroy or to cause the destruction of persons, objects, or institutions—'to ruin, to destroy, destruction.'"[255]

---

[253] *Epignosis* is a strengthened or intensified form of *gnosis* (*epi*, meaning "additional"), meaning, "true," "real," "full," "complete" or "accurate," depending upon the context. Paul and Peter alone use *epignosis*.

[254] Johannes P. Louw and Eugene Albert Nida, *Greek-English Lexicon of the New Testament: Based on Semantic Domains* (New York: United Bible Societies, 1996), 232.

[255] IBID, 231.

Some may wonder, though, about 2 Peter 3:7a. It says, "The heavens and earth that now exist are stored up for fire." Does this not support that the earth "shall be burned up"[256] (2 Pet. 3:10) as the KJV says. Does this not show that the earth will be burned up? See the footnote below, the reading *heurethesetai*, "be disclosed, "be exposed," or "be discovered" is the preferred reading. *Katakaesetai* (KJV), "be burned up" is the inferior reading and is not preferred. Moreover, the Bible sometimes uses the terms "heavens," "earth," and "fire" figuratively, as symbols. For example, at Genesis 11:1, it reads, "Now the whole earth had one language and the same words." Here we see Moses uses the word "earth" in a figurative sense, to mean all of human society.

Romans 2:7 Updated American Standard Version (UASV)

[7] to those who, by perseverance in good work, seek glory and honor and immortality, eternal life;

Paul tells us here that it is only the righteous, who will receive eternal life. Certainly, to suffer eternal torment is eternal life, which would contradict this verse.

Genesis 3:19 Updated American Standard Version (UASV)

[19] By the sweat of your face
   you shall eat bread,
till you return to the ground,
   for out of it you were taken;
for you are dust,
   and to dust you shall return."

God had made Adam from the dust of the ground. (Gen. 2:7) Adam had not been in existence prior to God creating him. Therefore, when God said that Adam would return to the dust, he meant that Adam was going to return to that nonexistent state. In other words, Adam would be as lifeless as the dust from which he had come.

Psalm 146:4 Updated American Standard Version (UASV)

[4] His spirit goes out, he returns to the earth;
   In that very day his thoughts perish.

Are we to understand that there is some spiritual being within us, which then departs from us at death? No, this is not the understanding, as the

---

[256]   The   preferred   is   "be   exposed"   or   "be   disclosed,"
(ℵ B K P 424ᶜ 1175 1739ᵗˣᵗ 1852 syrᵖʰ·ʰᵐᵍ arm Origen; while the less preferred reading is "be burned up," A 048 049 056 0142 33 614 *Byz Lect* syrʰ copᵇᵒ eth *al*

Psalmist next words were, "In that day have his thoughts perished," ("all his thinking ends," *NEB*). How, then, are we to understand this verse?

In the Hebrew Scriptures, we have *ruach*, and in the Greek New Testament, we have *pneuma*, both with the basic meaning "breath." This is why other translations read, "His breath goes forth."

Psalm 146:4 (ESV)	Psalm 146:4 (LEB)	Psalm 146:4 (HCSB)
[4] When his **breath departs**, he returns to the earth; on that very day his plans perish.	[4] His **breath departs**; he returns to his plot; on that day his plans perish.	[4] When his **breath leaves** him, he returns to the ground; on that day his plans die.

We will notice this further clarified when Moses informs us of what took place at the flood. However, we look at the literal translations first, followed by other literal translations that choose to define the use of the term "spirit." Note how we will use a footnote in the literal, and the others that chose to define.

Genesis 7:22 (NASB)	Genesis 7:22 ASV)	Genesis 7:22 (YLT)
[22] of all that was on the dry land, all in whose nostrils was the breath of the spirit of life **[breath of life]**, died.	[22] all in whose nostrils was the breath of the spirit of life **[breath of life]**, of all that was on the dry land, died.	[22] all in whose nostrils [is] breath of a living spirit **[breath of life]** -- of all that [is] in the dry land -- have died.

Other literal and semi-literal translations,

Genesis 7:22 (ESV)	Genesis 7:22 (LEB)	Genesis 7:22 (NRSV)
[22] Everything on the dry land in whose nostrils was the breath of life **["a breath of spirit of life"]** died.	[22] Everything in whose nostrils *was the breath of life* **["a breath of spirit of life"]**, among all that *was* on dry land, died.	[22] everything on dry land in whose nostrils was the breath of life **["a breath of spirit of life"]** died.

149

Therefore, *"ruach"* and "pneuma," i.e., "spirit" can refer to the breath of life that is active within both human and animal creatures. Then how do we explain Ecclesiastes 12:7?

Ecclesiastes 12:7 Updated American Standard Version (UASV)

⁷ and the dust returns to the earth as it was, and the spirit returns to God who gave it.

Are we to understand that a spiritual being within us, leaves us at death, and returns to God? No. We just learned that the "spirit" is the "breath of life," which sustains human and animal life. Once we lose our "breath of life," and are dead, the only hope of having it restored comes from God. Therefore, "the spirit returns to God," in that our only hope for living again, but this time for eternally, comes from God. It is only God, who can restore the "breath of life," which allows us to live again. Keep in mind too, this person was never in heaven with God, so the idea of him as a spirit person returning to God is not what is meant. How can he return to God, if he was never in heaven with God to begin with? Again, it is the "breath of life," which enables the person to live that returns to God, not literally, but in the sense of his having the power to restore it.

Ecclesiastes 12:7 (LEB)	Ecclesiastes 12:7 (NRSV)
⁷ And the dust returns to the earth as it was, and the breath returns to God who gave it.	⁷ and the dust returns to the earth as it was, and the breath returns to God who gave it.

All conservative Christians would point to the Bible as the final authority on all doctrine. This is true of our understanding of the *soul* as well. In the Hebrew Old Testament, the Hebrew word *nephesh* (translated "soul" in the UASV) is found 754 times, first in Genesis 1:20. In the Greek New Testament, the Greek word *psuche* (translated "soul" in the UASV) is found by itself 102 times, first in Matthew 2:20. In each case, a literal translation, looking to give its readers what God had said, should render this Hebrew and Greek word "soul," with the interpretive rendering in the footnote. By doing this, the reader of the Bible will be able to see how the word "soul" is used within the whole of the inspired, inerrant Word of God.

Can the Soul Die?

When we die, what happens to the soul? If you recall from above that the "soul" is the person, the being, the creature, i.e., us, and the **life** that we have. If you recall from above, the **Human soul** = body **[dust of the** ground] + active life force ("spirit") [Hebrew, *ruach*] within the trillions of human cells which make up the human body + breath of life [Hebrew, *neshamah*] that sustains the life force from God. In other words, the "soul" is we as a whole, everything that we are, so the soul or we humans can die. Let us look at a few verses, which make that all too clear.

Ecclesiastes 3:19-20 Updated American Standard Version (UASV)

[19] For the fate of the sons of men **[humans or people]** and the fate of beasts is the same. As one dies so dies the other; indeed, they all have the same breath and there is no advantage for man over beast, for all is vanity. [20] All go to the same place. All came from the dust and all return to the dust.

In other words, when we breathe our last breath, our cells begin to die. Death is the ending of all vital functions or processes in an organism or cell. When our heart stops beating, our blood is no longer circulating, carrying nourishment and oxygen (by breathing) to the trillions of cells in our body; we are what are termed, clinically dead. However, somatic death has yet to occur, meaning we can be revived, after many minutes of being clinically dead, if the heart and lungs can be restarted again, which gives the cells the oxygen they need.

After about three minutes of clinical death, the brain cells begin to die, meaning the chances of reviving the person is less likely as each second passes. We know that it is vital that the breathing and blood flow be maintained for the life force (*ruach chaiyim*) in the cells. Nevertheless, it is not the lack of breathing or the failure of the heart beating alone, but rather the active life force **("spirit") [Hebrew, ruach]** within the trillions of human cells which make up the human body + breath of life [Hebrew, *neshamah*] that sustains the life force from God.

Ps.104:29 (ESV)	Ps. 146:4 (ESV)	Eccl. 8:8 (ESV)
[29] When you hide your face, they are dismayed; when you take away their breath, they die and return to their dust.	[4] When his breath departs, he returns to the earth; on that very day his plans perish.	[8] No man has power to retain the spirit, or power over the day of death. There is no discharge from war, nor will wickedness deliver those who are given to it.

Again, …

Ezekiel 18:4 (ESV)	Leviticus 21:1 (ASV)	Numbers 6:6 (ASV)
4 Behold, all souls are mine; the soul of the father as well as the soul of the son is mine: the soul who sins shall die.	21 And Jehovah said to Moses, Speak to the priests, the sons of Aaron, and say to them, There shall none defile himself for the dead [Or "for a soul."] among his people;	6 All the days that he separates himself unto Jehovah he shall not come near to a dead body [Or "soul."].

Again, the death of a "soul" means the death of a person ...

1 Kings 19:4 (ASV)	Jonah 4:8 (ASV)	Mark 3:4 (ASV)
4 But he himself went a day's journey into the wilderness, and came and sat down under a juniper-tree: and he requested for himself that he [Or "his soul.]"might die, and said, It is enough; now, O Jehovah, take away my life [soul]; for I am not better than my fathers.	8 And it came to pass, when the sun arose, that God prepared a sultry east wind; and the sun beat upon the head of Jonah, that he fainted, and requested for himself that he might die [Or "that his soul might die."], and said, It is better for me to die than to live.	4 And he said to them, Is it lawful on the sabbath day to do good, or to do harm? to save a life [Or "soul."], or to kill? But they held their peace.

As you can see from the above texts, a "soul," or person can die. However, how are we to understand those texts that say the "soul" went out of a person, or came back into a person?

Soul Departing and Soul Coming into a Person

Genesis 35:18 Updated American Standard Version (UASV)

18 And as her soul was departing (for she was dying), she called his name Ben-oni; but his father called him Benjamin.

Are we to understand from this that Rachel had some inner being, a soul, which departed from her at death? No. We will recall from the texts from above that the term "soul" can also be used in reference to the life one has. Thus, this is a reference to her life that she had leaving her. Note the *Lexham English Bible*, "And it happened *that* when **her <u>life</u> was departing** (for she was dying), she called his name Ben-Oni. But his father called him Benjamin." (Bold and underline is mine) Therefore, it was her "life" that she had, which departed from her, not some inner being. When we take the time to ponder these things, it becomes all the more clear.

1 Kings 17:22 American Standard Version (ASV)

²² And Jehovah listened to the voice of Elijah; and the soul of the child came into him again, and he revived.

1 Kings 17:22 Updated American Standard Version (UASV)

²² And Jehovah listened to the voice of Elijah. And the soul of the child came into him again, and he revived.

Here again, the word "soul" is the "life" that someone has. The *New American Standard Bible* reads, "The **life** of the child returned to him and he revived." The *Lexham English Bible* reads, "The **life** of the child returned within him, and he lived." The *Holman Christian Standard Bible* reads, "The boy's **life** returned to him, and he lived." (Bold is mine)

John 11:11 (ESV)	1 Kings 2:10 (ESV)
¹¹ After saying these things, he said to them, "Our friend Lazarus has fallen asleep, but I go to awaken him."	¹⁰ Then David slept with his fathers and was buried in the city of David.

Notice that Lazarus' death is equated with being asleep in death, while King David is referred to as sleeping in death. This gives the reader a hope, as just as easily as you and I can awaken a person from sleep, Jesus is going to awaken people from death, a death like sleep. We are going to look at these verses a little differently that we have with the others. We will pause for a moment to see how a literal translation is best (which has already been demonstrated), with an interpretation in a footnote. Moreover, it is important that we read those footnotes. Otherwise, we can come to the wrong conclusions.

GLOSSARY of Bible Terms

Dead. A composition, lyrical or musical, expressing deep sorrow, such as the grief expressed because of the death of a friend or a loved one; a lamentation. – 2Sa 1:17; Ps 7:Sup.

Eternal. The Hebrew word *ôlām* 439x, according to its context, carries the thought of hidden time, long, everlasting, forever, eternity; from of old, ancient, lasting, for a duration, and times indefinite. The Greek word *aion* '121 x, according to context, denotes a period of time that is indefinite, eternity, age, the present age, forever, forever and ever, and time indefinite.

Gehenna. Hebrew Ge' Hinnom, literally, valley of Hinnom appears 12 times in the Greek New Testament books, and many translators render it by the word "hell." Most translations have chosen poorly not to use a transliteration, Gehenna or Geenna, as opposed to the English hell, ASV, AT, RSV, ESV, LEB, HCSB, and NASB. There is little doubt that the New Testament writers and Jesus used "Gehenna" to speak of the place of final punishment. What was Gehenna?

According to the *Holman Illustrated Bible Dictionary* (p. 632), Gehenna or the Valley of Hinnom was "the valley south of Jerusalem now called the Wadi er-Rababi (Josh. 15:8; 18:16; 2 Chron. 33:6; Jer. 32:35) became the place of child sacrifice to foreign gods. The Jews later used the valley for the dumping of refuse, the dead bodies of animals, and executed criminals."[257] We would disagree with the other comments by the Holman Illustrated Dictionary, "The continuing fires in the valley (to consume the refuse and dead bodies) apparently led the people to transfer the name to the place where the wicked dead suffer." This just is not the case.

In the Old Testament, the Israelites did burn sons in the fires as part of a sacrifice to false gods, but not for the purpose of punishment, or torture. By the time of the New Testament period, hundreds of years later, the only thing thrown in Gehenna was trash and the dead bodies of executed criminals. For what purpose were these thrown into Gehenna? It was used as an incinerator, a furnace for destroying things by burning them. Notice that any bodies thrown in Gehenna during the New Testament period were already dead. Thus, if anything, these people saw Gehenna as a place where they destroyed their trash and the bodies of dead criminals. Thus, if Jesus used this to illustrate the place of the wicked, it would have represented destruction as the punishment.

---

[257] http://biblia.com/books/hlmnillbbldict/Page.p_632

Grave. When lowercased, referring to an individual grave; when capitalized, the common grave of mankind, equivalent to the Hebrew "Sheol" and the Greek "Hades." It is described in the Bible as a symbolic place or condition wherein all activity and consciousness cease.—Ge 47:30; Ec 9:10; Ac 2:31.

Hades. Everyone knows that Hades was "the underground abode of the dead in Greek mythology."[258] However, as far as early Christianity, the Greek translation of the Old Testament, the Septuagint, uses the word Hades 73 times, employing it 60 times to translate the Hebrew word Sheol. Luke at Acts 2:27 write, "For you will not abandon my soul to Hades, or let your Holy One see corruption." Luke was quoting Psalm 16:10, which reads, "For you will not abandon my soul to Sheol, or let your holy one see corruption." Notice that Luke used Hades in place of Sheol. Therefore, Hades is the Greek equivalent of Sheol, as far as Christians and the Greek New Testament is concerned. In other words, Hades is also the abode of the dead in early Christian thought. Some translations choose to use a transliteration, Hades, as opposed to the English hell, ASV, AT, RSV, ESV, LEB, HCSB, and NASB.

Hell. Without being bogged down in doctrinal issues, let us just deal with the facts. "Hell" is the English translation for the Hebrew word Sheol and the Greek word Hades. Therefore, we need not ask, what Hell is. However, what did the word mean when it was first placed in English translations? Webster's Eleventh New International Dictionary, under "Hell" says: [Middle English, from Old English; akin to Old English helan to conceal, Old High German helan, Latin celare, Greek kalyptein] before 12th century"[259] The word "hell" meant to 'cover' over or 'conceal,' so it would have meant a place 'covered' or 'concealed,' such as a grave.

Lake of fire. A symbolic place that "burns with fire and sulfur," also described as "the second death." Unrepentant sinners, the Devil, and even death and the Grave (or, Hades) are thrown into it. The inclusion of a spirit creature and also of death and Hades, all of which cannot be affected by fire, indicates that this lake is a symbol, not of everlasting torment, but of everlasting destruction. – Rev. 19:20; 20:14, 15; 21:8.

Resurrection. The Greek word *anastasis* 42x, depending on the context means raising up; standing up, resurrection. – Ac 24:15; Php 3:11; Re 20:5-6; John 5:28-29; 11:25.

---

[258] http://biblia.com/books/mwdict11/word/hades
[259] http://biblia.com/books/mwdict11/word/hell

155

Sheol. Webster's Dictionary, "[Hebrew *Shĕ'ōl*] 1597: the abode of the dead in early Hebrew thought"[260] Collier's Encyclopedia (1986, Vol. 12, p. 28) says: "Since Sheol in Old Testament times referred simply to the abode of the dead and suggested no moral distinctions, the word 'hell,' as understood today, is not a happy translation." Some translations choose to use a transliteration, Sheol, as opposed to the English hell, AT, RSV, ESV, LEB, HCSB, and NASB. – Gen. 37:35; Ps 16:10; Ac 2:31.

---

[260] http://biblia.com/books/mwdict11/word/sheol

CHAPTER 8 Examining Nephesh and Psyche (Soul)

Death is the end of all functions of life, namely, the opposite of life. (Deut. 30:15, 19) Within Scripture, the same Hebrew words of the Old Testament and Greek words of the New Testament are used with humans, animals, and plants. (Eccles. 3:19; 9:5; John 12:24; Jude 12; Rev. 16:3) However, as we have already learned in the above, the Bible shows the essential purpose of the blood in preserving life, stating, "The soul [life] of the flesh is in the blood." (Lev. 17:11, 14; Gen. 4:8-11; 9:3, 4) The Bible says,

Genesis 7:21-24 Updated American Standard Version (UASV)

21 And every living thing that moved on the earth perished, the birds, and the domesticated animals, and the wild animals, and everything that swarmed on the earth, and all mankind; 22 everything in whose nostrils was the breath of the spirit of life among all that was on dry land, died. 23 And he blotted out every living thing that was upon the face of the land, from man to animals to creeping things and to birds of the sky, and they were blotted out from the earth; and only Noah was left, together with those that were with him in the ark. 24 The waters prevailed on the earth one hundred and fifty days.

Notice that the Bible says that both humans and animals died, i.e., perished. Literally, that means 'breathing out' the breath of life (Heb., *nishmath' chaiyim'*). (Gen. 7:21, 22; see Gen. 2:7.) Moreover, the Bible shows when both human and animals suffer somatic death (Death of the entire body), where there is a loss of "a breath of spirit of life," i.e., the "animating force; spirit." (Heb., *ruach chaiyim'*)—Gen 6:17; 7:15, 22; Eccles. 3:19

What is death?

Under this heading, we will repeat what was penned earlier, as repetition for emphasis. It is recommended that you read these few Scriptures and paragraphs again. When we die, what happens to the soul? If you recall from above that the "soul" is the person, the being, the creature, i.e., us, and the **life** that we have. If you recall from above, the **Human soul =** body **[dust of the ground]** + active life force **("spirit")** **[Hebrew, *ruach*]** within the trillions of human cells which make up the human body **+** breath of life [Hebrew, *neshamah*] that sustains the life force from God. In other words, the "soul" is we as a whole, everything that we are, so the soul or we humans can die. Let us look at a few verses, which make that all too clear.

Ecclesiastes 3:19-20 Updated American Standard Version (UASV)

[19] For the fate of the sons of men **[humans or people]** and the fate of beasts is the same. As one dies so dies the other; indeed, they all have the same breath and there is no advantage for man over beast, for all is vanity. [20] All go to the same place. All came from the dust and all return to the dust.

In other words, when we breathe our last breath, our cells begin to die. Death is the ending of all vital functions or processes in an organism or cell. When our heart stops beating, our blood is no longer circulating, carrying nourishment and oxygen (by breathing) to the trillions of cells in our body; we are what are termed, clinically dead. However, somatic death has yet to occur, meaning we can be revived, after many minutes of being clinically dead, if the heart and lungs can be restarted again, which gives the cells the oxygen they need.

After about three minutes of clinical death, the brain cells begin to die, meaning the chances of reviving the person is less likely as each second passes. We know that it is vital that the breathing and blood flow be maintained for the life force (*ruach chaiyim*) in the cells. Nevertheless, it is not the lack of breathing or the failure of the heart beating alone, but rather the active life force **("spirit") [Hebrew, ruach]** within the trillions of human cells which make up the human body + breath of life [Hebrew, *neshamah*] that sustains the life force from God.

Psalm 104:29 (ESV)	Psalm 146:4 (ESV)	Ecclesiastes 8:8 (ESV)
[29] When you hide your face, they are dismayed; when you take away their breath, they die and return to their dust.	[4] When his breath departs, he returns to the earth; on that very day his plans perish	[8] No man has power to retain the spirit, or power over the day of death. There is no discharge from war, nor will wickedness deliver those who are given to it.

Again, …

Ezekiel 18:4 (ESV)	Leviticus 21:1 (ASV)	Numbers 6:6 (ASV)
4 Behold, all souls are mine; the soul of the father as well as the soul of the son is mine: the soul who sins shall die.	21 And Jehovah said to Moses, Speak to the priests, the sons of Aaron, and say to them, There shall none defile himself for the dead [Or "for a soul."] among his people;	6 All the days that he separates himself unto Jehovah he shall not come near to a dead body [Or "soul."].

Again, the death of a "soul" means the death of a person …

1 Kings 19:4 (ASV)	Jonah 4:8 (ASV)	Mark 3:4 (ASV)
4 But he himself went a day's journey into the wilderness, and came and sat down under a juniper-tree: and he requested for himself that he [Or "his soul.] "might die, and said, It is enough; now, O Jehovah, take away my life [soul]; for I am not better than my fathers.	8 And it came to pass, when the sun arose, that God prepared a sultry east wind; and the sun beat upon the head of Jonah, that he fainted, and requested for himself that he might die [Or "that his soul might die."], and said, It is better for me to die than to live.	4 And he said to them, Is it lawful on the sabbath day to do good, or to do harm? to save a life [Or "soul."], or to kill? But they held their peace.

As you can see from the above texts, a "soul," or person can die, and the difference between clinical death and somatic death.

What Causes Human Death?

Genesis 2:16-17 Updated American Standard Version (ASV)

16 And Jehovah God commanded the man, saying, "From every tree of the garden you may freely eat, 17 but from the tree of the knowledge of good

and evil you shall not eat,[261] for in the day that you eat from it you shall surely die."[262]

Here we have the first mention of dying within Scripture. It would seem that the death of animals was already the case, as they were not designed to live forever. Thus, when God mentioned the sentence of death for disobeying, Adam knew full well what death was, as he likely had seen many animals die. When Adam disobeyed, he actually rebelled against the sovereignty of God, and this resulted in his death (Gen. 3:19; Jam. 1:14-15) From the moment that Adam ate, his sinful rebellion and its consequences, i.e., death, spread to all of his descendants.

Romans 5:12 (UASV)	Romans 6:23 (UASV)
[12] Therefore, just as through one man sin entered into the world, and death through sin, and so death spread to all men,[263] because all sinned—.	[23] For the wages of sin is death, but the free gift[264] of God is eternal life in Christ Jesus our Lord.

Some texts are often used to support the idea that physical death was all a part of God's plan; it was an eventuality for humans. One example would be Psalm 90:10, saying, "As for the days of our life, they contain seventy years, or if due to strength, eighty years" Another would be Hebrews 9:27, where Paul says, "inasmuch as it is appointed (Lit laid up) for men to die once and after this *comes* judgment ..."

Was physical death all a part of God's plan for Adam and Eve, since Hebrews 9:27 says, "inasmuch as it is appointed for men to die once and after this comes judgment"?

No, Hebrews 9:27 is not a reference to Adam and Eve, who were created by God so,

(1)   that Adam would procreate with Eve and fill the earth with perfect humans that would live forever,

(2)   that perfect Adam and Eve and their descendants would cultivate the Garden of Eden until we would have had a paradise earth, and

(3)   that perfect humanity would care for the animals.

---

[261] Lit *eat from it*
[262] Lit., *dying you* [singular] *shall die.* Heb., moth tamuth; the first reference to death in the Scriptures
[263] The Greek word *anthropoi* refers here to both men and women; also twice in verse 18
[264] Lit., "gracious gift." Gr., *kharisma*

Are we to believe that Satan could actually thwart God's intended purpose? Hardly! If Adam and Eve had chosen to obey God, which was possible with their free will, they were looking at being able to live as perfect humans forever. (Genesis 2:15-17) The context of Hebrews 9:27 is applicable to ancient Israel's high priest. On Atonement Day, the high priest foreshadowed Jesus Christ. – Hebrews 4:14-15.

Hebrews chapters 8 and 9 give the reader many details of the Mosaic Law that "serve as a copy and shadow of the heavenly things." (Heb. 8:5) This is especially true of the sacrificial process on the yearly Day of Atonement. It was on this one day each year that the high priest was allowed to enter into the Holy of Holies of the tabernacle. The Holy of Holies was the innermost sanctuary of the temple, which was "separated from the other parts of the temple by a thick curtain, the holy of holies was specially associated with the presence of Yahweh." (*Holman Illustrated Bible Dictionary*, 774) Before the high priest could enter, he had to prepare special incense. The *Holman Illustrated Bible Dictionary* states (387),

"The ceremony began with the sacrifice of a young bull as a sin offering for the priest and his family (Lev. 16:3, 6). After burning incense before the mercy seat in the inner sanctuary, the high priest sprinkled the blood from the bull on and in front of the mercy seat (16:14). The priest cast lots over two goats. One was offered as a sin offering. The other was presented alive as a scapegoat (16:5, 7–10, 20–22). The blood of the goat used as the sin offering was sprinkled like that of the bull to make atonement for the sanctuary (16:15). The mixed blood of the bull and goat were applied to the horns of the altar to make atonement for it (16:18). The high priest confessed all of the people's sins over the head of the live goat which was led away and then released in the wilderness (16:21–22). Following the ceremony, the priest again bathed and put on his usual garments (16:23–24). The priest then offered a burnt offering for the priest and the people (16:24)."

This offering, even if followed to the letter of the Law only lasted until the following year, as it had to be repeated year after year. Continuing his point, Paul said "Christ appeared as a high priest," but after his death and resurrection, "Christ has entered, not into holy places made with hands, which are copies of the true things, but into heaven itself, now to appear in the presence of God on our behalf." (Hebrews 9:11, 12, 24) Yes, Jesus' sacrifice did not need to be repeated, as "he has appeared once for all at the end of the ages to put away sin by the sacrifice of himself." (Heb. 9:25-26; Rom. 6:9) Paul then said,

Hebrews 9:27-28 Updated American Standard Version (UASV)

27 And just as it is appointed for man to die once, and after this comes judgment, 28 so Christ also, having been offered once to bear the sins of many, will appear a second time without reference to sin to those who eagerly await him for salvation.

After looking at the context, we can now better understand Hebrews 9:27. What most do not comment on when speaking of the priest going into the Holy of Holies each year to offer the atoning sacrifice, he was actually risking his life. If he had fallen short in any way, he would have never made it into the Holy of Holies, as he would have died before being allowed through the curtain. If he had not followed the process as laid out, or he had failed to walk with God aright throughout that previous year, neither he nor his sacrifices would have been accepted as atonement for the people. Therefore, if he fell short it would have meant a condemnation death for him and a condemnation for all he was offering sacrifices for, as they would have not been reconciled to God. Thus, the *judgment* mention in verse 27 was referring to the Day of Atonement and the typical priests.

It is clear that Jesus could have fallen short; otherwise, (1) Satan would have not bothered to tempt him, (2) and the Father would have never sent angels to strengthen him. Therefore, if Jesus had fallen short in any way, he would have not been resurrected on the third day, to go through the curtain into the Holy of Holies, heaven itself. He would have received the *judgment*. Nevertheless, because he was resurrected on the third day, we know that his life, ministry and sacrifice were perfect. When we look at the context of Hebrews 9:27, Paul makes the point that Jesus' sacrifice was superior to the priests that came before him.

We can also look at Hebrews 9:27 in an experiential way for humanity, in that, while Adam and Eve could have lived for an eternity, this has not proved the case for their descendants, as we have not had that opportunity as of yet.

As the reader knows, Adam and Even gave birth to their first child after sinning and being expelled from the Garden of Eden. Thus, "sin came into the world through one man, and death through sin, and so death spread to all men," and "the wages of sin is death." (Rom. 5:12; 6:23) The receiving of the death penalty by way of our ancestor Adam can only be given to us once. If one receives a resurrection, and uses his free will to sin or rebel at a future time, say during the millennium, death will then be the result of his own actions, not the sins of Adam. – Revelation 20:13-15.

On the other hand, those who receive a resurrection and remain faithful, they will receive a favorable judgment of eternal life. – Revelation 21:3-6.

In Summary, Hebrews 9:27 contextually refer to Jesus as the high priest, in contrast to the former priestly services, in ancient Israel. In addition, it also conveys the general experience of humanity that has received death by way of Adam's sin. Nevertheless, is **unbiblical** to use it as a means of predestination, saying Adam and Eve's physical death was all a part of God's plan.

Yes, these texts were written after the fall of man, after "sin came into the world through one man, and death through sin, and so death spread to all men. (Rom 5:12) We look at those who lived before the flood such as Methuselah, the father of Lamech and grandfather of Noah; he lived 969 years, the longest of Bible record. (Gen. 5:27) This is evidence that God's original intentions were for humans to live forever here on earth.

Humans are alienated from God and are in "slavery to corruption." (Rom. 8:21) This is because sin, missing the mark of perfection is at work within them, resulting in "the works of the flesh." (Gal 5:19-21) Paul tells us, "Let not sin therefore reign in your mortal body, to make you obey its passions." Then he asks, "Do you not know that if you present yourselves to anyone as obedient slaves, you are slaves of the one whom you obey, either of sin, which leads to death, or of obedience, which leads to righteousness?" (Rom. 6:12, 16, See 19-21) Satan "has the power of death" (Heb. 2:14-15) John called him a "murderer from the beginning." (John 8:44) This is not to say that Satan has the capacity to kill humans at will, but because he does so through deception and luring of humans into sin, by prompting or motivating wrongdoing that leads to corruption and death (2 Cor. 11:3), and also by engendering murderous thinking in the minds and hearts of humans. (John 8:40-44, 59; 13:2; See also James 3:14-16; 4:1, 2) Death is the "enemy" of humanity, and not what God had intended for us. (1 Cor. 15:26) The only ones who have ever desired death, even in imperfect bodies and an imperfect world, are those that have suffered immense pain. – Job 3:21, 22; 7:15; Rev. 9:6.

What is the Condition of the Dead?

When the Bible talks about the condition of the dead it presents it in five senses, (1) knowing nothing, (2) asleep like state, (3) powerless, (4) returning to the dust of the ground, (5) and awaiting a resurrection. If we examine both the Bible and religious history, the belief that a soul or spirit within us lives on after our physical death originates with Socrates and Plato. However, was it not Satan, who argued clear back in the Garden of Eden to Eve, saying that "You will not surely die."? **(Gen. 3:4, ESV) Yes, it was Satan that implied that Eve would not die in the flesh if she ignored God's prohibition on the tree og knowledge of good and bad.**

163

First Sense

Ecclesiastes 9:5, 10 Updated American Standard Version (UASV)

5 For the living know that they will die, but the dead know nothing, and they have no more reward, for the memory of them is forgotten. 10 Whatever your hand finds to do, do it with your might, for there is no work or thought or knowledge or wisdom in Sheol [gravedom], to which you are going.

Second Sense

John 11:11 (ESV)	1 Kings 2:10 (ESV)
11 After saying these things, he said to them, "Our friend Lazarus has fallen asleep, but I go to awaken him."	10 Then David slept with his fathers and was buried in the city of David.

Third Sense

Proverbs 2:18 (ESV)	Isaiah 26:14 (ESV)

18 for her house sinks down to death,
    and her paths to the departed;
	14 They are dead, they will not live;
	    they are shades, they will not arise;
	to that end you have visited them with destruction
	    and wiped out all remembrance of them.

Fourth Sense

Genesis 3:19 (ESV)	Ecclesiastes 3:19-20 (NASB)

19 By the sweat of your face
    you shall eat bread,
till you return to the ground,
    for out of it you were taken;
for you are dust,
    and to dust you shall return."
	19 For the fate of the sons of men and the fate of beasts is the same. As one dies so dies the other; indeed, they all have the same breath and there is no advantage for man over beast, for all is vanity. 20 All go to

	the same place. All came from the dust and all return to the dust.

Fifth Sense

John 5:28-29 (ESV)	Acts 24:15 (ESV)
[28] Do not marvel at this, for an hour is coming when all who are in the tombs will hear his voice [29] and come out, those who have done good to the resurrection of life, and those who have done evil to the resurrection of judgment.	[15] having a hope in God, which these men themselves accept, that there will be a resurrection of both the just and the unjust.

In death, Scripture shows us as being unable to praise God. The Psalmist tells us, "For in death there is no remembrance of you; in Sheol [gravedom] who will give you praise?" (Psa. 6:5) Isaiah the prophet writes, "For Sheol [gravedom] cannot thank you [God], death cannot praise you; those who go down to the pit cannot hope for your faithfulness. 'It is the living who give thanks to you, as I do today; a father tells his sons about your faithfulness.'" — Isaiah 38:18-19.

Passing Over from Death to Life

John 5:24 Updated American Standard Version (UASV)

[24] Truly, truly, I say to you, whoever hears my word and believes him who sent me has eternal life. He does not come into judgment, but has passed from death to life.

Regeneration is God restoring and renewing somebody morally or spiritually, where the Christian receives a new quality of life. This one goes from the road of death over to the path of life. (John 5:24) Here he becomes a new person, with a new personality, having removed the old person. (Eph. 4:20-24) **This does not mean** that the imperfection is gone, and the sinful desires are removed, but that he now has the mind of Christ, the Spirit and the Word of God to gain control over his thinking and his fleshly desires. Therefore, if one has truly experienced a conversion, it will be evident by the changes in one's new personality from the old personality, his life, and his actions. If this is the case, he will be fulfilling the words of Jesus, "let your light shine before others, so that they may see your good works and give glory to your Father who is in heaven." (Matt. 5:16)

Can we see one as truly a man of faith, a committed Christian, who attends the meetings, but he never carries out any personal study, never shares the gospel with another, never helps his spiritual brothers or sisters (physically, materially, mentally, or spiritually), nor helps his neighbor, or any of the other things one would find in a man of faith? James had something to say about this back in chapter 1:26-27, "If anyone thinks he is religious and does not bridle his tongue but deceives his heart, this person's religion is worthless. A Religion that is pure and undefiled before God, the Father, is this: to visit orphans and widows in their affliction, and to keep oneself unstained from the world." One who does not possess real faith, will not help the poor. He will not separate himself from worldly pursuits. He will favor those that he can benefit from (i.e., the powerful and wealthy), and ignore those that he cannot make gains from (i.e., orphans and widows). Moreover, he will not know the love of God, nor his mercy. – James 2:8-9, 13.

Titus 3:5 Updated American Standard Version (UASV)

[5] he saved us, not by deeds of righteousness that we have done, but because of his mercy, **through the washing of regeneration**[265] and renewal by the Holy Spirit,

The Greek word *polingenesia* means to a renewal or rebirth of a new life in Christ, by the Holy Spirit. Jesus told Nicodemus, "unless someone is born of … Spirit, he is not able to enter into the kingdom of God." (John 3:5). At the moment a person is converted, he is regenerated or renewed, passing over from death to life eternal. Jesus explains this in John 5:24, "the one who hears my word and who believes the one who sent me has eternal life, and does not come into judgment, but has passed from death into life." The principal feature of the rebirth of a new life in Christ, by the Holy Spirit, regeneration, is the passing over from death to life eternal.

At that point, the Spirit dwells within this newly regenerated one. From the time of Adam and Eve, God has desired to dwell with man. God fellowshiped with Adam in the Garden of Eden. After Adam's rebellion, he chose faithful men, to walk with him in their life course, to communicate

---

[265] **Regeneration (Rebirth), Born Again, Born of God, Born of the Spirit**: (Gr. palingenesiai; gennaō *anōthen*; gennaō *theos*; gennaō *pneuma*) This regeneration is the Holy Spirit working in his life, giving him a new nature, who repents and accepts Christ, placing him on the path to salvation. By taking in this knowledge of God's Word, we will be altering our way of thinking, which will affect our emotions and behavior, as well as our lives now and for eternity. This Word will influence our minds, making corrections in the way we think. If we are to have the Holy Spirit controlling our lives, we must 'renew our mind' (Rom. 12:2) "which is being renewed in knowledge" (Col. 3:10) of God and his will and purposes. (Matt 7:21-23; See Pro 2:1-6) All of this boil down to each individual Christian digging into the Scriptures in a meditative way, so he can 'discover the knowledge of God, receiving wisdom; from God's mouth, as well as knowledge and understanding.' (Pro. 2:5-6) As he acquires the mind that is inundated with the Word of God, he must also "be doers of the Word."–John 3:3; 6-7; 2 Corinthians 5:17; Titus 3:5; James 1:22-25.

166

with them. Enoch, Noah, and Abraham walked with God. In the Hebrew language, the tabernacle is called *mishkan* meaning "dwelling place." In both the tabernacle and the temple, God was represented as dwelling with the people in the Most Holy. He also dwelt with the people through the Son, "And the Word became flesh and dwelt among us, and we have seen his glory, glory as of the only Son from the Father, full of grace and truth." (John 1:14) After Jesus' ascension, God dwelt among the Christians, by way of the Holy Spirit, in the body of each individual Christian, which begins at conversion.

Death Thrown into the Lake of Fire

What is the Second Death

Although the expression "first death" does not occur, the concept is implied in Rev. 20:6, which states that "the second death has no power" over "the one who shares in the first resurrection." Sharing in the first resurrection would be impossible unless they had previously died. (Brand, Draper and Archie 2003, 1457)

We have been studying about the first death, namely Adamic death, that which we have inherited from Adam and Eve. If that was the first death, the second death must be distinct from that death. It is clear from the Scriptures that there is a resurrection hope from the first death, but not from the second death.

Revelation 2:11 Updated American Standard Version (UASV)

[11] He who has an ear, let him hear what the Spirit says to the congregations. The one who conquers will not be hurt by **the second death**.'

The ones who conqueror is guaranteed of immortal heavenly life, which cannot be affected by death. – 1 Corinthians 15:53-54.

Revelation 20:6 Updated American Standard Version (UASV)

[6] Blessed and holy is the one who has a part in the first resurrection; over these **the second deat**h has no power, but they will be priests of God and of Christ and will reign with him for a thousand years.

Again, the ones who conqueror that share in "the first resurrection" are guaranteed of immortal heavenly life, which cannot be affected by the second death, which will mean annihilation, destruction without hope of a resurrection for those who experience it.

¹³ And the sea gave up the dead which were in it, and death and Hades²⁶⁶ gave up the dead which were in them; and they were judged, every one of them according to their deeds. ¹⁴ Then death and Hades²⁶⁷ were thrown into the lake of fire. This is **the second death**, the lake of fire. ¹⁵ And if anyone was not found written in the book of life,²⁶⁸ he was thrown into the lake of fire.

Notice that death, which is what we inherited from our first parents Adam and Eve, as well as Hades (gravedom), is going to be "thrown into the lake of fire." Is not death and Hades abstract, are they able to be tormented and suffer forever. No. However, the fire does picture their eternal destruction, which will take place once they 'give up the dead who were in them.' Note that Paul clearly said, "The last enemy to be destroyed is death." (1 Corinthians 15:26)

The fire and burning within Scripture are merely representing annihilation or eternal destruction. Therefore, there is no eternal torment in Sheol (gravedom), Hades (equivalent of Sheol) hell (English translation), Gehenna (symbol of destruction), or the lake of fire (symbol of destruction). What about the parable of the sheep (righteous) and the goats (wicked), which has the goats, or the wicked going away into eternal punishment?

---

²⁶⁶ Hades is the standard transliteration into English of the corresponding Greek word haides, which occurs ten times in the UASV. (Matt. 11:23; 16:18; Lu 10:15; 16:23; Ac 2:27, 31; Rev. 1:18; 6:8; 20:13, 14.) It has the underlying meaning of 'a place of the dead, where they are conscious of nothing, awaiting a resurrection, for both the righteous and the unrighteous.' (John 5:28-29; Acts 24:15) It corresponds to "Sheol" in the OT. It does not involve torment and punishment.

²⁶⁷ Hades is the standard transliteration into English of the corresponding Greek word haides, which occurs ten times in the UASV. (Matt. 11:23; 16:18; Lu 10:15; 16:23; Ac 2:27, 31; Rev. 1:18; 6:8; 20:13, 14.) It has the underlying meaning of 'a place of the dead, where they are conscious of nothing, awaiting a resurrection, for both the righteous and the unrighteous.' (John 5:28-29; Acts 24:15) It corresponds to "Sheol" in the OT. It does not involve torment and punishment.

²⁶⁸ **Book of Life**: (Gr. *biblos tēs zōēs*) In biblical times, cities had a register of names for the citizens living there. (See Ps. 69:28; Isa. 4:3) God, figuratively speaking, has been writing names in the "book of life" "from the foundation of the world." (Rev. 17:8) Jesus Christ talked about Abel as living "from the foundation of the world," this would suggest that we are talking about the world of ransomable humankind after the fall. (Lu 11:48-51) Clearly, Abel was the first person to have his name written in the "book of life." The individuals who have their names written in the "book of Life" do not mean they are predestined to eternal life. This is evident from the fact that they can be 'blotted out' of the "book of life." (Ex 32:32-33; Rev. 3:5) Jesus ransom sacrifice alone gets one written in the "book of life," if they accept the Son of God. However, it is remaining faith to God that keeps them from being 'blotted' out of the "book of life." (Phil. 2:12; Heb. 10:26-27; Jam. 2:14-26) It is only by remaining faithful until the end that one can be retained permanently in the "book of life."–Matt. 214:13; Phil. 4:3; Rev. 20:15.

Revelation 21:8 Updated American Standard Version (UASV)

⁸ But as for the cowards and unbelievers, and the detestable, as for murderers, and the sexually immoral[269] persons and sorcerers and idolaters and all liars, their portion will be in the lake that burns with fire and sulphur, which is **the second death.**"

John speaks of a "lake that burns with fire and sulfur," where the wicked are thrown. It would seem that if hellfire were the truth, this would be the place. However, we are simply told by John, this is "the second death," which will mean annihilation, destruction without hope of a resurrection for those who experience it.

Do Humans Have a Soul that Is Apart from Us?

Ministers, pastors, elders, overseers, leaders of churches have made many comments to those who have lost their loved one prematurely, in a car accident, natural disaster, war, and the like. They make such comments, such as, "While we grieve for the loss of Julie Sanford, we know she is the one in a better place, and now she truly knows what joy, peace, and happiness are, because she is with the Lord." If we attended the funerals of different churches, we would find similar messages being given to the family of the loved one, who has died. What all of these messages have in common are, the belief in survival after death.

Some teach that the human soul is deathless and cannot die. These ones believe that we possess an immortal soul, which is death proof. One commentator, J. Warner Wallace, in an article entitled (What Happens to Our Souls When We Die?), writes, "There is good reason to believe our afterlife experience begins the minute we close our eyes for the last time here on earth. For those of us who are believers, the instant our earthly bodies die our souls will be united with Jesus in the afterlife." He goes on to write, "Each of us will leave our earthly bodies in the grave and our disembodied souls will go immediately into the presence of God or into Hades. Our destination is determined purely by our acceptance or rejection of God through our faith in Jesus Christ."[270]

Surviving Death

The belief in most of Christianity is that we have a soul, **not that** we are a soul, and the soul that we have does not die. In other words, they believe

---

[269] **Sexual Immorality**: (Heb. *zanah*; Gr. *porneia*) A general term for immoral sexual acts of any kind: such as adultery, prostitution, sexual relations between people not married to each other, homosexuality, and bestiality. – Num. 25:1; Deut. 22:21; Matt. 5:32; 1 Cor. 5:1.

[270] ttp://coldcasechristianity.com/2014/what-happens-to-our-souls-when-we-die/

that a soul within us is death proof, deathless, cannot die, i.e., is immortal. They observe that when a human body dies, it eventually turns into dust, (Gen. 3:19) but some part of the human must survive the body, and it is invisible to humans, untouchable, which some call the "soul," while others call this immaterial part of man "spirit." In order to get the theological position, we will quote Dr. Elmer Towns at length, He is a co-founder, with Jerry Falwell, of Liberty University, is a college and seminary professor, and Dean of the School of Religion, and Dean of Liberty University Baptist Theological Seminary.

Theologians often debate the question of whether man is a two-part being (dichotomy) or a three-part being (trichotomy). Some verses seem to teach that man consists only of a body and soul, while others apparently teach a third aspect to man, the spirit. Sometimes the Bible seems to use the terms "soul" and "spirit" interchangeably, yet at other times a distinction between the two is more clearly made. Part of the problem is solved when we study the verses more closely and realize there are actually two ways to look at man. When we consider the nature or makeup of man, he is a two-part being. He consists of both material (the body) and the immaterial (the soul). In activity or function, however, the body, soul, and spirit of man each has a function. The distinction and similarity of the soul and spirit can be seen in a biblical discussion of the Word of God.

"For the word of God is quick, and powerful, and sharper than any two-edged sword, piercing even to the dividing asunder of soul and spirit, and of the joints and marrow, and is a discerner of the thoughts and intents of the heart" (Heb. 4:12). The writer makes an interesting parallel. The joints and marrow are different in function, yet both are similar in that they are part of the bone structure of man. Thoughts and interests are also two distinct mental activities, yet they are similar in that they are activities of the mind. So the soul and spirit are distinct in function yet both are similar in immaterial composition. The writer is drawing five distinctions between things we may class together because of their similarity.

Soul. The Bible makes a clear distinction between the body and soul (Isa. 10:18). The term is used in the Bible to identify something that cannot be defined materially. The soul is that part of us that is life. At the creation of Adam, God "breathed into his nostrils the breath of life; and man became a living soul" (Gen. 2:7). Man did not have a soul, but he became a soul, and the life-principle was the breath (Hebrew ruah: spirit) of God. As a result, we say when man no longer has breath that he is dead. When Rachel died in childbirth, the Bible described it "as her soul was in departing, (for she died)" (Gen. 35:18). In the Old Testament, the word "soul" is used to speak of the whole person (Song of Sol. 1:7).

Spirit. A further consideration of the immaterial side of man will reveal additional aspects of truth in examining the spirit of man. The term "spirit" is sometimes used in Scripture to speak of the mind (Gen. 8:1) or breath (1 Thess. 2:8).

That part of man that survives death is called the "spirit" in the Bible. When Stephen was stoned to death, the Bible identifies his spirit as departing the body when his life ended. "And they stoned Stephen, calling upon God, and saying, Lord Jesus, receive my spirit" (Acts 7:59). This principle is seen in the biblical definition of death. "For as the body without the spirit is dead, so faith without works is dead also" (James 2:28).

Relationship between the soul and spirit. The "soul" and "spirit" sometimes appear to be used interchangeably in Scripture (Gen. 41:8, and Ps. 42:6; John 12:27 and 13:21), because they both refer to the life-principle. We do not say man is a spirit, but that he has a spirit. On the other hand, we say man is a soul. The soul seems to be related to man's earthly life while the spirit relates to man's heavenly life. The knowledge of God is received by man's spirit (1 Cor. 2:2–16) and interprets it for the total man. It is this spirit in man that is related to the higher things in man. The spirit of man is definitely related to the conversion experience. The apostle Paul acknowledged "The Spirit itself [the Holy Spirit] beareth witness with our spirit, that we are the children of God" – Romans 8:16.

Man is a unity. Man is the spiritual link between the life of God and the physical life of this planet. Man is a twofold being, possessing a dual nature in unity; a dual nature because he is spiritual, and he is physical. At times these two natures seem separate, but they operate as one. Man has one personality but possesses two natures that interact on each other. First, man's physical body is regulated by the material universe–he must eat, sleep, breathe, and live in dependence upon the earth. Man's body is an essential part of his constitution, so much so that he would not be man without a body. But in the second place, man is immaterial. This is the life of God that entered man when God breathed into him and he became a living soul. Man became immortal and will live forever because God, his source, is eternal. Since man was made in the image of God who created all things, man has creative abilities, to rule the physical earth.

Man with his dual nature is a unity. The material receives direction by the immaterial, and man's spiritual nature grows in harmony with physical well-being. God created man as a well-balanced unity. Those who harm their body sear their personality.

Sin entered God's perfect world as a foreign element and violated divine law. As a result, man was ruined spiritually and will die physically. God's purpose was thwarted and man's constitution was affected. The only thing that can restore his spiritual condition is the grace of God through the message of the gospel. Man's spiritual rebirth also guarantees for him a resurrected body that will again be made like his Maker.[271]

We would agree with some of Towns' point but would also disagree with much. We will not take the time to refute systematically what he has written, we will just deal with what the Bible really teaches, and that will do it for us. Before delving into what the Bible really teaches, we will comment on one thing that Towns said, "God's purpose was thwarted." He is talking about God's intended purposes for man, (1) that he procreates with Eve and fill the earth with perfect humans, (2) that he cultivated the Garden of Eden until we would have had a paradise earth, (3) that he cares for the animals. Now, are we to believe that Satan could actually thwart God's intended purpose?

THWART DEFINED: to prevent somebody or somebody's plan from being successful

Why not say that Satan sidetracked God purpose at best. If God had a purpose for man, are we to believe that one little act of Satan and Adam prevented him from seeing that purpose accomplished? God's purpose will be successfully accomplished through Jesus Christ. Satan merely delayed the inevitable fulfillment of God's will and purpose.

The Human Soul

Let us turn to *A Hebrew and English Lexicon of the Old Testament,*based on the Lexicon of William Gesenius and edited by three clergymen, Drs. Brown, Driver and Briggs, in its corrected edition of 1952. On page 659, under the Hebrew word *Néfesh,* this Lexicon is honest enough to make this admission, in column two: "2. The *néfesh* becomes a living being; by God's breathing *neshamáth hhayím*into the nostrils of its *basár;* of man Genesis 2:7; by implication of animals also Genesis 2:19; so Psalm 104:29, 30, compare 66:9; man is *néfesh hhayáh,* a living, breathing being Genesis 2:7; elsewhere *néfesh hhayáh* always of animals Genesis 1:20, 24, 30; 9:12, 15, 16; Ezekiel 47:9; . . . 3. The *néfesh* . . . is specifically: a. a living being whose life resides in the blood . . . (hence sacrificial use of blood, and its prohibition in other uses; . . .) . . . c. *Néfesh*is used for life itself 171 times, of animals Proverbs 12:10, and of man Genesis 49:3c . . . "[272]

---

[271] Towns, Elmer (2011-10-30). AMG Concise Bible Doctrines (AMG Concise Series) (Kindle Locations 3584-3630). AMG Publishers. Kindle Edition.
[272] In the above quotation the Hebrew words neshamáth hhayím mean "the breath of life." Basár means "flesh," and néfesh hhayáh means "a living soul," whether applied to animal or to man.

Let us turn also to the *Lexicon for the Old Testament Books,* by L. Koehler and W. Baumgartner, in its edition of 1953, which gives definitions in both German and English. On page 627 of its Volume 2, this Lexicon says, under *Néfesh: "the breathing substance, making man and animal living beings* Genesis 1:20, *the soul (strictly different from the Greek notion of soul) the seat of which is the blood*Genesis 9:4f; Leviticus 17:11; Deuteronomy 12:23 (249 times): 3. *néfesh hhayáh living being;* Genesis 1:20, 24 (= *animals*) 2:19 . . . 2:7; 9:10, 16. . . . 4. *soul = living being, individual, person . . . who kills a person* Numbers 31:19, . . . *destroy lives, persons* Ezekiel 22:27; . . . 7. *Néfesh breath = life* (282 times) . . . " And on page 628, column 1: *"Néfesh a dead one* (has developed from *a person*) Leviticus 21:1; Numbers 6:11; 9:10; Leviticus 22:4; Haggai 2:13; Numbers 5:2; 9:6f; 19:11, 13 . . . "

Many have wondered what happens to the soul after death. Do humans have a soul that is apart from them? What is the soul? Is the soul, some invisible force within us, which survives after death? While this seems farfetched to some, many believe this to be true. Many have heard the claims on television, in book and magazines, about those, who claim they have had so-called life-after-death experiences. Here is a question for you as a reader, before we look at the first Bile verse, 'Does the soul breathe to stay alive?' Likely, many would answer "no" to that question. Let us see what the Bible says.

A Soul Breathes

Genesis 2:7 American Standard Version (ASV)

[7] And Jehovah God formed man of the dust of the ground, and breathed into his nostrils the breath of life; and man **became a living soul**.

The Christian apostle Paul, writer of fourteen books of the Bible, supports Moses' writings, saying, "So also it is written: 'The first man Adam became a living soul' … The first man was from the earth, a man of dust." (1 Cor. 15:45, 47, *UASV*)

Human soul = body **[dust of the ground] +** active life force **("spirit") [Hebrew, *ruach*]** within the trillions of human cells that make up the human body **+** breath of life [Hebrew, *neshamah*] that sustains the life force from God.

Genesis 2:7 tells us that God formed man out of the "dust of the ground." In other words, he was formed from the elements of the soil. This body needed life and so God caused the trillions of cells in his body to come to life, giving him the force of life. *Ruach* "spirit" is the active life force that Adam now possessed. However, for this life force to continue to feed these

173

trillions of cells, there needed to be oxygen, sustained by the breathing. Therefore, we all know what God did next: he "breathed into his nostrils the breath [*neshamah*] of life." At this point, Adam's lungs would sustain the breathing the life force into those body cells.

If we are to understand fully what the "soul" is, we must investigate what the Hebrew and Greek words mean. The Hebrew word translated "soul" is *nephesh*. What does "nephesh" mean? The *Holman Illustrated Bible Dictionary* says,

> In the Hebrew OT, the word generally translated "soul" is *nephesh*. The word occurs over 750 times, and it means primarily "life" or "possessing life." It is used of both animals (<u>Gen. 9:12</u>; Ezek. 47:9) and humans (<u>Gen. 2:7</u>). The word sometimes indicates the whole person, as for instance in Gen. 2:7 where God breathes breath (*neshamah*) into the dust and thus makes a "soul" (*nephesh*). A similar usage is found in Gen. 12:5 where Abram takes all the "souls" (persons) who were with him in Haran and moves on to Canaan. Similarly in Num. 6:6 it is used as a synonym for the body—the Nazirite is not to go near a dead *nephesh* (Lev. 7:21; Hag. 2:13). (Brand, Draper and Archie 2003, 1523)

Soul as "a living creature"

The American Standard Version has our literal rendering of *nephesh* at Genesis 2:7, "and man became **a living soul**." The English Standard Version offers an interpretation of *nephesh*, "and the man became **a living creature**." (LEB same) The Holman Christian Standard Bible offers an interpretation of *nephesh*, "and the man became **a living being**." (NASB same) You will notice that Genesis 2:7 makes it all too clear that Adam was not given a soul, he does not have a soul, but that he **became** a living soul, i.e., a living creature, a living being. Therefore, the "soul" is the person, the creature, the being, not what we have. When we look at the Hebrew Old Testament using a literal rendering, this is born out.

Leviticus 5:1 Updated American standard Version (UASV)

5 "If a soul [*nephesh*, **soul**] **sins** in that he hears a public adjuration to testify, and though he is a witness, whether he has seen or come to know the matter, yet does not speak, he will bear his error;[273]

---

[273] **Error**: (Heb., 'āwōn; Gr. anomia, paranomia) The Hebrew word awon essentially relates to erring, acting illegally or wrongly. This aspect of sin refers to committing a perverseness, wrongness, lawlessness, law breaking, which can also include the rejection of the sovereignty of God. It also focuses on the liability or guilt of one's wicked, wrongful act. This error may be deliberate or accidental; either willful deviation

Leviticus 23:30 Updated American standard Version (UASV)

30 As for any soul [*nephesh*, **soul**] **who does any work** on this same day, that person I will destroy from among his people.

Deuteronomy 24:7 Updated American standard Version (UASV)

7 "If a man is caught kidnapping a soul [*nephesh*, **a soul**] of his brothers of the sons of Israel, and he deals with him violently or sells him, then that thief will die; so you shall purge the evil from among you.

Judges 16:16 New American Standard Bible (NASB)

16 It came about when she pressed him daily with her words and urged him, that his **soul was annoyed** to death.

Job 19:2 Updated American Standard Version (UASV)

2 How long will you **torment my soul**, And break me in pieces with words?

Psalm 119:28 New American Standard Bible (NASB)

28 My **soul weeps** because of grief;
Strengthen me according to Your word.

We notice here in the above verses that a soul sins, a soul works, a soul can be kidnapped, a soul can get annoyed, a soul can be tormented, and a soul can weep. These things happened to persons, to creatures, to beings, not inanimate objects within the human body, which is supposed lives on after death. *The Holman Illustrated Bible Dictionary* says,

> **New Testament** Greek word *psuche* carries many of the same meanings as the Hebrew *nephesh*. Often the soul is equated with the total person. Romans 13:1 says, "Everyone [soul] must submit to the governing authorities" equating "soul" (one) with "person" (cp. Acts 2:41; 3:23). There will be "affliction and distress for every human being [soul] who does evil, first to the Jew, and also to the Greek" (Rom. 2:9 HCSB). Soul in the NT also indicates the emotions or passions: "But the Jews who refused to believe stirred up and poisoned the minds [*psuche*] of the Gentiles against the brothers" (Acts 14:2 HCSB). In John 10:24 the Jews asked Jesus, "How long are You going to keep us [our souls] in

---

of what is right or unknowingly making a mistake. (Lev. 4:13-35; 5:1-6, 14-19; Num. 15:22-29; Ps 19:12-13) Of course, if it is intentional; then, the consequence is far more serious. (Num. 15:30-31) Error is in opposition to the truth, and those willfully sinning corrupt the truth, a course that only brings forth flagrant sin. (Isa 5:18-23) We can be hardened by the deceitfulness of sin. – Ex 9:27, 34-35; Heb. 3:13-15.

suspense?" Jesus also told the disciples that they should love God with all of their souls (Mark 12:30), indicating something of the energy and passion that ought to go into loving Him. (Brand, Draper and Archie 2003, 1523)

When we look at the Greek New Testament using a literal rendering, "soul," the basic idea inherent in the word as the Bible writers used it, namely, that it is a living person, a living creature, or a living being; or, the life that a person or an animal has as a soul.

John 12:27 New American Standard Bible (NASB)

²⁷ "Now **My soul has become troubled**; and what shall I say, 'Father, save Me from this hour'? But for this purpose I came to this hour.

Acts 2:43 American Standard Version (ASV)

⁴³ And **fear came upon every soul**: and many wonders and signs were done through the apostles.

Romans 13:1 New American Standard Bible (NASB)

13 Every person [*psuche*, **soul**] is to be in subjection to the governing authorities. For there is no authority except from God, and those which exist are established by God.

1 Thessalonians 5:14 Lexham English Bible (LEB)

¹⁴ And we urge you, brothers, admonish the disorderly, console the **discouraged** [oligo*psuche*, literally "those of little **soul**," i.e., "discouraged."], help the sick, be patient toward all *people*.

1 Peter 3:20 New American Standard Bible (NASB)

²⁰ who once were disobedient, when the patience of God kept waiting in the days of Noah, during the construction of the ark, in which a few, that is, eight persons [*psuchai*, **souls**], were brought safely through *the* water.

We notice here in the above verses that a soul can become troubled, fear can come upon a soul, a soul is to be in subjection to the governmental authorities, a soul can get discouraged, and souls can be delivered through a flood. These things happen to a person, a creature, a being, not an inanimate object within the human body, which supposed lives on after death. We note to from our quote of *The Holman Illustrated Bible Dictionary*, animals are "souls" too.

Genesis 1:24 American Standard Version (ASV)	Numbers 31:28 American Standard Version (ASV)
24 And God said, Let the earth bring forth living creatures [*nephesh*, soul] after their kind, cattle, and creeping things, and beasts of the earth after their kind: and it was so.	28 And levy a tribute unto Jehovah of the men of war that went out to battle: one soul of five hundred, both of the persons, and of the oxen, and of the asses, and of the flocks:

Soul as the Life of the Creature

"Soul" is used in Scripture as a reference to the life that a living person, a living creature, a living animal has. This does not negate what we learned in the above. We are living "souls," i.e., living persons. It does not change a thing to use "soul" in the sense of our possessing "life." Below are a few examples.

Exodus 4:19 American Standard Version (ASV)

19 And Jehovah said to Moses in Midian, "Go, return into Egypt, for all the men are dead who sought your life [***nephesh*, soul**]."[274]

Joshua 9:24 American Standard Version (ASV)

24 And they answered Joshua, and said, Because it was certainly told thy servants, how that Jehovah your God commanded his servant Moses to give you all the land, and to destroy all the inhabitants of the land from before you; therefore we feared greatly for our lives [***nephesh*, souls**] because of you, and have done this thing.

2 Kings 7:7 American Standard Version (ASV)

7 Wherefore they arose and fled in the twilight, and left their tents, and their horses, and their asses, even the camp as it was, and fled for their life [***nephesh*, soul**].

Proverbs 12:10 American Standard Version (ASV)

10 A righteous man regards the life [***nephesh*, soul**] of his beast; But the tender mercies of the wicked are cruel.

Matthew 20:28 American Standard Version (ASV)

---

[274] Lit. all the men who were **seeking your soul** are dead.

[28] even as the Son of man came not to be ministered to, but to minister, and to give his life [*psuche*, **soul**] a ransom for many.

Philippians 2:30 New American Standard Bible (NASB)

[30] because he came close to death for the work of Christ, risking his life [*psuche*, **soul**] to complete what was deficient in your service to me.

Now, we do not want to misrepresent the *Holman Illustrated Bible Dictionary*, by quoting two paragraphs, where this author would agree, and not go on to the next paragraph, where they would disagree with this author. There are two positions, when it comes to the biblical position of the body and the soul. **We would <u>disagree</u>** with the first, which is "**holistic dualism**—that there is a difference between body and soul, but the two are linked together by God such that humans are not complete when the two are separated." Our position that **we would agree** with, would be the second, which is the "**monistic view** that the soul is not separable from the body at all. Nearly all who have held the second view have also believed that after death Christians 'go to sleep' and await the resurrection." (Bold mine, more on this below) *The Holman Illustrated Bible Dictionary* holds to the holistic dualism position, as they write,

It is also the case that the NT speaks of the soul as something that is distinguishable from the physical existence of a person. Jesus made this point when He observed, "Don't fear those who kill the body but are not able to kill the soul; but rather, fear Him who is able to destroy both soul and body in hell" (Matt. 10:28 HCSB). James seems to have the same thing in mind when he concludes his letter, "He should know that whoever turns a sinner from the error of his way will save his life [soul] from death" (James 5:20 HCSB; cp. Rev. 6:9; 20:4). This may be the idea found in Mark 8:36, "For what does it benefit a man to gain the whole world yet lose his life [soul]?" (HCSB). Scripture clearly teaches that persons continue to exist consciously after physical death. Jesus pointed out that as the God of Abraham, Isaac, and Jacob, He is the God of the living. These still live, their souls having returned to God (Eccles. 12:7). (Brand, Draper and Archie 2003, 1523)

We will take their texts one at a time, offering the text, and then offering a thought that will clarify what was meant by the author.

Matthew 10:28 Holman Christian Standard Bible (HCSB)

[28] Don't fear those who kill the body but are not able to kill the soul; rather, fear Him who is able to destroy both soul and body in hell.[7]

What is meant by this is, man can kill the body alone, but he cannot kill "life," as in everlasting life. The prospect of life is in the hands of God alone.

He can kill both the body, which is used to represent what we have here and now, but he can also kill any prospect that we have at everlasting life. Again, man can kill the body; he cannot kill the person for an eternity, as the hope of a resurrection is in hands of God.

James 5:20 Holman Christian Standard Bible (HCSB)

20 let him know that whoever turns a sinner from the error of his way will save his life **[soul]** from death and cover a multitude of sins.

First, we should point out that, the 'life **[soul]** that is saved from death' is, not the one doing the helping, but rather, it is the sinner. Our works do not save us; we are saved by the loving-kindness of God, in offering his Son as a ransom sacrifice for all, who trust in that sacrifice. (Acts 4:12) The person who was saved was walking down the path of eternal death, from where there is no hope for eternal life. When the one Christian helped the sinner turn back from his error, by spreading love and counsel, as well as prayer, he helped this sinner stay on the path of life, eternal life, by way of the atonement sacrifice of Christ.

Mark 8:36 Holman Christian Standard Bible (HCSB)

36 For what does it benefit a man to gain the whole world yet lose his life **[soul]**?

Here again, it is not referring to the person's life in this present imperfect age, but eternal life that is to come after Jesus brings the last enemy to nothing, death. We will deal with Ecclesiastes 12:7 below.

Can the Soul Die?

When we die, what happens to the soul? If you recall from above that the "soul" is the person, the being, the creature, i.e., us, and the **life** that we have. If you recall from above, the **Human soul** = body **[dust of the ground]** + active life force **("spirit") [Hebrew, *ruach*]** within the trillions of human cells which make up the human body + breath of life [Hebrew, *neshamah*] that sustains the life force from God. In other words, the "soul" is we as a whole, everything that we are, so the soul or we humans can die. Let us look at a few verses, which make that all too clear.

Ecclesiastes 3:19-20 New American Standard Bible (NASB)

19 For the fate of the sons of men **[humans or people]** and the fate of beasts is the same. As one dies so dies the other; indeed, they all have the same breath and there is no advantage for man over beast, for all is vanity. 20 All go to the same place. All came from the dust and all return to the dust.

In other words, when we breathe our last breath, our cells begin to die. Death is the ending of all vital functions or processes in an organism or cell. When our heart stops beating, our blood is no longer circulating, carrying nourishment and oxygen (by breathing) to the trillions of cells in our body; we are what are termed, clinically dead. However, somatic death has yet to occur, meaning we can be revived, after many minutes of being clinically dead, if the heart and lungs can be restarted again, which gives the cells the oxygen they need.

After about three minutes of clinical death, the brain cells begin to die, meaning the chances of reviving the person is less likely as each second passes. We know that it is vital that the breathing and blood flow be maintained for the life force (*ruach chaiyim*) in the cells. Nevertheless, it is not the lack of breathing or the failure of the heart beating alone, but rather the active life force **("spirit") [Hebrew, ruach]** within the trillions of human cells which make up the human body **+** breath of life [Hebrew, *neshamah*] that sustains the life force from God.

Psalm 104:29 (ESV)	Psalm 146:4 (ESV)	Ecclesiastes 8:8 (ESV)
29 When you hide your face, they are dismayed; when you take away their breath, they die and return to their dust.	4 When his breath departs, he returns to the earth; on that very day his plans perish.	8 No man has power to retain the spirit, or power over the day of death. There is no discharge from war, nor will wickedness deliver those who are given to it.

Again, ...

Ezekiel 18:4 (ESV)	Leviticus 21:1 (ASV)	Numbers 6:6 (ASV)
4 Behold, all souls are mine; the soul of the father as well as the soul of the son is mine: the soul who sins shall die.	21 And Jehovah said to Moses, Speak to the priests, the sons of Aaron, and say to them, There shall none defile himself for the dead **[Or "for a soul."]** among his people;	6 All the days that he separates himself unto Jehovah he shall not come near to a dead body **[Or "soul."]**.

Again, the death of a "soul" means the death of a person ...

180

1 Kings 19:4 (ASV)	Jonah 4:8 (ASV)	Mark 3:4 (ASV)
4 But he himself went a day's journey into the wilderness, and came and sat down under a juniper-tree: and he requested for himself that he **[Or "his soul.]** "might die, and said, It is enough; now, O Jehovah, take away my life [soul]; for I am not better than my fathers.	8 And it came to pass, when the sun arose, that God prepared a sultry east wind; and the sun beat upon the head of Jonah, that he fainted, and requested for himself that he might die **[Or "that his soul might die."]**, and said, It is better for me to die than to live.	4 And he said to them, Is it lawful on the sabbath day to do good, or to do harm? to save a life **[Or "soul."]**, or to kill? But they held their peace.

As you can see from the above texts, a "soul," or person can die. However, how are we to understand those texts that say the "soul" went out of a person, or came back into a person?

Soul Departing and Soul Coming into a Person

Genesis 35:18 English Standard Version (ESV)

18 And as her soul was departing (for she was dying), she called his name Ben-oni; but his father called him Benjamin.

Are we to understand from this that Rachel had some inner being, a soul, which departed from her at death? No. You will recall from the texts from above that the term "soul" can also be used in reference to the life one has. Thus, this is a reference to her life that she had leaving her. Note the *Lexham English Bible*, "And it happened *that* when **her <u>life</u> was departing** (for she was dying), she called his name Ben-Oni. But his father called him Benjamin." (Bold and underline is mine) Therefore, it was her "life" that she had, which departed from her, not some inner being.

1 Kings 17:22 American Standard Version (ASV)

22 And Jehovah listened to the voice of Elijah; and the soul of the child came into him again, and he revived.

Here again, the word "soul" is the "life" that someone has. The *New American Standard Bible* reads, "The **life** of the child returned to him and he revived." The *Lexham English Bible* reads, "The **life** of the child returned

181

within him, and he lived." The *Holman Christian Standard Bible* reads, "The boy's **life** returned to him, and he lived." (Bold is mine)

John 11:11 (ESV)	1 Kings 2:10 (ESV)
[11] After saying these things, he said to them, "Our friend Lazarus has fallen asleep, but I go to awaken him."	[10] Then David slept with his fathers and was buried in the city of David.

Notice that Lazarus' death is equated with being asleep in death, while King David is referred to as sleeping in death. This gives the reader a hope, as just as easily as you and I can awaken a person from sleep, Jesus is going to awaken people from death, a death like sleep. We are going to look at these verses a little differently that we have with the others. We will pause for a moment to see how a literal translation is best (which has already been demonstrated), with an interpretation in a footnote. Moreover, it is important that we read those footnotes. Otherwise, we can come to the wrong conclusions.

Souls Have Blood

As we know by now, the Bible's viewpoint is that the living human creature is the human soul. In addition, though, the Bible states that the human soul has blood.

Jeremiah 2:34 Updated American Standard Version (UASV)

[34] Also on your skirts is found **the blood of the souls** of the innocent poor; you did not find them breaking in. But in spite of all these things,

God says,

Genesis 9:5 Updated American Standard Version (UASV)

[5] Surely I will require **your blood of your souls**; from every beast I will require it. From every beast[275] will I require it. And at the hand of man, even at the hand of every man's brother, will I require the **soul**[276] of man.[277]

The Creator himself shows us the level of dependence of the human soul upon the blood stream by saying,

Leviticus 17:11 Updated American Standard Version (UASV)

---

[275] Lit *from the hand of*

[276] Heb., *nephesh,* as in 2:7; Gr., *psuche.*

[277] The Creator of the heavens and the earth, Adam and Eve views blood as standing for life.

182

[11] For the soul of the flesh is in the blood, and I have given it to you upon the altar to make atonement for your souls; for it is the blood that makes atonement by the soul.[12]

Leviticus 17:14 Updated American Standard Version (UASV)

[14] "For as for the soul of all flesh, its blood is *identified* with its soul. Therefore I said to the sons of Israel, 'You are not to eat the blood of any flesh, for the soul of all flesh is its blood; whoever eats it shall be cut off.'

Deuteronomy 12:23 Updated American Standard Version (UASV)

[23] Only be sure not to eat the blood, for **the blood is the soul**, and you shall not eat the soul with the flesh.

Souls can Eat Fat and Blood

Human souls can eat both blood and Fat, but God prohibited it. Nevertheless, the point is that human souls can eat fat and blood. All of the different points being made with these Scriptures are that the soul is the person, not some entity inside of us that goes to another realm somewhere when we die.

Leviticus 7:25 Updated American Standard Version (UASV)

[25] For whoever eats the fat of the animal from which an offering by fire is offered to Jehovah, even **the soul who eats** shall be cut off from his people.

Leviticus 7:27 Updated American Standard Version (UASV)

[27] Any **soul who eats** any blood, that soul must be cut off from his people.'"

The human soul can also eat the dead animal souls. Thus, we see in this one verse that animals are souls as well and that if any Israelite violated certain parts of the Mosaic Law he would be cut off by expelling him or even executing. However, the text refers to the soul being cut off.

Leviticus 17:15 Updated American Standard Version (UASV)

[15] And every **soul who eats** what dies of itself or what is torn by beasts, whether he is a native or a sojourner, shall wash his clothes and bathe himself in water and be unclean until the evening; then he shall be clean.

Human Souls Desire to Eat Meet

Deuteronomy 12:20 Updated American Standard Version (UASV)

20 "When Jehovah your God enlarges your territory, as he has promised you, and you say, 'I will eat meat,' because your soul craves to eat meat, your soul may eat meat whenever you desire.

Deuteronomy 23:24 Updated American Standard Version (UASV)

24 "When you enter your neighbor's vineyard, then you may eat grapes until you satisfy your soul, but you shall not put any in your basket.

Proverbs 27:7 Updated American Standard Version (UASV)

7 A soul who is full loathes honey,
but to the soul who is hungry everything bitter is sweet.

The reader may wonder why this author is using a translation that is not even fully complete at the time of penning this book. It is because the "so-called" literal translations (ESV, HCSB, even the NASB) are letting their readers down.

Leviticus 17:11 (ESV)	Leviticus 17:11 (HCSB)	Leviticus 17:11 (NASB)
11 For the life of the flesh is in the blood, and I have given it for you on the altar to make atonement for **your souls**, for it is the blood that makes atonement by the life.	11 For the life of a creature is in the blood, and I have appointed it to you to make atonement on the altar for[a] your lives, since it is the lifeblood that makes atonement.	For the [a]life of the flesh is in the blood, and I have given it to you on the altar to make atonement for **your souls**; for it is the blood by reason of the [b]life that makes atonement.'
	Footnotes:	**Footnotes:**
	[a] Leviticus 17:11 Or *to ransom*	[a] Leviticus 17:11 Lit *soul*
		[b] Leviticus 17:11 Lit *soul*

Only the NASB, at least, places the literal rendering in the footnote, when it should be in the main text. Leviticus 17:11 is indicative of all the verses above. This has allowed the reader to see they are not getting what they were promised, i.e., a literal translation. We have shown the translations and their footnotes. We have only looked at the ESV, HCSB, and the NASB. First, *nephesh* "soul" or souls" appear three times in Leviticus 17:11. The NASB used the corresponding English "souls" once but does not stay faithful to their literal translation philosophy the other two times. However, unlike the others, they at least offer the reader a footnote, so he will know what was actually in the main text. The HCSB does not remain faithful to their claim of being literal one time out of the three, nor do they offer the reader a footnote. The ESV used the corresponding English "souls" once but does not stay faithful to their literal translation philosophy the other two times. Worse still, they **did not** offer the reader a footnote, so he will know what was actually in the main text.

Why should we be so the concerned over the literal rendering versus an interpretative rendering? Why should we be so worried over the necessity of being constant? One might ask. How can I know the truth about the Hebrew term *nephesh* (translated "soul" by the USAV) and the Greek term *psuche* (translated "soul" by the USAV)? If we look to the dynamic equivalent (interpretive) translations and the literal translations, we will discover that they use more than thirty English words when they translate *nephesh* and *psuche*. What English readers are not aware of, because most do not even add a footnote, which most English readers bypass anyway; there is just one Hebrew word and one Greek word behind all of those different English words.

We are not suggesting that the interpretation translation is incorrect, just inappropriate. Genesis 35:18 in the ESV says, "And as **her soul was departing** (for she was dying), she called his name Ben-oni; but his father called him Benjamin.)" First, notice that the ESV translators are not shy about using the rendering "soul" here, whereas they use an interpretive word in most other places, with no footnote. Why? Would it be because, to the average reader, Genesis 35:18 appears to support that we do have an immaterial part of humans that leaves when we die? Would it be that if we rendered *nephesh* and *psuche* as "soul" in all the other places, it would negate such an idea? Now, the interpretive translations here actually explain what is meant. These translations render the phrase "her soul was departing" as "her life was departing" (LEB), "With her last breath" (HCSB), and "her life went from her" (BBE). We can clearly see that no immaterial part of Rachel survived her body after her death. She was dead, awaiting a future resurrection.

Yes, we cannot fully understand what the Bible authors meant by their use of *nephesh* and *psuche*, if the translator is not consistent in his rendering of those terms. When a serious Bible reader has a translation that shows

- that we do not have a soul,
- but that we are souls,
- animals are souls,
- souls eat food,
- souls have blood,
- souls die,
- and dead bodies are even called souls,

they will come to understand that the Bible scholars who say the immortal soul concept **is _not_ found** in God's Word but is found in Greek literature **are correct**, as opposed to those scholars, like Elmer Towns, who claim an immaterial part of the human is found within the Scriptures. Now, even though the dynamic equivalent translations are correct as to the meaning, it is clear that the literal translation consistently rendered, with the interpretive rendering in a footnote will give us a clear understand of the soul. Thus, let us take a few more moments contrasting the dynamic equivalent translation with the literal translation.

Dynamic Equivalent Translations Hide the Truth

1 Kings 2:10 Essentially Literal Translation (ASV, RSV, ESV, NASB)

And <u>David slept</u> with his fathers, and was buried in the city of David.

And <u>David slept</u> with his fathers, and was buried in the city of David.

Then <u>David slept</u> with his fathers and was buried in the city of David.

Then <u>David slept</u> with his fathers and was buried in the city of David.

1 Kings 2:10 Though-for-Thought Translation (GNB, CEV, NLT, MSG)

<u>David died</u> and was buried in David's City.

Then <u>he died</u> and was buried in Jerusalem.

Then <u>David died</u> and was buried with his ancestors in the City of David.

Then <u>David joined his ancestors</u>. He was buried in the City of David.

One could conclude that the thought-for-thought translations are conveying the idea in a more clear and immediate way, but is this really the case? There are three points that are missing from the thought-for-thought translation:

In the scriptures, "sleep" is used metaphorically as death, also inferring a temporary state where one will wake again, or be resurrected. That idea is lost in the thought-for-thought translation. (Ps 13:3; John 11:11-14; Ac 7:60; 1 Cor. 7:39; 15:51; 1Th 4:13)

David's sleeping with or lying down with his father also conveys the idea of having closed his life and having found favor in God's eyes as did his forefathers.

When we leave out some of the words from the original, we also leave out the possibility of more meaning being drawn from the text. Missing is the word *shakab* ("to lie down" or "to sleep"), *'im* ("with") and 'ab in the plural ("forefathers").

Psalm 13:3 American Standard Version (ASV)

Consider *and* answer me, O Jehovah my God: Lighten mine eyes, lest I sleep the *sleep of* death

John 11:11-14 Updated American Standard Version (UASV)

¹¹ After saying these things, he said to them, "Our friend Lazarus has fallen asleep, but I go to awaken him." ¹² The disciples said to him, "Lord, if he has **fallen asleep**, he will get well." ¹³ Now Jesus had spoken of his death, but they thought that he meant taking rest in sleep. ¹⁴ Then Jesus told them plainly, "**Lazarus has died,**

Acts 7:60 Updated American Standard Version (UASV)

⁶⁰ Then falling on his knees, he cried out with a loud voice, "Lord, do not hold this sin against them!" Having said this, **he fell asleep.** [I.e., he died]

1 Corinthians 7:39 Updated American Standard Version (UASV)

³⁹ A wife is bound to her husband as long as he lives. But if her husband dies [lit (*koimethe*) falls asleep [i.e., asleep in death], she is free to be married to whom she wishes, only in the Lord.

1 Corinthians 15:51 Updated American Standard Version (UASV)

⁵¹ Behold, I tell you a mystery; we will not all **sleep [in death]**, but we will all be changed,

1 Thessalonians 4:13 Updated American Standard Version (UASV)

¹³ But we do not want you to be ignorant,[278] brothers, about those who are **asleep [in death]**, so that you will not grieve as do the rest who have no hope.

---

[278] Or *uninformed*

Those who argue for a though-for-thought translation will say the literal translation "slept" or "lay down" is no longer a way of expressing death in the modern English-speaking world. While this may be true to some extent, the context of chapter two, verse 1: "when David was about to die" and the latter half of 2:10: "was buried in the city of David" really resolves that issue. Moreover, while the reader may have to meditate a little longer, or indulge him/herself in the culture of different Biblical times, they will not be deprived of the full potential that a verse has to convey. (*Translating Truth*, Grudem, Ryken, Collins, Polythress, & Winter, 2005, 21-22) Therefore, we offer a word of caution here. The dynamic equivalent can and does obscure things from the reader by overreaching in their translations.

His Spirit Goes Forth and He Returns to the Earth

Psalm 146:4 Young's Literal Translation (YLT)

[4] His spirit goes forth; he returns to his earth, In that day have his thoughts perished.

Are we to understand that there is some spiritual being within us, which then departs from us at death? No, this is not the understanding, as the Psalmist next words were, "In that day have his thoughts perished," ("all his thinking ends," *NEB*). How, then, are we to understand this verse?

In the Hebrew Scriptures, we have *ruach*, and in the Greek New Testament, we have *pneuma*, both with the basic meaning "breath." This is why other translations read, "His breath goes forth."

Psalm 146:4 (ESV)	**Psalm 146:4** (LEB)	**Psalm 146:4** (HCSB)
[4] When his **breath departs**, he returns to the earth; on that very day his plans perish.	[4] His **breath departs**; he returns to his plot; on that day his plans perish.	[4] When his **breath leaves** him, he returns to the ground; on that day his plans die.

You will notice this further clarified, when Moses informs us of what took place at the flood. However, we look at the literal translations first, followed by other literal translations that choose to define the use of the term "spirit." Note how we will use a footnote in the literal, and the others that chose to define.

Genesis 7:22 (NASB)	**Genesis 7:22** (ASV)	**Genesis 7:22** (YLT)
[22] of all that was on the dry land, all in whose	[22] all in whose nostrils was the breath of the	[22] all in whose nostrils [is] breath of a living

nostrils was the breath of the spirit of life **[breath of life]**, died.	spirit of life **[breath of life]**, of all that was on the dry land, died.	spirit **[breath of life]** — of all that [is] in the dry land — have died.

Other literal and semi-literal translations,

Genesis 7:22 (ESV)	**Genesis 7:22** (LEB)	**Genesis 7:22** (NRSV)
²²Everything on the dry land in whose nostrils was the breath of life **["a breath of spirit of life"]** died.	²²Everything in whose nostrils *was the breath of life* **["a breath of spirit of life"]**, among all that *was* on dry land, died	²²everything on dry land in whose nostrils was the breath of life **["a breath of spirit of life"]** died.

Therefore, "*ruach*" and "pneuma," i.e., "spirit" can refer to the breath of life that is active within both human and animal creatures. Then how do we explain Ecclesiastes 12:7?

Ecclesiastes 12:7 English Standard Version (ESV)

⁷and the dust returns to the earth as it was, and the spirit returns to God who gave it.

Are we to understand that a spiritual being within us, leaves us at death, and returns to God? No. We just learned that the "spirit" is the "breath of life," which sustains human and animal life. Once we lose our "breath of life," and are dead, the only hope of having it restored comes from God. Therefore, "the spirit returns to God," in that our only hope for living again, but this time for eternally, comes from God. It is only God, who can restore the "breath of life," which allows us to live again. Keep in mind too, this person was never in heaven with God, so the idea of him as a spirit person returning to God is not what is meant. How can he return to God, if he was never in heaven with God to begin with? Again, it is the "breath of life," which enables the person to live that returns to God, not literally, but in the sense of his having the power to restore it.

Ecclesiastes 12:7 (LEB)	**Ecclesiastes 12:7** (NRSV)
⁷And the dust returns to the earth as it was, and the breath returns to God who gave it.	⁷and the dust returns to the earth as it was, and the breath returns to God who gave it.

All conservative Christians would point to the Bible as the final authority on all doctrine. This is true of our understanding of the *soul* as well. In the Hebrew Old Testament, the Hebrew word *nephesh* (translated "soul" in the UASV) is found 754 times, first in Genesis 1:20. In the Greek New Testament, the Greek word *psuche* (translated "soul" in the UASV) is found by itself 102 times, first in Matthew 2:20. In each case, a literal translation, looking to give its readers what God had said, should render this Hebrew and Greek word "soul," with the interpretive rendering in the footnote. By doing this, the reader of the Bible will be able to see how the word "soul" is used within the whole of the inspired, inerrant Word of God.

CHAPTER 9 Gender-Inclusive Language in Bible Translation

The reader of this book has continuously read interpretive and translation principles that are not only sound but also aid the Christian in understanding the Bible more fully. One such interpretive principle is about the meaning that we are after, what the author meant by the words that he used as should have been understood by his initial intended audience.

When we look at the controversy over gender-inclusive language and the use of plurals, the above principles come into play, as does the historical-grammatical approach, which means that God personally chose the time, the place, the language, and the culture into which his Word was being inspirationally penned. Who are we to disrespect that because we wish to appease the modern man or woman, who may be offended? Their offense is nothing more than self-centeredness, refusing to wrap their mind around the idea that the Creator of all things chose the setting, the language, and time in which his Word was to be introduced to man.

D. A. Carson in the publication: *The Challenge of Bible Translation* wishes to address the issue of gender-inclusive language and singular and plurals forms, in which he addresses comments made by Wayne A. Grudem and Vern S. Poythress. We will be addressing Carson's comments.

The Chief Translation Principle Is Accuracy

The chief principle that supersedes all others is accuracy, accuracy, and accuracy! In the above, we define Biblical meaning as the original author's intended meaning, by the words he chose to use; therefore, the translator seeks to accurately represent the exact wording and personal style of the original text and find the corresponding English equivalent as far as the differences in grammar, syntax, and idiom will allow. In other words, he seeks 'to render the *words* of the original language text into an English equivalent (corresponding) word or phrase as *accurately* as possible.' The translator wants to re-express what the original language text says into an English equivalent, leaving it up to the reader, to determine the meaning for himself. Therefore, it seeks to allow the reader to see the original text through the English equivalent.

Liberal-progressive Christianity has taken the driver's seat of the car of Christendom and has conservative Christianity riding in the back seat, if not the trunk. The liberal-progressive mindset of homosexuality being an accepted alternative lifestyle, the belief that the Bible is nothing more than a book by man, and inspiration is not being led by "Holy Spirit," but simply being moved to pen something extraordinary, no different than a Shakespeare or even a John Grisham novel. Therefore, they accept the Bible as being full of errors, and that Adam and Eve are nothing more than allegorical (fictional) persons.

What these gender-inclusive translators fail to understand is this: to deviate, in any way, from the pattern, or likeness of how God brought his Word into existence, merely opens the Bible up to a book that reflects the age and time of its readers. If we allow the Bible to be altered because the progressive woman's movement feels offended by masculine language, it will not be long before the Bible gives way to the homosexual communities being offended by God's Words in the book of Romans; so modern translations will then tame that language, so as to not cause offense. I am certain that we thought that we would never see the day of two men, or two women being married by priests, but that day has been upon us for some time now. In fact, the American government is debating whether to change the definition of marriage. Therefore, I would suggest that the liberal readers do not take my warning here as radicalism, but more as reality.

Additionally: One has to consider the whole scope of translation issues. Let us look at the arguments directly from a modern thought-for-thought translation: Eugene Peterson:

> While I was teaching a class on Galatians, I began to realize that the adults in my class weren't feeling the vitality and directness that I sensed as I read and studied the New Testament in its original Greek. Writing straight from the original text, I began to attempt to bring into English the rhythms and idioms of the original language. I knew that the early readers of the New Testament were captured and engaged by these writings and I wanted my congregation to be impacted in the same way. I hoped to bring the New Testament to life for two different types of people: those who hadn't read the Bible because it seemed too distant and irrelevant and those who had read the Bible so much that it had become 'old hat.'

As we can see, the focus here is on the reader and trying to appease them, both new and old readers alike. Let us take a quick look at the words of the apostle Peter before commenting:

2 Peter 3:16 Updated American Standard Version (UASV)

¹⁶ as also in all his [the apostle Paul's] letters, speaking in them of these things, in which are some things **hard to understand**, which the untaught and unstable distort, as they do also the rest of the Scriptures, to their own **destruction**.

The Bible is a very complex and deep book. There are literally dozens of books available on how to interpret the Bible. Some of these books are over 600 pages long, with very small print. To read these books, one has to have a dictionary in one hand and their hermeneutics book in the other. Do we, not find it a bit ironic that one has to slow down and meditatively ponder through a book on how to understand the Bible, yet we wish to put the Bible itself, in third to sixth-grade language. Many of the words in these hermeneutic books are foreign to the lay reader: amanuensis, chiasm, exegesis, contextualization, criticism, didactic, etymology, genre, hermeneutics, hyponoia, metaphor, metonymy, pericope, perspicuity, proof-text, rhetoric, semantics, structuralism, synecdoche and so on. How many of these words do we think the new Bible reader knows offhand, without going to a dictionary?

Herein is where the real problem lies. In the first century, all Christians were evangelizers. All Christians were obligated to be teachers of the good news, to make disciples. (Matthew 24:14, 28:19-20; Ac 1:8) Bible scholar John R. W. Stott noted:

> Our failure to obey the implications of this command is the greatest weakness of evangelical Christians in the field of evangelism today. He added: We tend to proclaim our message from a distance. We sometimes appear like people who shout advice to drowning men from the safety of the seashore. We do not dive in to rescue them. We are afraid of getting wet.

Imagine this scenario: if every member of Christendom took on their responsibility to teach new persons, there would be no need to write a Bible translation on the sixth- grade level. Another factor to consider is, 'why are we so bent on adjusting God's Word to appease man that we neglect to be respectful of God's choice of when, how, and in what way his Word was to be made known?'

Hebrews 2:6 (English Standard Version)	Hebrews 2:6 (Today's New International Version)
6 It has been testified somewhere, "What is man, that you are mindful of him? or the <u>son of man</u>, that you care for him?	6 But there is a place where someone has testified: "What are mere mortals that you are mindful of them, human beings that you care for them?
Psalm 8:4 (English Standard Version) [8:5 in the Hebrew text]	**Psalm 8:4** (Today's New International Version) [8:5 in the Hebrew text]
4 What is man, that you are mindful of him? and the son of man that you care for him?	4 what are mere mortals that you are mindful of *them*, human beings that you care for them?

In the Gospel accounts, the expression "son of man" is found over 80 times, with no scholar in denial that every instance it is applied Jesus Christ, being used by him to refer to himself. (Mt 8:20; 9:6; 10:23) There are several occurrences outside the Gospels, one being our above Hebrews 2:6.

The apostle Paul applied Psalm 8 as prophetic of Jesus Christ. In the book of Hebrews (2:5-9), Paul quoted the verses, which read, "What is man [*enohsh*] that you are mindful of him, and the son of man [*benadham*] that you care of him? Yet you have made him a little lower than the heavenly beings ["angels" Septuagint; "a little lower than angels," at Hebrews 2:7] and crowned him with glory and honor. You have given him dominion over the works of your hands; you have put all things under his feet." (Ps 8:4-6; compare Ps 144:3, ESV) There is no doubt that Paul was applying this prophetic Psalm to Jesus, and stating that it had been fulfilled in him, as Jesus was made "a little lower than angels," and becoming a mortal "son of man," in order that he may die and thereby "taste death for everyone." (Heb. 2:8-9) The TNIV has removed Christ from this prophecy at Psalm 8:4 and its application to him by Paul, with its mere mortals, them, human beings, and them. How do Carson and other gender inclusive translators rationalize such a move? Carson writes:

> In Psalm 8, the overwhelming majority of commentators see the expression as a **gentilic**, parallel to the Hebrew word for "man" in the preceding line. . . . In the context of the application of Psalm 8:4 to Jesus in Hebrews 2, one should at least recognize that the nature of the application to Jesus is disputed. Scanning my commentaries on Hebrews, over three-quarters of them do not think that "son of man" here functions as a messianic title but simply

as a **gentilic**, as in Psalm 8.[279] If this exegesis is correct (and I shall argue elsewhere and at length that it is), Jesus is said to be "son of man," not in function of the messianic force of that title in Daniel 7:13-14, but in function of his becoming a human being – which all sides recognize is one of the major themes of Hebrews 2. (Scorgie, Strauss, & Voth, 2003, bolding mine)

The **gentilic criterion** requires one of two constructions: (1) It must end with, *hireq-yod* or (2) take the definite article.

Biblia Hebraica Stuttgartensia [Literal English Translation]

you remember him that and <u>son of man</u> you remember him that man what (is)

Take note that *ben-adam* of Genesis 8:4 fit neither of the gentilic criterions: (1) It must end with, *hireq-yod* or (2) take the definite article. In addition, Carson claims 'most commentators hold that it is not a messianic title, but apply it to the messiah.' In response to that, we would suggest that we skip what most people think because much of mankind's tragedies have come by way of what people have thought to be the case, when, in fact, they were just plain wrong. Also, why block the reader from the possibility? Why not let the reader have the literal words, instead of a translator's interpretation of, and allow the reader to decide through their own exegesis, what the writer of Hebrews meant by those words. Moreover, the writer of Hebrews would likely have been aware of Matthew's Gospel written in Hebrew and the Greek edition as well, in which "son of man" is used some 31 times. In addition, the readers of the book of Hebrews, the Jewish Christians, would be reading the Greek phrase *huios anthrōpou* ("son of man") in the Greek Septuagint at Psalm 8 as well. Moreover, by now the Gospels had been published **orally** for almost 30-years and Matthew in written form for about 15-years, making known that Jesus referred to himself as *huios anthrōpou* ("son of man"). If Jesus applied this title to himself, it should be evident that the writer of Hebrews was doing no less, and at least the original readers had a chance to reach this conclusion because the exact words were not hidden from them.

The TNIV and its plural "human beings" for *huios anthrōpou* ("son of man") go beyond translation and gets into playing the role of a commentary. First, we have the rendering of a singular as a plural. Second, "human beings" inappropriate though it may be is meant to convey the idea of humankind, but we have a word that is left out: *huios* (son) in the Greek of Hebrews 2:6

---

[279] *This writer has found about forty of them that think otherwise. Moreover, the principle of scholarship is that you never count anything, with the majority winning, or being right. For example, I do not say a certain reading in the manuscripts is correct, because the majority of the manuscripts have that reading. I choose the best reading based on evidence.*

and *bēn* (son) in the Hebrew of Psalm 8:4. In this, we are losing the father-son relationship.

Those who speak and read English enjoy the benefit of having more than 100 different English translations. If one translation does not fit our preconceived notion of what a particular passage says, we can simply choose another, and another, until we find a translation that reads the way we want. If we search through the translations until we find the rendering of our choice; then, what have we learned that we already did not know? God's Word is a revelation from our heavenly Father, about himself, his will and purposes, to us, his creation. It was written in such a way, to …

(1) Help the reader draw closer to his Creator

(2) Comprehend the issues within creation

(3) Understand why we are here and how we are to achieve a good life while we are still within Satan's system of things

(4) Direction to help us achieve life in the new heavens and earth to come under Christ and his kingdom

We are to mold ourselves to God's Word, to achieve the best possible life now and a hope at everlasting life when this age of wickedness ends. How is that to be done if our translators are busy adjusting his Word to suit the modern reader; instead, of our adjusting ourselves to fit His Word? God's Word was rendered to reflect his choosing of the time, the place, the language, and the culture? It seems that sales and the need to please man [or woman in this case] have taken on more significance than the accurate message of God's Word.

CHAPTER 10 Theological Bias in Bible Translation

John 8:58 is one of the most hotly debated verses in the Bible, so our investigation begins and ends here.

UASV	ESV, LEB, HCSB, RSV	NLV	CEV
Jesus said to them, "Most truly I say to you, *Before* Abraham came to be, I have been *in existence*."	Jesus said to them, "Truly, truly, I say to you, *before* Abraham was, I am."	Jesus said to them, "For sure, I tell you, **before Abraham was born**, I was and am and always will be!"	Jesus answered, "I tell you for certain that even **before Abraham was**, I was, and I am."
NLT	**NAB**	**TEV, GNT**	**NASB, ASV**
Jesus answered, "I tell you the truth, *before* **Abraham was even born**, I AM!	Jesus said to them, "Amen, amen, I say to you, *before* **Abraham came to be**, I AM."	"I am telling you the truth," Jesus replied. "*Before* **Abraham was born**, 'I AM'."	Jesus said to them, "Truly, truly, I say to you, **before Abraham was born**, I am."

John 8:58 American Translation (AT) Jesus said to them, "I tell you, I existed *before* **Abraham was born!**"

Throughout this entire publication, we have preached the importance of the literal translation philosophy. However, we have repeatedly said that there are two exceptions to the literal, philosophical position, **(1)** if the rendering ends up nonsensical, or **(2)** the rendering presents misinformation. As you can see from the above, there are several different things going on:

(1) Some are trying to remain to what they believe is literal (RSV, ESV, and LEB),

(2) Others are trying to get at the sense of what Jesus meant by the words that he used and how he used them (ASV, UASV, and NASB).

(3) Some are demonstrating theological bias (NLT, NAB, TEV and GNT).

Before we begin our investigation, first, let us consider some sound advice from the chief translator of the Good News Bible (TEV) Robert Bratcher:

> "At least it can be agreed that any translation, in order to be considered good, should satisfy three requirements: **(1)** it should handle textual matters in an informed and responsible way. . . . **(2)** Its exegesis of the original texts should be theologically unbiased ... **(3)** Its language should be contemporary; it should conform to normal English usage. – Bratcher 1978, pp 115-116.

First, we do not have to worry about any textual problem with John 8:58. However, his very translation, the Today's English Version (TEV) violated point number 2, in that his team's exegesis was certainly theologically biased here at John 8:58. As to point number 3, we have already stated our position on that through this publication. Now, before we delve into how the NLT, NAB, TEV, and GNT are theologically biased here, let us look at the original Greek.

εἶπεν αὐτοῖς Ἰησοῦς, Ἀμὴν ἀμὴν λέγω ὑμῖν, πρὶν Ἀβραὰμ
Said to them Jesus   truly truly I say to you before Abraham

γενέσθαι ἐγὼ εἰμί
to become I am

We likely recall that an interlinear study tool is not interested in grammar and syntax, but rather only in the lexical English corresponding equivalent. Therefore, the first person, personal pronoun *ego* would be rendered "I" and the present, active, indicative, verb *eimi* would be rendered "am." It is not until we bring our lexical glosses over into English that we begin our investigation of the grammar and syntax.

Grammar and Syntax

- **πρὶν**: Adjective Adverb ["before"] (adverbial past time expression)

- **Ἀβραὰμ**: Noun Accusative ["Abraham"] (Direct Object)

- **γενέσθαι**: Verb Infinitive Aorist Middle-Deponent [came to be] (past tense)

- **ἐγὼ**: Noun Pronoun Nominative ["I"] (Subject)

- **εἰμί**: Verb Indicative Present Active ["I am"]

Having [before Abraham / came to be / I am] as far as English word order is fine, but we are violating verb compatibility, mixing a present tense with a past tense; which is not grammatically correct. In both Greek and English, we would put or find our past tense first, followed by the present tense; logically reasoning that the past happened before the present. However, the adverb "before" affects this decision, for it informs us that the action expressed by our present tense verb ("am") not only began in the past, but it was before our past tense verb ("came to be"), and up unto our past tense verb and still in progress at the time this clause was uttered.

Lexical-Syntactical Analysis and Comparison

In this stage, we will continue with our look at individual words (lexicology), but we will also take a deeper look into our new stage of how these words are dealt with in concert with each other (syntax). However, to avoid theological bias, we will look at two other examples of this same grammatical construction in the Gospel of John first, staying outside of the highly theologically charged John 8:58 at this time, to see how other translations deal with the grammatical construction before rendering John 8:58.

John 14:9

λέγει αὐτῷ ὁ Ἰησοῦς, Τοσούτῳ χρόνῳ μεθ' ὑμῶν
Says to him the Jesus   in such   time with you

εἰμι καὶ οὐκ   ἔγνωκάς   με,
I am and not you have known me

Literal: So much time with you I am

The "I am" present indicative of John 14:9 is 'modified' by the past time expression "so much time." How do our translations render this verse? Do they ignore the grammar rules, using present tense ("I am"), or do they follow the grammar rules that we are about to discuss, and use a perfect tense ("have been")? Our translations below do follow the grammar rule.

ESV	NASB	ASV	HCSB
Have I been with you so long	Have I been so long with you	Have I been so long time with you	Have I been among you all this time

John 15:27

καὶ ὑμεῖς δὲ μαρτυρεῖτε, ὅτι ἀπ'   ἀρχῆς   μετ' ἐμοῦ ἐστε
also you but   testify   that from beginning with me you are

The "you are" present indicative of **John 15:27** is 'modified' by the past time expression "from the beginning."

ESV	NASB	ASV	HCSB
you have been with me from the beginning	you have been with Me from the beginning	ye have been with me from the beginning	you have been with Me from the beginning

Greek Grammar

At this point, it is time to visit the Greek grammars, looking for this particular construction that we have found in John 8:58, as well as all throughout the Gospel of John. The grammar rule for a present tense that is

200

found positioned with an adverbial expression of past time and duration is largely known as a PPA

Moulton's references Ernest De Witt Burton in his *Syntax of the Moods and Tenses in N.T. Greek*, 'The Tenses,' par.17, p.10, we can read: "17. **The Present of Past Action still in progress [PPA]**. The Present Indicative, accompanied by an adverbial expression denoting duration and referring to past time, is sometimes used in Greek, as in German, to describe an action which, beginning in past time, is still in progress at the time of speaking. <u>English idiom requires the use of the Perfect in such cases.</u>" Bold and underline is mine.

A Manual Grammar of the Greek New Testament, by Dana and Mantey, MacMillan, 1927, p. 183, says, "Sometimes the progressive present is retroactive in its application, denoting that which has begun in the past and continued into the present. For the want of a better name, we may call it the present of duration. This use is generally associated with an adverb of time, and may best be rendered by the English perfect. "Ye have been (present tense) with me from the beginning" John 15:27."

A Grammar of New Testament Greek, by J. H. Moulton, Vol. III, by Nigel Turner, Edinburgh, 1963, p. 62, says, "The Present which indicates the continuance of an action during the past and up to the moment of speaking is virtually the same as Perfective, the only difference being that the action is conceived as still in progress . . . It is frequent in the N[ew] T[estament]: Lk 2^{48} 13^7 . . . 15^{29} . . . Jn 5^6 8^{58} . . . "

Greek Grammar for Colleges, by Herbert Weir Smyth, New York, 1920, pp. 422-423: "The present, when accompanied by a definite or indefinite expression of past time, is used to express an action begun in the past and continued in the present. The 'progressive perfect' is often used in translation. Thus,... **I have been long** (and am still) **wondering.**"

The Expository Times, 1996, page 302 by Kenneth McKay says, "The verb 'to be' is used differently, in what is presumably its basic meaning of 'be in existence', in John 8:58: *prin Abraam genesthai ego eimi*, which would be most naturally translated 'I have been in existence since before Abraham was born', if it were not for the obsession with the simple words 'I am'. If we take the Greek words in their natural meaning, as we surely should, the claim to have been in existence for so long is in itself a staggering one, quite enough to provoke the crowd's violent reaction."

As we can see, the translations have been following the grammar rule known as PPA, the Present of Past Action still in progress, where in a present indicative ("I am" or "you are"), which is accompanied by an adverbial expression ("so much time" or "from the beginning"), is rendered with the

201

perfect tense of "have been." The PPA is describing an action that began in the past and has run up unto the time of writing or speaking. Let us pause and look at two more examples.

John 8:24

ἐὰν γὰρ μὴ πιστεύσητε ὅτι ἐγώ εἰμι, ἀποθανεῖσθε ἐν
if   for not you might trust that I   am   you will die in

ταῖς ἁμαρτίαις ὑμῶν
the   sins   of you

We have an implied predicate nominative ("he") that comes after the "I am."

ESV	NASB	ASV	HCSB
for unless you believe that I am **he** you will die in your sins.	for unless you believe that I am **He,** you will die in your sins.	for except ye believe that I am **he,** ye shall die in your sins.	for unless you believe that I am **He,** you will die in your sins."

Notice that all of these translations recognize the implied predicate nominative ("he") that comes after the "I am."

John 4:26

26 λέγει αὐτῇ ὁ Ἰησοῦς, Ἐγώ εἰμι, ὁ   λαλῶν   σοι
Says to her the Jesus   I   am the one speaking to you

Here in John chapter 4, you have Jesus being spoken to by a Samaritan woman. She is inquiring about the coming Messiah, and Jesus does something with the Samaritan woman that he has not done even with his disciples, He discloses who he really is, "I am the one" [i.e., the Messiah]. The ESV, like the other translations that we have considered, is aware that there is an implied predicate pronoun in the sentence "I am [he] the one speaking to you."

ESV	NASB	ASV	HCSB
Jesus said to her, "I who speak to you am **he**."	Jesus said to her, "I who speak to you am **He**."	Jesus saith unto her, I that speak unto thee am **he**.	"I am **He**," Jesus told her, "the One speaking to you."

The predicate nominative is supplied from context in the English translation.

John 13:19

ἵνα πιστεύσητε ὅταν γένηται ὅτι ἐγώ εἰμι
that you might trust when it might become because I __am__

The Lexham English Bible writes in a footnote, "Here the predicate nominative (*"he"*) is understood but must be supplied in the translation." Again, our other translations recognize this.

ESV	NASB	ASV	HCSB
I am telling you this now, before it takes place, that when it does take place you may believe that I am **he**.	From now on I am telling you before it comes to pass, so that when it does occur, you may believe that I am **He**.	From henceforth I tell you before it come to pass, that, when it is come to pass, ye may believe that I am **he**.	I am telling you now before it happens, so that when it does happen you will believe that I am **He**.

Jesus is merely pointing to himself as a fulfillment of the prophecy in which one of his closest disciples would betray him. (See John 13:18 and Psalm 41:9)

Context, Context, Context

The most important interpretation rule is the context. All along, our grammar has been telling us about the PPA rule. The PPA is describing an action that began in the past and had run up unto the time of writing or speaking. The question is, do we find the context of John 8:58 as being in harmony with our grammar. Well, let us look at the verse(s) that come before and after our verse. In verse 57, the Jews ask a question in reference to Jesus statement in verse 56: "Your father Abraham rejoiced that he would see my day. He saw it and was glad." Thus, they reasonably ask, "You are not yet fifty years old and have you seen Abraham?" It is all too clear that we have a question that is based on age, not Jesus' identity.

John 8:56-59 New American Standard Bible (NASB)	**John 8:56-59** Updated American Standard Version (UASV)
[56] Your father Abraham rejoiced to see My day, and he saw *it* and was	[56] Your father Abraham rejoiced that he would see my day. He saw it and

glad." [57] So the Jews said to Him, "You are not yet fifty years old, and have You seen Abraham?" [58] Jesus said to them, "Truly, truly, I say to you, before Abraham was born, I am." [59] Therefore they picked up stones to throw at Him, but Jesus hid Himself and went out of the temple.	rejoiced." [57] So the Jews said to him, "You are not yet fifty years old, and have you seen Abraham?" [58] Jesus said to them, "Truly, truly, I say to you, I have been in existence since before Abraham was born." [59] So they picked up stones to throw at him, but Jesus hid himself and went out of the temple.

Clearly, John 8:58 has no meaning in the way of expressing existence or some kind of identity. Why are we even saying this? Because the theologically biased translators attempt to argue that that the "I am" is not predicated. In other words, for them the "I am" is absolute, a reference to what they perceive to be the divine name in Exodus 3:14.[280] These translators believe that the "I AM" as they render it is a title for Jesus, which ties him into Exodus 3:14, which is rendered, "God replied to Moses, 'I AM who I AM. Say this to the people of Israel: I AM has sent me to you.'" Notice that the NLT capitalizes the "I AM" in both John 8:58 and Exodus 3:14. There is no objective reason to capitalize the "I AM." It is completely subjective, in that their agenda is to tie Jesus in with Exodus 3:14. However, that alone is a problem, because Exodus 3:14 is referring to the Father, and John 8:58 is referring to Jesus, his length of existence actually. Therefore, the Son and the Father are two separate persons. Moreover, the context is not about the person of Jesus or his title, but the length of his existence, i.e., how long he has been around.

Bible Background

Our historical-cultural question is addressed in verse 59, where we find the Jews seeking to stone Jesus for his response. What was there about Jesus' response that would result in their attempting to stone him? First, to claim to have been in existence since before Abraham and up unto this point; would mean Jesus was/is a divine person. Bible scholar Kenneth L. McKay wrote: "to claim to have been in existence for so long is in itself a staggering one, quite enough to provoke the crowd's violent reaction." – McKay: *The Expository Times*, 1996, p. 302.

Our "am" present indicative is 'modified' by the adverbial past time expression of *prin* (before), an adverb. In other words, "**Before** Abraham came to be." As many grammarians have suggested, getting the exact sense of the original Greek, it is best to render the present indicative "am" as the perfect indicative "have been." It is not only best, but also required as was

---

[280] **Exodus 3:14 New Living Translation (NLT)** [14] God replied to Moses, "I AM who I AM. Say this to the people of Israel: I AM has sent me to you."

said; the present indicative "am" is 'modified' to the perfect indicative "have been."

As was said earlier, a translation should reflect the meaning of the original Greek in English by way of being unbiased, accurate, clear, and natural. Is a translation *unbiased* to follow a grammatical construction in other parts of John when there is no theological significance at stake, but to abandon this grammar at John 8:58? Is it *unbiased* to capitalize **εἰμί** (*eimi*) as "I AM" when there is absolutely no authority for such a decision? Is a translator *accurately* communicating the correct sense when he ignores the grammar and the context and takes it upon himself to render a verse based on his preconceived understanding? Is it *clear* if the reader is blocked by the translator's choice and is unable to achieve the correct mental understanding of the original writer? Does the translation that reads, "Before Abraham came to be, I AM," sound *natural* in our English language and is it appropriate?

Final Analysis

The final analysis is to ask how John 8:58b should be translated into English? Let us look for the bounds that we have set forth here in this chapter: grammatical, coherent and conveying what was meant, as well as the avoidance of intentional theological bias. Our objective is to follow the principle mentioned in Dr. Robert H. Stein's lectures, i.e., 'render it as it should be, if it supports a doctrinal position, so be it. However, if it does not support a doctrinal position, so be it as well. God does not need our help in conveying a doctrine. No doctrine is built on any one Scripture.'

John 8:58

Jesus said to them, "Amen, amen, I say to you, *before* **Abraham came to be,** I AM."

[This is the most common rendering minus the capitalization of the "I AM." However, it falls short in many areas. First, it is not grammatically correct, because the English present come before some past time. This makes it incoherent, meaning that it does not convey the sense that Jesus was attempting to express. It has elements of theological bias because of the capitalization of the "I AM."]

John 8:58

Jesus said to them, "Truly, truly, I say to you, *before* **Abraham came to be,** I am."

[Again, this rendering falls short in at least two areas. First, it is not grammatically correct, because the English present come before some past time. This makes it incoherent, meaning that it does not convey these sense that Jesus was attempting to express.]

John 8:58

Jesus said to them, "Truly, truly, I say to you, *before* **Abraham came into being,** I was."

[This rendering is grammatically correct, making it coherent, and possesses some semblance of what Jesus meant. However, Jesus entire thought was that he was in existence prior to Abraham and had been living up unto his present conversation.]

John 8:58

Jesus said to them, "Most truly I say to you, *Before* **Abraham came to be,** I have been *in existence*."

[This is the least favored by most translators, even though they use "have been" with the same grammatical construction elsewhere in the Gospel of John. An earlier edition of the New American Standard Bible had "I have been" as a marginal note. It is not grammatical as far as English goes because a perfect cannot appear with specifying adverbials. However, it is coherent in that the reader now fully understand what Jesus meant about his being in existence prior to Abraham's being born and has existed up unto his current conversation. It is also the recommended rendering by the grammarians because of the present indicative "I am," which is accompanied by an adverbial expression "before," so it should be rendered with the perfect tense of "have been."]

The problem that we have is that we must set aside our desire to be literal here because the Greek and English have two different aspects. While there is a distaste for "**Before Abraham came to be,** I have been in existence," it must be the preferred choice because it conveys the entire sense of what Jesus meant to convey, although it is ungrammatical in English. There is no theological baggage of trying to tie it to any other text, nor some avoidance of a grammar rule because it does not fit our preconceived ideas. One way to deal with the issue would be to adopt the dynamic equivalent rendering by K. L. McKay, "I have been in existence before Abraham was born."[281]

---

[281] K. L. McKay, A New Syntax of the Verb in New Testament Greek, and the Gospel of John, 91.

CHAPTER 11 A Worthy Translation is Faithful

What exactly do we mean by faithful, and faithful to what or whom? By faithful, we mean unwavering to the original, to the author himself. However, there are times when translation committees choose to be unfaithful to the original text. Obviously, theological bias should not affect its rendering.

Romans 9:5 (RSV)	Romans 9:5 (NLT)
5 to them belong the patriarchs, and of their race, according to the flesh, is the Christ. God who is over all be blessed forever. Amen.	5 Abraham, Isaac, and Jacob are their ancestors, and Christ himself was an Israelite as far as his human nature is concerned. And he is God, the one who rules over everything and is worthy of eternal praise! Amen.

Romans 9:5: The Revised Standard Version takes *ho on* ["the one who is"] as the opening of a separate, stand-alone sentence or clause that is independent of Christ, which is referring to God (the Father) and pronouncing a blessing upon him for the provisions he made. Here and in Ps 67:19 in the LXX[282] the predicate *eulogetos* [blessed"] occurs after the subject *Theos* ["God"]. Textual scholar, Bruce M. Metzger made the following point:

> On the other hand, in the opinion of others of the Committee, none of these considerations seemed to be decisive, particularly since nowhere else in his genuine epistles does Paul ever designate ho khristos ["the Christ"] as Theos ["God"]. In fact, on the basis of the general tenor of his theology it was considered tantamount to impossible that Paul would have expressed Christ's greatness by calling him God blessed forever.[283]

A detailed study of the construction in Romans 9:5 is found in *The Authorship of the Fourth Gospel and Other Critical Essays,* by Ezra Abbot, Boston, 1888, pp. 332-438. On pp. 345, 346 and 432 he says:

> "But here *ho on* ["the one who is"] is separated from *ho khristos* ["the Christ"] by to kata *sarka* ["according to the

---

[282] Septuagint (Greek translation of the Hebrew Old Testament)

[283] Bruce Manning Metzger and United Bible Societies, *A Textual Commentary on the Greek New Testament, Second Edition a Companion Volume to the United Bible Societies' Greek New Testament (4th Rev. Ed.)* (London; New York: United Bible Societies, 1994), 461-62.

flesh"], which in reading *must* be followed by a pause,—a pause which is lengthened by the special emphasis given to the kata *sarka* ["according to the flesh"] by the *to* ["the"]; and the sentence which precedes is complete in itself grammatically, and requires nothing further logically; for it was only as to the flesh that Christ was from the Jews. On the other hand, as we have seen (p. 334), the enumeration of blessings which immediately precedes, crowned by the inestimable blessing of the advent of Christ, naturally suggests an ascription of praise and thanksgiving to God as the Being who rules over all; while a doxology is also suggested by the Amen ["Amen"] at the end of the sentence. From every point of view, therefore, the doxological construction seems easy and natural. . . . The naturalness of a pause after *sarka* ["flesh"] is further indicated by the fact that we find a point after this word in all our oldest MSS. that testify in the case,—namely, A, B, C, L, . . . I can now name, besides the uncials A, B, C, L, . . . at least twenty-six cursives which have a stop after *sarka* ["flesh"], the same in general which they have after *aionas* ["forever"] or Amen ["Amen"]."

Therefore, Romans 9:5 in the Revised Standard Version is correct in its ascribing praise and thanksgiving to God (the Father).

The problem is compounded by the fact that there is practically no punctuation in the ancient manuscripts and we must decide for ourselves whether it is better to put a comma or a full stop after "flesh"; the former ascribes deity to Christ, the latter makes for a doxology to the Father. The grammatical arguments almost all favor the first position, but most recent scholars accept the second on the grounds that Paul nowhere else says explicitly that Christ is God; he may come near it, but, they say, he always stops short of it.[284]

Acts 20:28 (RSV)	Acts 20:28 (NLT)
[28] Take heed to yourselves and to all the flock, in which the Holy Spirit has made you overseers, to care for the	[28] So guard yourselves and God's people. Feed and shepherd God's flock, his church, purchased with his

---

[284] Leon Morris, *The Epistle to the Romans* (Grand Rapids, Mich.; Leicester, England: W.B. Eerdmans; Inter-Varsity Press, 1988), 349.

church of God which he obtained with the blood of his own Son.	own blood, over which the Holy Spirit has appointed you as elders.

Acts 20:28:[285] The RSV reads that the church was purchased with "the blood of his [God's] own Son." On the other hand, the NLT reads that the church was purchased with "God's . . . own blood." Before we can begin determining which of these two renderings is correct, it should be noted that we have two textual problems within this verse. As we are a publication for the lay reader, we will cover the issues, but if any wishes a more technical answer, see *A Textual Commentary on the Greek New Testament* (2nd ed.), by Bruce M. Metzger (1993), or *the New Testament Text and Translation Commentary* by Philip W. Comfort (2008).

Acts 20:28a has three different readings within the Greek New Testament manuscripts: variant (1) "the church of God," variant (2) "the church of the Lord," and variant (3) "the church of the Lord and God." Variant 1 has the better manuscript support and is the choice of the Textus Receptus of 1551, Westcott and Hort text of 1881, the text of Nestle-Aland and the Greek New Testament of the United Bible Society of 1993. The expression "the church of the Lord" is found nowhere in the New Testament. "the church of God" is found eleven times, all by the Apostle Paul, and Luke, the writer of Acts, who was Paul's traveling companion.

The textual criticism principle of what reading led to the other will be discussed in two parts. There is no doubt that variant 3 is simply a conflation (combination of variant 1 and variant 2). If "the church of the Lord" is the original reading, it could be that a copyist familiar with Paul made the change to "the church of God." On the other hand, if "the church of God" is the original reading, there is the slight chance that a copyist was influenced by the Greek Old Testament (Septuagint), and changed it to "the church of the Lord."

However, our other principle of textual criticism, 'the more difficult reading is to be preferred' (more difficult to understand), seems to be most helpful. This principle is also related to 'the reading that led to the other,' as the copyist would have moved to an easier reading. The reason being is that it was the tendency of scribes to make difficult readings easier to understand. There is no doubt that "the church of God" is the most difficult reading. Why? The following clause, which will be dealt with shortly could have been

---

[285] * J. H. Moulton in A Grammar of New Testament Greek, Vol. 1 (Prolegomena), 1930 ed., p. 90, says: "Before leaving ἴδιος [*idios*] something should be said about the use of ὁ ἴδιος [*ho idios*] without a noun expressed. This occurs in Jn 111 131, Ac 423 2423. In the papyri we find the singular used thus as a term of endearment to near relations . . . . In Expos. VI. iii. 277 I ventured to cite this as a possible encouragement to those (including B. Weiss) who would translate Acts 2028 'the blood of one who was his own.'"

taken as "which he purchased with his own blood." This would almost certainly cause pause for any copyist, asking himself, 'does God have blood?' Thus, the original was "the church of God," which was changed to "the church of the Lord," because the idea of saying 'God had blood' would have been repugnant. All things being considered (internal and external evidence), the correct reading is "the church of God."

Acts 20:28b has two different readings within the Greek New Testament Manuscripts:

(1) [literally, the Greek reads "which he purchased with the blood of his own"] "which he [God] purchased with the blood of his own [Son]" or "which he [God] purchased with his own blood" and,

(2) [literally, the Greek reads "which he purchased with the own blood"] "which he purchased with his own blood"

Variant one has the best manuscript evidence by far, and there is no question that it is the original reading. Therefore, we will not use space debating the two but will spend our time determining how it should be understood. Textual scholar Bruce Metzger had this to say,

> This absolute use of ho *idios* ["his Own"] is found in Greek papyri as a term of endearment referring to near relatives. It is possible, therefore, that "his Own" (*ho idios*) was a title that early Christians gave to Jesus, comparable to "the Beloved"; compare Ro 8:32, where Paul refers to God "who did not spare tou idiou huiou ["his own Son"] in a context that clearly alludes to Gn 22:16, where the Septuagint has agapetou huiou ["beloved Son"].
>
> It may well be, as Lake and Cadbury point out, that after the special meaning of ho *idios* ["his Own"] (discussed in *the previous comment) had dropped out of Christian usage, tou* idiou ["of his own"] of this passage was misunderstood as a qualification of haimatos ("his own blood"). "This misunderstanding led to two changes in the text: *tou haimatos tou idiou* ["the blood of his own"] was changed to *tou idiou haimatos* ["his own blood"] (influenced by Heb. ix. 12?), which is neater but perverts the sense, and *Theou* ["God"] was changed to *kuriou* ["Lord"] by the Western revisers,

who doubtless shrank from the implied phrase 'the blood of God.'"[286]

In the end, we must draw the conclusion from all of the evidence; the Revised Standard Version has followed the evidence, with its rendering: "Take heed to yourselves and to all the flock, in which the Holy Spirit has made you overseers, to care for the church of God which he obtained with the blood of his own Son." On the other hand, it seems that the New Living Translation publisher or committee has allowed theological bias, once again, to blind them from the evidence, as their rendering makes clear: "So guard yourselves and God's people. Feed and shepherd God's flock, his church, purchased with his own blood, over which the Holy Spirit has appointed you as elders. Dr. Robert H. Stein said in a lecture at Southern Baptist Theological Seminary, 'God does not need our help [in translation]. Simply render it as it should be, whether it supports your position or not.'

Another translation that is no longer being used, but can illustrate a lack of faithfulness to the original is Moffatt's *New Translation of the Bible*. Repeatedly he arranges chapters and verses in a way to suit himself in both the Hebrew Scriptures and the Christian Greek Scriptures. Particularly in what he does with the book of Isaiah is open to censure, rearranging the chapters and verses to suit himself. The Dead Sea Scroll of Isaiah, going back, as it does, about a thousand years earlier than the accepted Masoretic text, leaves Dr. Moffatt without any justification whatsoever for such rearranging of Isaiah. This makes it difficult to find certain Bible texts.

---

[286] Bruce Manning Metzger and United Bible Societies, *A Textual Commentary on the Greek New Testament, Second Edition a Companion Volume to the United Bible Societies' Greek New Testament (4th Rev. Ed.)* (London; New York: United Bible Societies, 1994), 427.

CHAPTER 12 Review of Rolf J. Furuli, The Role of Theology and Bias in Bible Translation

Dr. Mark A. House

Director of Online Biblical Greek Studies Reformed Theological Seminary

Review of Rolf J. Furuli: *With a Special Look at the New World Translation of Jehovah's Witnesses* **(Second Edition; Stavern, Norway: Awatu Publishers, 2011).**

Reviewed by Dr. Mark A. House

Dr. Rolf Furuli lectures in Semitic languages at the University of Olso, where he has taught courses in Hebrew and a number of related languages. His previous publications include studies in the Hebrew verbal system—the subject of this 2005 doctoral dissertation—in which he has proposed a new system for the classification of Hebrew verbs. More recently, Furuli has produced two volumes that compare Hebrew Bible chronology with the records of other ancient Near Eastern cultures in the interest of reassessing the date of the Babylonian exile.

The Role of Theology and Bias in Bible Translation (hereafter abbreviated *RTB*) is a revision and expansion of the author's work by the same name that was published in 1999 by Elihu Books, a publisher dedicated to promoting works that reflect the theological perspective of the Jehovah's Witness denomination. Furuli's association with the Jehovah's Witnesses explains his interest in focusing his work particularly on the *New World Translation* (*NWT*), the Bible released in 1961 by the Watchtower Bible and Tract Society, the administrative organization of the Jehovah's Witnesses, and the preferred version among the group's adherents. The second edition of Furuli's work (*RTB²*) is published by Awatu Publishers, which the author has described as a joint venture by scholars desiring to circumvent certain undesirable features of Norwegian academic publishing. (My internet search of Awatu Publishers revealed only two titles, both by Furuli, so apparently, the scholarly consortium is still in its early stages of development.)

My attempt to obtain a review copy of the first edition (*RTB¹*) led to the discovery that there may be a legal dispute brewing between Furuli and Elihu Books, whose owner contends that he holds the rights to any revision of the book and that publishing a second edition through another publisher represents copyright infringement. For his part, Furuli contends that Elihu holds the publishing rights only to the first edition and that the publisher has fallen short of its obligation to continue distribution of the book. A resolution of the dispute is pending, and I mention it only because it may be relevant to a potential reader's purchasing decision.

Although I did not have the opportunity to compare the two editions of *RTB*, the expansion represented in *RTB²* appears to have been significant, without affecting the original chapter structure. The Amazon listing for the title features only *RTB¹*, which is described as being 300 pages in length, while *RTB²* has 475 pages. An email from the author explained that the changes to *RTB²* were driven by his subsequent experience in translating several ancient Near Eastern documents into Norwegian. Although the essential argument and many of the illustrations and examples remain intact, *RTB²* offers clearer argumentation. According to the author, the greatest area of expansion has been in the fifth chapter, which addresses the question of whether the *NWT* is consistent in following the translation principles laid out in the work's Preface. In particular, Furuli interacts with recent works that address the issue of the *NWT*'s use of "Jehovah" in its translation of the Greek word *kurios* in many New Testament contexts. In *RTB¹* Furuli took a neutral stance toward the New Testament use of "Jehovah" while in *RTB²* he advocates it.

RTB² is a relatively recent work, so I wasn't surprised at my inability to find a scholarly review of it in the ATLA Religion Database. More surprising was my inability to locate in the same database a review of *RTB¹*, a letdown somewhat alleviated by my discovery of a few informed reviews of *RTB¹* on its Amazon page (http://www.amazon.com/Role-Theology-Bias-Bible-Translation/dp/0965981444). One of these was authored by Robert M. Bowman, Jr. (listed in *RTB*'s Author Index as Robert E. Bowman), whose 1989 book, *Jehovah's Witnesses, Jesus Christ, and the Gospel of John* (Grand Rapids: Baker, 1989)—a work critical of the *NWT*—is discussed numerous times in *RTB*. Bowman's key criticism is that in *RTB¹* Furuli advocates a "concordant" (or literal) approach to translation that has been discredited by modern linguists. He goes on to note that not even the *NWT* uses a consistently concordant approach. In fairness, although Furuli does make a clear distinction between literal and idiomatic translations in his early chapters of *RTB²*, he advocates only that translations should be as literal *as possible*. He concedes that sometimes, due to the differences between the "presuppositional pool" of the source culture and that of modern culture, a less literal approach is unavoidable. Yet in departing from literal renderings, translators should be careful "that one particular interpretation should not be forced upon the readers" (*RTB²*, 65).

Another thoughtful reviewer of *RTB¹*, Luis Carlos Reyes, critiqued the work on more purely linguistic grounds. He contended that the book's primary shortcoming lies in Furuli's acceptance of the "code model of communication," illustrated in the "triangles of signification" used in the book (RTB², 28–33). The code model assumes that once the translator has decoded the communicator's words, he has sufficient information to recover his or her intended meaning. "Relevance theory," however, advocates a second level—"utterance interpretation," which fills the gap between what the words themselves imply and what the communicator intends. In linguistics this is often referred to as the distinction between "semantics" and "pragmatics," and in common parlance it boils down to the difference between the static dictionary meanings of a word and the meanings it takes on when shaped by particular contexts. Reyes contends that especially in theological texts the contextual meaning of a word may at times even go against what would normally be required by the grammatical or syntactical "code." As stated earlier, Furuli advocates literal renderings whenever possible, contending that "pragmatic renderings" leave the reader "wholly dependent upon the translator" (RTB², 82). But again, in all fairness, Furuli does discuss the advantages of idiomatic translation, admitting that they are "unsurpassed when it comes to giving readers an immediate understanding of the text," so long as they remain faithful to the meaning of the original (83).

In formulating my own assessment of RTB, it was important to recognize from the outset that the author approaches the subject of Bible translation from a particular theological perspective. The exegetical and translational issues discussed in the book consistently touch on theological themes and biblical texts important in the ongoing theological debate between the Witnesses and "orthodox"[287] traditional Catholics and Protestants—the trinity, the deity of Christ, the existence of hell, the separate existence of the human soul apart from the body, the shape of the wood on which Jesus was executed, the pronunciation of the Hebrew personal name for God (the Tetragrammaton), and the use of "Jehovah" in the New Testament. The reader should be aware that RTB is not so much a discussion of the principles of Bible translation in general, but is rather something more like a compendium of translation issues and texts that relate to a particular religious group and the translation that reflects their views.

So pervasive is the undercurrent of theological concern in RTB that one reviewer of the first edition suggested that the book should be titled "New

---

[287] Here and throughout I use "orthodox" not in the denominational sense (as in Greek Orthodox), but to refer to Protestant, Catholic, or Orthodox groups that adhere (whether implicitly or explicitly) to the "orthodox" confessions of the early Christian centuries. I am aware that this term biases these groups' beliefs as orthos, or "straight," thereby implicitly branding their opponents' beliefs as crooked. However, it seems to be the most familiar term by which to lump together these otherwise very diverse groups for purposes of discussion.

World Translation Defended." Another refers to Furuli as a Jehovah's Witness "apologist." Such assessments are corroborated by the fact that there are no substantial criticisms of the *NWT* to be found anywhere in the book, though there are a couple of occasions where Furuli challenges material in the *NWT* footnotes. To be fair, Furuli does on occasion suggest that other translational options than those chosen by the *NWT* translators might serve just as well to represent the meaning of the text. Still, his unwillingness to directly critique anything in the biblical text of the *NWT* leads me to suspect that he holds the version sacrosanct, much as many "King James only" advocates view their treasured version.

I am not claiming that theological convictions necessarily bias a scholar's academic work to the extent that it becomes invalid. I certainly have my own theological convictions, and yet I am hopeful that in most cases they do not disable me from giving the views of others a fair hearing or representing them accurately. But in a book dedicated to exposing and removing theological bias from the translation process, it is especially important that the author be fully aware and up front about his own theological biases. Yet nowhere in *RTB* does Furuli discuss his apparent relationship to the Witnesses or the implications of that relationship as they relate to his academic assessment of the *NWT*.

Looking at the book in an overview, the first three chapters lay the groundwork for translation theory that will be used in the later chapters to discuss particular translational questions as they relate to the *NWT*. The fourth and fifth chapters deal with translational questions related to specific doctrinal issues such as the trinity and the divine name. Chapter 6 treats a number of disputed passages that impact beliefs related to Christology and Pneumatology. The final chapter sums up the previous discussions as to their impact on particular types of Bible translations.

The first chapter defends literal translation by explicating the relationship between words and meaning. Furuli supports the notion the word is the basic unit of meaning and bemoans the fact that modern translations have moved increasingly father away from word-by-word translation in favor of paraphrase or idiomatic translation. Carefully avoiding the "etymological fallacy" that places too strong an emphasis on the meaning of words in history, he instead highlights the distinctions represented in C. K. Ogden's "triangle of signification." Communicators form *concepts* in their mind that are represented by particular verbal *signs,* and these signs points to particular *referents.* The challenge for the translator is to use the appropriate sign in the target language that will reproduce the concept of the original communicator in the mind of the recipient of the communication. Literal translations leave it to the reader, whenever possible, to link the concept to the appropriate referent, whereas idiomatic translations take the recipient directly to the referent, bypassing the recipient's role in the translation process. To oversimplify, literal translations tell what the biblical writer *said,* while idiomatic translations tell what the translator feels the writer *meant.*

Chapter 2 takes the reader through studies of a number of words that serve to illustrate the concepts taught in the first chapter. Predictably, the ideas dealt with are all crucial the debate between the Witnesses and orthodox believers. One Greek word Furuli examines is *hades,* which in the *NWT* is consistently left untranslated. In particular, he argues that the translation "hell" reflects an anachronistic infusion of preconceived theological content. Arguing that the Bible nowhere teaches that "persons continue to live after death," Furuli rejects translations such as "underworld," "netherworld," or "world of the dead" and opts instead for "the grave" or for the transliteration *hades* (43). Despite the author's appeal to a popular theological dictionary to support his theological conclusions, orthodox believers will likely reject his premise that the Bible is devoid of information about the continuing state of humans after death and will opt instead for the primary definition of the most recent edition of the Bauer Greek Lexicon (BDAG): "'Hades,' then the nether world, *Hades as place of the dead.*"[288] Other words examined in the chapter include *kosmos* ("world"), *sarx* ("flesh"), *nephesh,*and *psyche* (the Hebrew and Greek words for "soul").

Chapter 3 walks the reader through the process of Bible translation, covering the various forms of linguistic analysis, situation analysis (often referred to as historical or cultural analysis), the process of transmission from the source language to that of the receptor language, the planes (or levels) of transmission (word, phrase, sentence, paragraph, etc.), and the final formulation. This material provides a good summary of the kind of information found in textbooks on Bible translation, and none of it is particularly controversial. That is until Furuli inserts an excursus that brings forth what he considers a prime example of an improper "formulation" common to virtually all English Bible translations—the rendering of the Greek word *stauros* as "cross."

---

[288] "ᾅδης," in F. W. Danker, W. Bauer, W. F. Arndt, and F. W. Gingrich, eds., *Greek-English Lexicon of the New Testament and Other Early Christian Literature* (BDAG; 3d ed.; Chicago, 2000), emphasis added. BDAG's primary definition seems to assume that readers will identify "hades" with "the nether world" and "the place of the dead." This certainly comports with my experience that most modern English speakers equate "hades" and "hell." Indeed, "hades" is often used as a euphemism for "hell," as in the expression, "It's hotter than hades." This raises the question whether the NWT's practice of transliterating the Greek word as hades really accomplishes the translators' purpose of avoiding the theological baggage inherent in a word like "hell."

Those familiar with the teaching of the Witnesses will again recognize a familiar point of dispute. The group contends that Jesus was not executed on a "cross"—a wooden beam with a cross-member—but on a vertical stake. Thus they oppose rendering *stauros* as "cross," opting instead for the translation universally adopted by the *NWT*—"torture stake." The related verb *stauroō* (traditionally translated "crucify") is rendered "impale." Furuli contends that "cross" and "crucify" are renderings that are hopelessly irradiated with church tradition, calling to mind a long history of the use of the cross as a pervasive symbol for orthodox Christianity. He presents detailed historical and linguistic evidence that first-century Roman "crucifixion" was done using a vertical pole without a cross-member. Evidence for the use of cross-pieces in Roman crucifixion postdates the NT, he argues, thus making the use of "cross" and "crucify" anachronous.

Furuli's historical analysis of early Roman execution practices is both careful and thorough. He rightly points out that there has been a considerable discussion among historians regarding the precise nature of Roman executions and that the evidence is divided as to precisely when cross-pieces began to be used. Furthermore, his point is well taken that traditional renderings of the *stauroō* word group bias the historical question in a particular direction. Since people universally identify a "cross" with a particular shape, it is impossible to use the language of "cross" and "crucify" without calling that shape to mind.

The deeper question is how important this issue is in communicating the New Testament's message concerning the meaning of Christ's brutal death to modern readers. If Furuli is right that cross-pieces were not used in first-century Roman executions, then the worst that can be said is that the church has embraced a historically incorrect visible image and has incorporated that image into its religious symbolism.

Suppose that in a particular part of the world all the sheep were black instead of the predominantly white sheep the prevailed in ancient Palestine. Were people from that part of the world to read in their Bibles that Christ is "the lamb of God," they would naturally form a visual image of a black lamb, whereas people in other parts of the world might form the visual image of a white lamb. Yet despite the difference in these mental images, both groups would be able, to the extent that they were biblically literate, to grasp the meaning of the lamb imagery. That is, the difference in color would not in itself interfere with their ability to appreciate the deeper theological significance of what they are visualizing.

Similarly, the shape of the "cross" has no significant effect on the deeper theological significance of Christ's "crucifixion" as portrayed in the New

Testament. It should be noted that there are deep theological differences between the Witnesses and orthodox Christians as to the role Jesus' death plays in salvation, and indeed as to the very nature of salvation itself. But those theological differences do not hinge on the shape of the instrument used to bring about Christ's death.

But what about the alternative translations to "cross" and "crucify" adopted by the *NWT*? Some will no doubt recoil from the perceived inelegance of the language of *impaling on a torture stake,* particularly in New Testament passages where the images are used in symbolic and deeply theological ways, such as when Paul says, "But far be it from me to boast except in the *torture stake* of our Lord Jesus Christ, by which the world has been *impaled* to me, and I to the world" (Gal 6:14, NRSV, modified). It could certainly be argued that our perception of the language as clumsy merely reflects how deeply we have become so steeped in the traditional language of crucifixion.

But some have raised a deeper issue with the *NWT*'s use of "impale," in that the common meaning that English speakers associate with that word relates to hanging someone on a pole by piercing their body with the pole itself—certainly not what the New Testament describes in connection with Christ's execution. Furuli responds to this objection by citing a specialized meaning for "impale" as "to fix in an inescapable and helpless position" (92, n. 30). While this definition nicely covers the metaphorical meaning of the word as used, for instance, in the expression, *to impale on the horns of a dilemma,* it is hardly the image brought to mind by the common usage of the word. So, if "crucify" is guilty of conjuring the wrong mental image of the *shape* of the "cross," "impale" is guilty of conjuring the wrong mental image of the *process* of Christ's execution.

In the fourth chapter of *RTB*, Furuli addresses what many would deem to be the heart of the theological dispute between Jehovah's Witnesses and orthodox believers—what he consistently refers to as "the Trinity doctrine." Witnesses hold to a form of teaching similar to that advocated by Arius, the fourth-century bishop who denied the deity of Christ and the existence of the Trinity. Since this is a book on Bible translation, the author is particularly concerned to show how Trinitarian theology has colored the translation of particular biblical texts and how the *NWT* has avoided such theological bias. Yet this chapter seeks to lay the groundwork for that discussion by examining the Greek philosophical background for the theological discussions of the early church fathers.

Furuli's historical survey of the development of the understanding of the early church's thinking regarding the Trinity seeks to link Trinitarian theology with Greek philosophy and thereby to discount its legitimacy. There

218

can be no doubt that much of the language used in the early church's formulations of the doctrine of the Trinity was borrowed from the philosophical discussions of the day, but many will question what amounts to an argument of guilt by association with everything Greek. Rather than engaging directly with the church fathers on the language they used to avoid contradiction in their understanding the triune nature of God, he repeatedly charges them with logical inconsistency and accuses them of seeking to resolve their irrationality by an appeal to mysticism.

Examples of Furuli's insensitivity to the finer distinctions of the Trinitarian discussion can be seen in his insistence that the early apologist Justin Martyr advocated "the difference between Jesus Christ and God" (114) and that church father Origen believed that "Jesus was different from and subordinate to God" (118). This way of stating the issue implies that neither of these early Christian writers believed Jesus Christ himself to be God, which is simply not the case. Had he said that these men considered Jesus as different from and subordinate to *the Father,* his statement would have been more astute.

A similar lack of finesse arises in his discussion of Tertullian's views. Furuli quotes Tertullian's careful statement that "the connection of the Father in the Son, and of the Son in the *Paraclete* [i.e., the Holy Spirit], produces three coherent persons who are yet distinct One from Another." Yet he goes on to explain the church father's position as "showing that the Father and the Son are two distinct beings" (115). Such a statement ignores Tertullian's concern to develop language that affirmed the unity of the Father, Son, and Spirit *in essence,* while at the same time upholding their distinctness *as persons.*

Readers coming from an orthodox perspective will be most disturbed by some of Furuli's blanket statements near the end of the chapter, such as that "there is no passage in the Bible that even hints that Jesus (the Word of the Son) is eternal," and that "there is no passage that states that Jesus was divine (a spirit being) and human *at the same time*" (145, emphasis original).

By far the longest chapter in the book is the fifth, which raises the question of whether the *NWT* follows its own translational principles, particularly in its use of "Jehovah" to translate the Greek word *kurios* in New Testament passages referring to the Father (as opposed to Jesus). Furuli's argument, in a nutshell, is that the original translators of the Old Testament into Greek (the Septuagint) retained in some form the use of the Tetragrammaton—the four-letter personal name of God used frequently throughout the Hebrew Bible, often translated as "Jehovah" or "Yahweh." He carefully and effectively counters the argument that the original translators, out of a growing reluctance to speak or write God's name, replaced it with the Greek word *kurios* ("Lord").

He brings forth evidence from other early translations of the Old Testament that show that the name of God was still widely used up through the first century A.D. , when the New Testament documents were being written. He sees the so-called *nomina sacra*—the abbreviations of sacred names used consistently in the earliest manuscripts of the New Testament— as evidence that the original documents have been tampered with, replacing all the occurrences of the divine name (in whatever form it occurred) with the abbreviation KS (for *kurios*). To correct this tampering, the *NWT* translators have used their discretion in restoring the divine name to its rightful place in the New Testament text.

Furuli should be commended for his careful work in demonstrating how historical evidence has served to dismantle the longstanding argument that the divine name had ceased to be used in the centuries prior to the writing of the New Testament. There is clear evidence that *in some quarters* there was a tendency to avoid us of the divine name, but this was by no means universal. Whatever one may think is the reason for the absence of the divine name from the New Testament, it can no longer be credibly maintained that the name had fallen into complete disuse in the first century. Even if there was a reluctance in some quarters to pronounce the name when the Old Testament was being read in the synagogues, the early documents indicate that it was still being used in writing.[289]

However, even if it could be shown that the divine name was in common use during the time in which the New Testament was being written, the fact remains that there is not a stitch of actual, documentary evidence that any of the New Testament documents themselves were originally written using the divine name. Furuli is correct in his statement that the earliest papyri and uncial manuscripts consistently used the abbreviation KS in place of the Greek word *kurios,* and there are various explanations as to why this was the case. It may be that the copyists used the abbreviations out of respect for the divine name, but it may also be that they were using a form of simple shorthand for reproducing common biblical words. The fact is that *kurios* is abbreviated in these early manuscripts both in passages that refer to God generally and in those that refer specifically to Jesus Christ. So, the more likely

---

[289] Furuli's documentation of the use of the divine name in magical and pagan contexts shows that indeed it had not disappeared in first-century non-Jewish contexts. However, such use would likely have been considered by the Jews as a blasphemous abuse of God's name, and thus could conceivably have strengthened Jewish resolve to protect the divine name by never pronouncing it publicly.

explanation is that whether out of respect or convenience, the abbreviated for KS was used consistently as a form of shorthand.[290]

In making his case for the use of the divine name in the New Testament, Furuli at times seems to assume that the New Testament documents represent translation Greek, and that the loss of the divine name may be the result of translating from a particular writing's original Aramaic or Hebrew form into Greek. It seems clear that many of the New Testament writers spoke Aramaic, and perhaps even Hebrew. Jesus is sometimes quoted by the Gospel writers as having made an utterance in Aramaic. Some have even argued that Matthew's Gospel was originally written in Aramaic, though other scholars have disputed this based on the fact that the language of the extant Matthew does not seem to be translation Greek. However, few have disputed that the bulk of the New Testament documents were originally penned in Greek by fluent Greek speakers. Thus there is little justification for saying that the divine name was somehow lost in translation.

In addition, Furuli argues that the use of the abbreviation KS represents a corruption of the New Testament text. He writes that "we cannot deny that these abbreviations show that a tampering with the NT text has occurred because the abbreviations cannot be original.... We have a corrupt text!" (238). However, there is little basis for this argument. It is true that we do not possess the autographs (originals) of any New Testament document, and that the copies we do possess show some evidence of error on the part of the copyists. However, we simply do not know whether or not the original writers may have abbreviated the word *kurios* as the copyists have done. Whether they did so or not, it seems clear that there would have been no question among early readers that KS consistently represented the word *kurios,* and thus the abbreviation can hardly be said to represent a textual corruption that leaves the reader's mind in doubt as to the original wording.

Chapter 6 of *RTB* contains analyses of several New Testament passages commonly used by orthodox believers to defend the deity of Christ. In each case, Furuli is concerned to demonstrate how the *NWT* represents a more accurate rendering. Perhaps the most notorious of these is the *NWT*'s translation of John 1:1: "In [the] beginning the Word was, and the Word was with God, and the Word was a god." The *NWT*'s translation of theos as "a god" is based on the fact that the Greek word occurs without the article and is therefore interpreted as an indefinite noun. Furuli rightly points out that Colwell's rule, which states that a definite predicate nominative, when it

---

[290] The same thing, by the way, can be said for the consistent abbreviation of theos, the Greek word for God, in the uncial manuscripts. Furuli does not suggest any connection between these abbreviations and the use of the divine name.

precedes the verb, usually occurs without the article, can indeed be used to show that *theos* could be definite, but it cannot be used to prove that it is definite. He also correctly cites evidence that *theos,* used without the article, sometimes has a qualitative thrust ("the Word was divine"). It may even be the case that "the occurrence without the article must have some semantic significance" (291), although the point of Colwell's rule is that normally this is not the case. Nevertheless, biblical scholars and translators have nearly universally rejected the *NWT's* use of the indefinite translation "a god" as foreign both to the immediate context of the Johannine prologue and to the theology of John's Gospel as a whole. Furuli's appeal to the handful of other biblical texts that refer to lesser "gods" scarcely warrants importing such a notion into the context of John 1.

Furuli's discussion of Philippians 2:6 serves well to demonstrate the role of theology in Bible translation. Traditional renderings of this verse represent Christ as refusing to hold on tenaciously to his divine prerogatives, rather letting them go for the sake of the incarnation. The *NWT,* by contrast, represents Christ as refusing to try to seize divine prerogatives that weren't his own. The issue hinges on the translator's understanding of the Greek word *harpagmos,* which can refer either to the act of robbery or to booty one might seize in a robbery. Was "equality with God" something Christ refused to try to seize or something he was willing to give up? This passage has huge implications for one's Christology, and yet its correct interpretation has been debated by biblical scholars for generations. After a lengthy discussion of the linguistic evidence on both sides of the interpretive question, Furuli concedes that while it is normally dangerous to let one's theology color one's translation, "linguistic evidence is not decisive, so theology must play a role in the translators' choice." (351) Not surprisingly, his conclusion is that the *NWT* has correctly translated based on its correct theology.

The final chapter of *RTB* presents a summation of the author's assessment of the arguments of the *NWT's* critics and a review of his responses to the accusation of bias on the part of the *NWT* translators. It also contains a discussion of various tools readers can use to go beyond their translation, including the *New World Translation Reference Edition* (NWTref), the *Kingdom Interlinear Translation* (based on the *NWT),* the literal *Schocken Bible,* Vine's *Expository Dictionary,* and Pick's *Dictionary of Old Testament Words.* Furuli also recommends a number of grammars for students wishing to study biblical languages. A footnote referencing Daniel Wallace's *Greek Grammar beyond the Basics,* perhaps the most influential advanced grammar of the current generation, expresses Furuli's view that the work is "biased in favor of the Trinity doctrine" (391). One has to wonder why Furuli does not recommend any more recent Bible study resources.

I appreciated the fact that in his Appendix, Furuli gives us a glimpse into his seminal work on the Hebrew and Greek verbal systems, although I am not sure of its relevance to his volume. The glossary of words and expressions is a helpful addition, particularly for readers unfamiliar with grammatical or linguistic terminology. The book has author and Scripture indices, but I did find myself wanting a subject index at a few points.

All in all, *RTB* is a good read for the serious student who wants to interact with the theological views of the Jehovah's Witnesses and the exegetical basis for those views from the perspective of a scholar who holds those views and is able to defend them. Often evangelical critics of "the cults" approach such groups without a depth of knowledge of what they believe or the biblical texts they use to support those beliefs. As a result, their arguments are often shallow and unfair. Readers of Furuli's book will come away with a far better appreciation for the nuanced arguments that lie behind many of the Witnesses' theological positions and far greater ability to interact intelligently with those who have similar views.

Although there is plenty of good information on the theory and practice of Bible translation in this book, I would not recommend *RTB* for someone generally seeking greater knowledge in this area. Although Furuli is strongly critical of the theological bias in Bible translations and Bible study aids written from the perspective of those who hold to "the Trinity doctrine," his work has a strong theological bias of its own and serves more as an apologetic for the views of a particular group than as a impartial work dealing with the science of Bible translation. This is seen most profoundly in his reluctance to critique any aspect of the *New World Translation* (other than its supportive footnotes).

Dr. Mark House is Professor of Biblical Studies at New Geneva Theological Seminary in Colorado Springs, CO, and an adjunct professor at Reformed Theological Seminary Virtual Campus in Charlotte, NC. He is the editor of the *Compact Greek-English Lexicon of the New Testament* (Hendrickson) and coeditor of *An Analytical Lexicon of New Testament Greek* (Hendrickson, forthcoming). Dr. House has a Ph.D. from Fuller Theological Seminary in New Testament Studies.

CHAPTER 13 How Can You Share Your Faith When the Jehovah's Witnesses Come Knocking?

What result would I get if I were to ask any church audience, "How many have had the Jehovah's Witnesses Come a Knocking on Your Door or have seen them witnessing on the streets?" There would be a high 90% that would raise their hands in 235+ lands around the world. All Jehovah's Witnesses have a personal obligation to spend at least a few hours each month spreading the good news and talking about God's Word as they understand it. Each year, they spend about 2 billion hours evangelizing their communities around the world in 357 languages. Here is what you need to know to effectively share your faith with JWs when they come knocking. I have only two words for you, BE PREPARED. You need to understand who they really are, what their life mission is, how they carry out their ministry, and to what extent. This article offers that and much more.

Just how effective are these Witnesses in their ministry? There are some Christian apologists on social media that like to boast about how they undermine and debunk the Witnesses that come to their door. Many times they are being disingenuous or even downright dishonest. Let's look at an online example of what I believe to be a severe case of exaggeration. I will quote a REAL online person who thinks he is an apologist. I will insert bracketed [...] comments within what he is saying and response after.

Steve the Apologist, as we shall call him, says, "On one occasion I invited two Jehovah's Witnesses into my house and the rookie girl began her spiel. **[Notice the disrespectful tone]** After a few minutes of discussion, the man knew I was too strong for her, so he took over. **[Notice the haughty spirit]** I challenged him with a passage in John 20:28 concerning Thomas when he called Jesus Lord and God. **[The verse says in the JW Bible (NWT),** In answer Thomas said to him: "My Lord and my God! Notice, it is the same, so there would be a ready answer by any Witness]** The gentleman refused to answer this verse as he continually tried to get me to leave John and look at other passages. [This is doubtful, as they have an answer right there in their book that they use when evangelizing, the Reasoning From the Scriptures. I will give you the answer he would have had below in my response.] I asked him politely can we stay on this verse and not hop around? At that moment, the young girl agreed with me and said to her partner we should answer John 20:28. [Again, not likely that the girl would interrupt the more experienced Witness, especially to publicly disagree] Almost immediately the man leaped up angrily and said we are going. [Very like untrue, Witnesses do not get angry in their ministry. They have had urine thrown on them, attacked by dogs, beaten, and much worse and never **angered.**] They both hurriedly went out of my door. I am certain the young girl was chastised for her agreement with me. [Never would that happen, ever.] You can bet the next time a situation like this arises, she will keep her mouth shut and obediently follow his lead. [Hardly]"

RESPONSE: The above is nothing more than a boasting session of, 'see how smart I am' from Steve the apologist. Here is what the Witness would have had right there for him to respond to the John 20:28 verses. Read it and see if you think he had no answer. Moreover, the Trinity verses are dealt with thousands of times in their literature. Judge for yourself just how honest Steve the Apologist was being to his online readers.

Reasoning from the Scriptures, p. 213 Jesus Christ

Does Thomas' exclamation at John 20:28 prove that Jesus is truly God?

John 20:28 (RS) reads: "Thomas answered him, 'My Lord and my God!'"

There is no objection to referring to Jesus as "God," if this is what Thomas had in mind. Such would be in harmony with Jesus' own quotation from the Psalms in which powerful men, judges, were addressed as "gods." (John 10:34, 35, RS; Ps. 82:1-6) Of course, Christ occupies a position far higher than such men. Because of the uniqueness of his position in relation to Jehovah, at John 1:18 (NW) Jesus is referred to as "the only-begotten god." (See also Ro, By.) Isaiah 9:6 (RS) also prophetically describes Jesus as "Mighty God," but not as the Almighty God. All of this is in harmony with Jesus' being described as "a god," or "divine," at John 1:1 (NW, AT).

The context helps us to draw the right conclusion from this. Shortly before Jesus' death, Thomas had heard Jesus' prayer, in which he addressed his Father as "the only true God." (John 17:3, RS) After Jesus' resurrection, Jesus had sent a message to his apostles, including Thomas, in which he had said: "I am ascending . . . to my God and your God." (John 20:17, RS) After recording what Thomas said when he actually saw and touched the resurrected Christ, the apostle John stated: "These are written that you may believe that Jesus is the Christ, the Son of God, and that believing you may have life in his name." (John 20:31, RS) So, if anyone has concluded from Thomas' exclamation that Jesus is himself "the only true God" or that Jesus is a Trinitarian "God the Son," he needs to look again at what Jesus himself said (vs. 17) and at the conclusion that is clearly stated by the apostle John (vs. 31).

225

Below I will let you know who you are going to meet at your door and how well they are trained in their evangelism. Mind you, they expend much time and effort in learning how to effectively evangelize and to know when to walk away. What is their goal, purpose, mission? They seek to **start a conversation** with you wherever possible. They are trained to **stimulate interest** in current affairs, world affairs, the Bible, life, the life to come, hopes, and dreams. Once they have your interest, they are well-trained in **motivating you to** want to **learn more**.

Do not live in denial, their ways are charming and interesting, and their literature is overwhelmingly designed to **draw you into** what they call, **the truth**. Once they have you motivated, they seek to **start a Bible study** with you, where you will study a book in conjunction with the Bible, like *The Truth That Leads to Eternal Life* in 1981; then, in 1989 they move to *You Can Live Forever in Paradise on Earth*, and in 1995 *Knowledge That Leads to Everlasting Life*. In 2006, they began using *What Does the Bible Really Teach?* Once they have you fully interested and growing in knowledge as they know it, they want to get you to **their congregation meetings** at the Kingdom Hall, what they call their church. They also want to get you to their website, https://www.jw.org/en/. Use the language drop-down on their website, and you will see, that it is available in hundreds of languages. It is one of the most visited sites in the world. How should we talk about and to the Jehovah's Witnesses in person or on social media?

1 Peter 3:15 Updated American Standard Version (UASV)

[15] but sanctify Christ as Lord in your hearts, always **being prepared to make a defense** to anyone who asks you for a reason for the hope that is in you; yet do it with **gentleness** and **respect;**

Colossians 4:6 Updated American Standard Version (UASV)
[6] Let your speech always be **gracious, seasoned with salt**, so that you may know **how you ought to answer** each person.

JWs base their practices on the biblical interpretations of Charles Taze Russell (1852–1916), founder (c. 1881) of the Bible Student movement, and of successive presidents of the Watch Tower Society, Joseph Franklin Rutherford (in office 1917–1942) and Nathan Homer Knorr (in office 1942–1977). Since 1976 practices have also been based on decisions made at closed meetings of the group's Governing Body. The group disseminates instructions regarding activities and acceptable behavior through *The Watchtower* magazine and through other official publications, and at conventions and congregation meetings.

Jehovah's Witnesses endeavor to remain "separate from the world," which they regard as a place of moral contamination and under the control of Satan. Witnesses refuse to participate in any political and military activity and limit social contact with non-Witnesses. Members practice a strict moral code, which forbids premarital and homosexual sex, adultery, smoking, drunkenness and drug abuse, and blood transfusions. A system of judicial committees maintains discipline within congregations, exercising the power to expel members who breach organizational rules and to demand their shunning by other Witnesses. The threat of shunning also serves to deter members from dissident behavior.

Evangelizing Work

Members are expected to participate regularly in evangelizing work and to attend all congregation meetings, as well as regular large-scale conventions – highly structured events based on material from Watch Tower Society publications.

JW Unbaptized Publishers (UP) are persons who are not yet baptized, but who have requested and been granted approval to join in the congregation's formal ministry. ... To qualify as an unbaptized **publisher**, an individual must already be "an active associate of **Jehovah's Witnesses**," who regularly attends congregation meetings, participating in those meeting (answering questions in the Book study and Watchtower study. These ones are not left alone, as they are in training. When Witnesses meet to go out and evangelize, they will pair the up with the most experienced person working that day, a pioneer or an elder.

JW Baptized Publishers (BP) are members who have been publicly baptized following conversion to the Jehovah's Witness faith. Witnesses do not practice infant baptism, and previous baptisms performed by other denominations are not considered valid. Prior to baptism, they are required to respond to a series of questions to assess their suitability and to make a personal dedication to serve God. Baptisms are typically performed at assemblies and conventions. From the moment of baptism, the organization officially considers the person to be a member of Jehovah's Witnesses, an ordained minister, and a publisher. These are not as experienced, and they too will work alongside the more experienced. It depends on how long they have been a Witness on whether you can draw them into an interchange of ideas or a deeper Bible discussion. Do not be misled, if you are not well-grounded in the Word of God yourself, they will be the more knowledgeable and the more experienced. They do not fear other Bibles other than their New World Translation (NWT).

JW Auxiliary Pioneers (AP) are the next level up from a publisher. The AP commits to at least **30 hours a month** (360 yearly) preaching (used to be 60 for decades), and they are a baptized publisher. This can be done on a one-month-only basis, or Regular **Auxiliary** (RA) basis, so every month until the Witness decides that he or she does not want to do it at that level anymore. Now, we are entering into the more knowledgeable and the more skilled JW, so you have to really be grounded in the Bible yourself.

JW Regular Pioneer (RP) makes a commitment of an average of seventy **hours** of preaching activity each month (used to be 90 hours), totaling 840 **hours** for the year. For the elders in the congregation to recommend someone for the appointment of a **regular pioneer**, a publisher must be baptized for at least six months and be considered an exemplary member of the congregation. If this person has been a RP for some time, they are going to be highly trained in overturning your argumentation.

Special Pioneers (SP) are assigned by a branch to perform a special activity, such as preaching in remote areas, which may require at least 130 hours per month. Special pioneers receive a stipend for very basic living expenses. Generally, few people run into one of these Witnesses because they are sent to special places but it is possible. This Witness is going to be extremely trained, skilled, and effective.

Missionaries are sent to foreign countries to preach. They spend at least 130 hours per month preaching. Before assignment to a location, missionaries may receive training at Gilead School. Missionaries receive a stipend for basic living expenses. The same holds true here, these will be extremely trained, skilled, and effective.

JW Elders & Ministerial Servants. Each congregation has a body of elders, who are responsible for congregational governance, pastoral work, selecting speakers and conducting meetings, directing the public preaching work and creating "judicial committees" to investigate and decide disciplinary action for cases that are seen to breach scriptural laws. There are no secular educational requirements for elders; however, training programs are offered for elders within the organization. Elders are considered "overseers" based on the biblical Greek term, ἐπίσκοπος (*episkopos*, typically translated "bishop"). Prospective elders are recommended from among ministerial servants and former elders by the local elder body for appointment by the circuit overseer. These are going to be very highly trained in evangelism work, and it will be no easy task to evangelize them.

JW Circuit Overseers. This is like Paul was. The Governing Body directly appoints *circuit overseers* as its representatives to supervise activities within circuits. *Headquarters representatives* visit groups of branch offices to provide instruction and report the branch's activities to the Governing Body. These Witnesses are going to be the most trained Jehovah's Witness you will likely ever come across. Yes, the headquarters has workers that are researchers for their publication, who may contain more knowledge than a circuit overseer but are likely not more skilled at the art of persuasion. This person might have been born to Jehovah's Witness parents, the mother being a pioneer, the father an elder. They might have been baptized early. They may have become a pioneer as a teenager, a ministerial servant in their early twenties, an elder before thirty, and a circuit overseer in their forties.

When They Come Knocking

JWs Work In Pairs. They will always come to your door in pairs that could consist of any of the combinations above. It could be two publishers, a pioneer and an unbaptized publisher, two elders, circuit overseers, and an elder. Every aspect of their life is to make disciples, to reason, explain, prove, and persuade. Every moment is a learning situation.

JW Literature. The Watch Tower Bible and Tract Society produces a significant amount of printed and electronic literature, primarily for use by Jehovah's Witnesses. Their best-known publications are the magazines, *The Watchtower* and *Awake!* **The Watchtower Announcing Jehovah's Kingdom** is an illustrated religious magazine, published monthly by Jehovah's Witnesses via the Watch Tower Bible and Tract Society of Pennsylvania. Along with its companion magazine, *Awake!*, Jehovah's Witnesses distribute *The Watchtower—Public Edition* in their door-to-door ministry. *Awake!* is an illustrated religious magazine published every four months (used to be twice a month) by Jehovah's Witnesses via the Watch Tower Bible and Tract Society of Pennsylvania. It is considered to be a companion magazine of *The Watchtower* and is distributed by Jehovah's Witnesses in their door-to-door ministry, with a total worldwide circulation of over 93 million copies in 221 languages per issue. The Watch Tower Bible and Tract Society produces religious literature primarily for use by Jehovah's Witnesses. The organization's international writing, artwork, translation, and printery workforce are all baptized Jehovah's Witnesses. Since 2001, the literature produced by the Watch Tower Society is said to have been "published by Jehovah's Witnesses." Prior to 1931, the Watch Tower Society produced literature for the Bible Student movement. All of their literature is designed for education with a mild leaning toward helping with evangelism to a primary focus on helping their evangelism.

Christian Literature. JWs are not supposed to accept any religious literature that was not published by the Watchtower Bible & Tract Society. This does not mean that they will not consider it in your home. If it is an anti-Jehovah's Witness book, they almost always will not look at that. However, there are thousands of JWs that are well-educated in Christian literature outside the organization, like biblical Hebrew and Greek, textual studies hermeneutics, theology, and so on. So, do not be surprised if you happen upon the right Witness.

Skilled in the Art of Reasoning, Persuasion, Explain, Proving. All Witnesses are trained in this way. The literature is geared this way. The meetings are designed this way. They are trained to reason with you using logic, and leading questions, and will easily overturn most objections they come across. The more skilled Witness that you come across, the more difficult it will be to cope with their skills. Some might see my tone thus far as showing too much respect for what they feel to be a cult. There is respect just like one military special forces, say the Navy SEALs might have for the Israeli special forces, the elite commando, counterterrorist, antiterrorist, and recon units.

Overturning Your Objections. One tool they have is the book they have had for decades, Reasoning From the Scriptures. Page 7 of How to Use "Reasoning From the Scriptures" says that "This publication has not been prepared for the purpose of helping anyone to "win arguments" with people who show no respect for the truth. Rather, it provides valuable information that is meant to be used in reasoning with individuals who will allow you to do so. Some of them may ask questions to which they really want satisfying answers. Others, in the course of conversation, may simply state their own beliefs, and they may do so with some conviction. But are they reasonable persons who are willing to listen to another viewpoint? If so, you can share with them what the Bible says, doing so with the conviction that it will find a welcome response in the hearts of lovers of truth." The Witnesses always see themselves as the teachers and you as the student. It does not matter if you have an MDiv and a Ph.D. As long as you are respectful and show interest, they will keep returning, affording you the opportunity to witness to the Witnesses. I hope this brief insight into the Witnesses will help you not to underestimate them, and push you to dig deeper to evangelism those that come knocking.

This video is from the official **Jehovah's Witness website (jw.org)**. It may seem like such a video would be highly edited to make things seem better than they are, but this is reflective of what it would really look like. This video will give you a deeper insight into the lives of Jehovah's Witnesses and why they are so well-prepared.

JW Personal Study, Family Study, & Meetings. Jehovah's Witnesses hold meetings for worship twice each week. (Hebrews 10:24, 25) At these meetings, which are open to the public, they examine what the Bible says and how we can apply its teachings in our life as they understand it. Most of our services include audience participation, much like a classroom discussion. Meetings begin and end with song and prayer. You don't have to be one of

Jehovah's Witnesses to attend their meetings. They invite everyone to come along. Seats are free. No collections are ever taken.

This video is from the official **Jehovah's Witness website (jw.org)**. This video will give you a deeper insight into the lives of Jehovah's Witnesses and why they are so well-prepared, enabling you to be better prepared to discuss your faith with them.

Meetings for worship and study are held at Kingdom Halls and are open to the public. Witnesses are assigned to a congregation in which "territory" they reside and are expected to attend weekly meetings as scheduled by the Watch Tower Society and congregation elders. The meetings are largely devoted to the study of the Bible and Witness doctrines. During meetings and in other formal circumstances, Witnesses refer to one another as "Brother" and "Sister." Sociologist Andrew Holden claims meetings create an atmosphere of uniformity for Witnesses, intensify their sense of belonging to a religious community, and reinforce the plausibility of the organization's belief system. He says they are also important in helping new converts adopt a different way of life. According to *The Watchtower*, one role of the frequency and length of meetings is to protect Witnesses from becoming "involved in the affairs of the world."

The form and content of the meetings are established by the denomination's Brooklyn headquarters, generally involving a consideration of the same subject matter worldwide each week. Two meetings each week are divided into five distinct sections, lasting a total of about four hours. Meetings are opened and closed with hymns and brief prayers delivered from the platform. Witnesses are urged to prepare for all meetings by studying Watch Tower literature from which the content is drawn and looking up the scriptures cited in the articles. Kingdom Halls are typically functional in character and contain no religious symbols. Each year, Witnesses from several congregations, which form a "circuit," gather for two one-day assemblies; several circuits meet once a year for a three-day "regional convention," and every few years the Governing Body of Jehovah's Witnesses holds "international conventions" in selected cities around the world. These larger gatherings are usually held at rented stadiums or auditoriums. Their most important and solemn event is the celebration of the "Lord's Evening Meal," or "Memorial of Christ's Death."

Weekend Meeting

The weekend meeting, usually held on Sunday, comprises a 30-minute public talk by a congregation elder or ministerial servant and a one-hour question-and-answer study of a Bible-based article from *The Watchtower* magazine, with questions prepared by the Watch Tower Society and the answers provided in the magazine. Members may use their own words to express the ideas in the printed material, though personal ideas derived from independent study are discouraged.

Midweek Meeting

The midweek meeting, typically held in the evening, includes various question-and-answer sessions based on Watch Tower Society publications, Bible reading, and sample presentations of how to use Watch Tower Society literature for Bible studies and public preaching.

Assemblies and Conventions

Each year, Jehovah's Witnesses hold two one-day "Circuit Assemblies," held in each circuit worldwide. Each circuit comprises several congregations in a geographical area. These are held either in Assembly Halls owned by Jehovah's Witnesses, or in rented facilities, such as public auditoriums. Once a year, Jehovah's Witnesses gather at larger assemblies called "Regional Conventions" which are usually three days long (Friday to Sunday). These conventions consist primarily of Bible-based sermons, including demonstrations and experiences of their preaching work. They also often feature video presentations and live, full-costume dramatic plays re-enacting biblical accounts—such as Moses and the Plagues of Egypt, and Lot in Sodom and Gomorrah—or contemporary settings based on biblical principles. Every few years, "International Conventions" are held in selected cities, with visiting delegates from other countries. Attendance at some of these international conventions has exceeded one hundred thousand; the 1958 international convention in New York at Yankee Stadium and the Polo Grounds had a peak attendance exceeding 253,000.

Evangelism of the Jehovah's Witnesses

Jehovah's Witnesses believe they are under an obligation to God to "give witness" by participating in organized and spontaneous evangelizing and proselytizing work. (Matt. 24:14; 28:19-20; Ac 1:8) Prospective members are told they have a moral obligation to serve as "publishers" by "regular and zealous" participation in the Witnesses' organized preaching work, disseminating Watch Tower doctrines as evangelists of "the Truth." Qualifying as an "unbaptized publisher" is a requirement for baptism, and baptism is regarded as an automatic ordination as a minister. Watch Tower publications describe house-to-house visitations as the primary work of Jehovah's Witnesses in obedience to a "divine command" to preach "the Kingdom good news in all the earth and (make) disciples of people of all the nations." Children usually accompany their parents and participate in public ministry. In addition to taking part in organized door-to-door preaching, Witnesses are taught that they should seek opportunities to "witness

232

informally" by starting conversations with people they meet during routine activities such as shopping or on public transport and directing the conversation towards their beliefs.

Witnesses are told that they should put the interests of God's Kingdom first in their lives and that other secular and recreational pursuits should remain secondary to spiritual matters. Witnesses are frequently instructed through Watch Tower Society publications, and at meetings and conventions, to increase the quality and quantity of their preaching efforts. Watch Tower Society publications suggest that endurance in public preaching is a requirement for Witnesses to attain salvation, and that evangelizing frees them from blood guilt regarding individuals who might die at Armageddon without having heard about God's kingdom.

Members who commit themselves to evangelize for 840 hours per year (an average of 70 hours per month) are called *regular pioneers*. Those who commit themselves to evangelize for 50 hours for one month are called *auxiliary pioneers*, which they may do for consecutive months. Some Witnesses volunteer for missionary service and may be invited to receive specialized training at the Watchtower Bible School of Gilead. These individuals dedicate, on average, more than 120 hours per month to their work. Members who are not able to 'pioneer' are told they may maintain the "pioneer spirit," by spending as much time as they can in preaching and supporting the efforts of pioneers.

Specialized "territory" maps of residential and commercial areas are prepared within the boundaries of each congregation's territory and distributed to publishers who are responsible for preaching within that area. Witnesses are instructed to fill out monthly report slips on their preaching activity, listing the hours spent, publications placed with householders, and the number of "return visits" made to households where interest had been shown formerly. The reports are used to help measure the "spirituality" of individuals and to establish the eligibility of men as congregation elders and ministerial servants. A Witness who fails to report for a month is termed an "irregular publisher;" one who has not turned in a field service report for six months consecutively is termed an "inactive publisher."

Witnesses have, in the past, used a wide variety of methods to spread their faith, including information marches, where members wore sandwich boards and handed out leaflets, to sound cars (car-mounted phonographs), and syndicated newspaper columns and radio segments devoted to sermons. Between 1924 and 1957, the organization operated a radio station, WBBR, from New York. Since 2011, the Witnesses have engaged in "public witnessing" in metropolitan districts and fairs using tables, carts, and literature displays. The Watch Tower Society operates a website, JW.org, which provides access to Watch Tower Society literature and video streaming.

Jehovah's Witnesses Literature

Jehovah's Witnesses make extensive use of Watch Tower Society literature, including books, magazines, booklets, and handbills, to spread their beliefs and to use as textbooks at their religious meetings. The publications are produced in many languages, with a small selection available in 500 languages. Their primary journal, *The Watchtower,* is published simultaneously in nearly two hundred languages, and along with *Awake!,* available in audio and electronic formats. Issues of both publications are compiled annually into bound volumes, and are added yearly to the *Watchtower Library* CD-ROM, which contains many Witness publications from 1950 onward, and is officially available to baptized members only. New books, brochures, and other items are released at their annual conventions. Additionally, a number of audio cassettes, videocassettes, and DVDs have been produced explaining the group's beliefs, practices, organization, and history. Some of these also provide dramas based on biblical accounts. Since 1942 all Watch Tower literature has been published anonymously.

Publications were sold to the public until the early 1990s, from which time they were offered free of charge, with a request for donations. The change in policy was first announced in the United States in February 1990, following the loss of a case before the US Supreme Court by Jimmy Swaggart Ministries on the issue of sales tax exemption for religious groups. The Watch Tower Society had joined the case as an Amicus curiae, or "friend of the court." The court ruling would have resulted in the Watch Tower Society having to pay millions of dollars in sales tax if sales of their literature had continued.

Witnesses are urged to prepare for congregation meetings by studying the assigned Watch Tower literature, and are expected to read all magazines and books published by the Society. One analysis noted that each year Witnesses are expected to read more than 3,000 pages of the Society's publications, according to its suggested program for personal study. Much of the literature is illustrated extensively, with sociologist Andrew Holden observing utopian, post-Armageddon images of happy Witnesses in bright sunshine and pristine environments, often playing with formerly wild animals such as lions and tigers, in contrast to dark-colored images of unfavorable activities such as murders, burglaries and promiscuity that highlight the moral dangers outside the organization.

Conversion to the Jehovah's Witnesses

Individuals seeking to be baptized as Jehovah's Witnesses are required to follow a systematic, catechistical Bible study course, usually in their home, for several months. They will be expected to attend meetings at the Kingdom Hall and must also demonstrate a willingness to carry out the doorstep ministry. Before baptism, they will be questioned by elders to determine that they understand and accept the beliefs of the Witnesses, and also that they accept Jesus' ransom sacrifice and repent of sins, and have made a personal dedication to God. Baptisms are normally performed in pools at assemblies and conventions. At these baptisms, candidates make "public declaration" of their prior dedication to God. The speaker asks the candidates the following two questions.

1. "On the basis of the sacrifice of Jesus Christ, have you repented of your sins and dedicated yourself to Jehovah to do his will?"

2. "Do you understand that your dedication and baptism identify you as one of Jehovah's Witnesses in association with God's spirit-directed organization?"

After candidates agree to both questions, they line up to undergo water immersion, usually in quick succession, often with hundreds baptized at large conventions.

Sociologist James Beckford reported two significant distinguishing features of the conversion process when related by Jehovah's Witnesses. He said they typically spoke of their conversion experience as a steady progression of mental states in which Witnesses "'work for' their conversion by a methodical confrontation with intellectual obstacles and by a deliberate program of self-reform. Conversion is not represented as something which *happened* to them; it is framed as something that they *achieved*." Beckford noted that those he interviewed regarded sudden, emotional upheavals in religious consciousness as suspect: "Experiences which smack of sudden or idiosyncratic illumination/revelation cannot be reconcilable with either the tenor of God's historical practice or the nature of his special covenant with the Watchtower Society."

He also found a striking contrast with other churches in the common attribution of responsibility for conversion to "a spiritual guide ... the person who acted as the intermediary with the Watchtower movement and who supervised the initial process of learning and reforming." Beckford cited an interview "representative of many" in which a convert recalled initially resisting the Watch Tower Society's teachings until he was "talked into making a serious study of the scriptures ... I had plenty of objections and was sure the Witnesses were wrong, but (the Witness leading the personal Bible study sessions) showed me how the facts of the Bible could not be faulted."

This video is from the official **Jehovah's Witness website (jw.org)**. This video will give you a deeper insight into the lives of Jehovah's Witnesses and why they are so well-prepared, enabling you to be better prepared to discuss your faith with them.

Construction

International and regional building teams frequently undertake constructions of Kingdom Halls over the course of one or two weekends, termed "quick-builds". Larger construction projects, including building regional Assembly Halls and Bethel offices, factories, residences, warehouses, and farm facilities, are also performed almost entirely by volunteer members.

Funding of the Jehovah's Witnesses

Jehovah's Witnesses fund their activities, such as publishing, constructing and operating facilities, evangelism, and disaster relief via donations. There is **no tithing or collection**, but on exceptional occasions, members are reminded to donate to the organization; Witnesses typically provide an opportunity for members of the public to make donations as they encounter them in their preaching work. Donation boxes labeled for several purposes are located in Kingdom Halls and other meeting facilities. Generally, there are contribution boxes for local operating expenses, a Kingdom Hall fund for helping Witnesses around the world to build Kingdom Halls, and a general fund for the "Worldwide Work", which includes the printing of literature, organization of conventions, supporting missionaries and disaster relief, and other operating expenses of the organization.

The accounts (including donations) and the financial operation of the local congregation are reviewed monthly and posted on a congregation notice board. Donations are also accepted via mail, and the Watch Tower Bible and Tract Society can be named as a beneficiary to an estate, and also accepts donations in the form of life insurance policies, pension plans, bank accounts, certificates of deposit, retirement accounts, stocks and bonds, real estate, annuities, and trusts.

Spiritual Warfare

Watch Tower Society publications teach that Witnesses are engaged in "spiritual, theocratic warfare" against false teachings and wicked spirit forces, they say try to impede them in their preaching work. Based on their interpretation of Ephesians 6:10–20, they believe their "spiritual war" is fought with truth, righteousness, the "good news of peace," faith, the hope of salvation, God's word, and prayer. They have advocated the use of "theocratic war strategy" to protect the interests of God's cause, which would include hiding the truth from God's "enemies" by being evasive or withholding truthful or incriminating information from those not entitled by law to know. *The Watchtower* told Witnesses: "It is proper to cover over our arrangements for the work that God commands us to do. If the wolfish foes draw wrong conclusions from our maneuvers to outwit them, no harm has been done to them by the harmless sheep, innocent in their motives as doves."

Conclusion

In a future article, we will tackle some of the beliefs of Jehovah's Witnesses. For now, this article and the two below should suffice in giving the reader an unbiased, non-dogmatic, objective look into the Witnesses' organization, enabling the reader to be better prepared in their quest to witness to the Jehovah's Witnesses. If you have an appreciation of just how prepared the Witnesses truly are; then, you will not come to the door unprepared when they come knocking.

CHAPTER 14 How Can Christian Apologists Effectively Witness to Jehovah's Witnesses?

Apologists Exposing False Prophecies of Watchtower Organization Jehovah's Witnesses 1878, 1914, 1918, 1925, and 1975

Is it best to spend much time trying to expose historical problems or is there a better way. Most Christian apologists are pretty much on par with the history they present about Jehovah's Witnesses, but I would offer them some feedback. Their messages are usually a little conspiratorial. They like to add qualifiers to what they say that makes things more extreme and dire than they really are. Some have suggested that the Jehovah's Witnesses organization has been lying to their people.

The Witnesses are not trying to hide the fact that they have been wrong several times in their predictions. In fact, they have stated it several times over the years in the watchtower and awake Magazines in the 1980s and 1990s. They did so for a while for the generation most immediately impacted by the misinterpretation.

When evangelizing, think of how it feels when a Muslim apologist or an atheist is dragging you over the coals for the history of Christianity. The Muslim and the atheist like to qualify things in the worst light possible.

Also, make sure that when you set the criteria that are supposed identifying markers of false Christianity that so-called "true Christianity" is not guilty of the same things or even worse.

Yes, the Witnesses were showing signs of Obsessive-Compulsive Disorder (OCD) about end times prophecy and the Second Coming of Christ but so is most of Christianity. The irony is, how did the Witnesses get so interested in end times, the Second Coming, and Bible chronology?

It was actually by the teachings of an **American Baptist preacher**. Yes, it's true. In the early 19th century, William Miller (1782 – 1849), an American Baptist preacher, was OCD about end times, the Second Coming, and Bible chronology. Where did Miller get his interest in end times, from a Joshua Vaughan Himes (1805–1895) pastor of the First Christian Church in Boston?

William Miller, the Baptist preacher set the date of the second coming of Christ to 1844, which became known as the Big or Great Disappointment. His followers would go on and set yet another date. When the end did not occur as expected in the 1840s, new heirs of his message emerged, including the Advent Christians (1860), the Seventh-day Adventists (1863) and other Adventist movements.

The Great Disappointment in the Millerite movement was the reaction that followed Baptist preacher William Miller's proclamations that Jesus Christ would return to the Earth by 1844, what he called the Advent. His study of the Daniel 8 prophecy during the Second Great Awakening led him to the conclusion that Daniel's "cleansing of the sanctuary" was cleansing of the world from sin when Christ would come, and he and many others prepared, but October 22, 1844, came and they were disappointed.

When the founder of Jehovah's Witnesses, Charles Taze Russel (1852 – 1916) was a teenager, he became an atheist because of the hellfire doctrine and several other things. One day, when walking down the street at night, he heard singing from a basement. Russel went down to investigate and met the Adventists. He became closely involved with them. They were still OCD about end times, the Second Coming, and Bible chronology.

Some of the major influences on young Charles Taze Russel were Henry Grew (1781 – 1862) a Christian teacher, George Stetson (1815 – 1879) a Christian pastor, and George Storrs (December 13, 1796 – 1879) a Christian teacher, N. H. Barbour (1824 – 1905) an Adventist, William Henry Conley (1840 – 1897) a Pittsburgh philanthropist and industrialist. He provided organizational and financial support to religious institutions in the United States.

Thus, at a very early age, Russell caught the bug of end times, the Second Coming, and Bible chronology from older religions, men from different Christian denominations, some of who had found it from William Miller, the Baptist preacher. Of course, this is not to excuse the setting of false dates.

John Calvin was OCD about eternal security, and today most Calvinist-minded Christians from several different denominations are just as OCD about the doctrinal view. One can argue another time about whether it is biblically true or not.

Do the Christians you meet today know their church history and the horrific things that have been done in the name of Christ? No. Every time you talk to an atheist, and you tell them about Christ and Christianity, are you in a rush to tell them about the things done in the name of Christ: the wars, the slaughter of men, women, and children, sexual abuses, and so on? You likely know about these things in the history of "true Christianity." Do you rush to share those things? There are hundreds of millions of churchgoers that do not know these things, does that make it conspiratorial that they do not know? Does it mean that there is a grand coverup? I think not. Consider for a moment, there are numerous books on the history of Christianity that expose their own bad history, so there is no real coverup.

The message of this blog post is that we as Christian apologetic evangelists need to be empathetic and realistic when we are trying to share what true and false Christianity looks like. We should simply teach the truth of God's Word because the very things we shine the light on might be used in return for far worse behavior.

CHAPTER 15 CHRISTIAN APOLOGETIC EVANGELISM: What Will You Say to a Jehovah's Witness?

NOT ALL CHRISTIAN APOLOGETICS ARGUMENTS ARE EQUAL: Some Arguments Have Liabilities When They Are Used

We will use some arguments often raised about Jehovah's Witnesses as our text case. J. Warner Wallace is a leading Evangelical Christian apologist today. On his blog, he has the article titled, "10 Important Questions for the Jehovah's Witness Worldview."[291] Therein Wallace writes,

One way to examine the Jehovah's Witnesses' perspective is simply to see how well they would answer a few important philosophical and theological questions as we examine what the Jehovah's Witness religion teaches. The following questions are designed to challenge the Jehovah's Witness claims about reality and help you to initiate a discussion with your friends or family who may hold this worldview:

Philosophical Questions

Let's begin with some questions springing from basic philosophical concerns:

A primary concern in asking questions that undermine another's faith is to never ask any question that also applies to your side of the fence as well. Before we look at the 10 questions, let us consider some basics.

The Greek Term Apologia

Apologetics: (Gr. *apologia*) The term literally means "to defend" and is used in the biblical sense to refer to ones who defend the Christian faith, the Bible, and God in speech or in written form. The Christian apologist attempts to prove that the Christian faith, the Bible, and God are reasonable, logical, necessary and right. – Ac 25:16; 2 Cor. 7:11; Phil. 1:7, 16; 2 Tim. 4:16; 1 Pet. 3:15

Two Kinds of Apologetics

There are two basic kinds of apologetics. There is negative apologetics and positive apologetics.

Negative Apologetics

---

[291]   https://coldcasechristianity.com/writings/some-important-questions-for-the-jehovahs-witness-worldview/

In negative apologetics, the Christian apologist is playing defense. We can use sports as an analogy. Whether it be baseball, football, or basketball, when we are playing defense, we cannot score any points. The only task we have while playing defense is to prevent the other team from scoring any points. Therefore, the atheist, agnostic, or Bible critic that has some kind of problem with the Christian faith, the Bible, or God raises issues that they believe undermine the Christian beliefs. They are on the offense, trying to score points. In playing defense, the Christian apologist only needs to show that this objection that was raised is not valid, it is unreasonable, illogical. There is no real substance to it. In this scenario, the burden of proof is on the unbeliever who is raising the issues. Negative apologetics is always easier than positive apologetics.

Burden of Proof

The burden of Proof: The burden of proof in a criminal trial is on the prosecution. The defense attorney only needs to undermine the argument(s) for guilt by the prosecution are not valid. The burden of proof in a trial of the Christian faith is on the unbeliever bringing the case. Either their arguments are valid, or they are not. The Christian apologist need not prove his innocence so to speak, just that the case against him has no merit. The burden of proof falls on the one making the claims. If the Christian is witnessing to another, he has the burden to prove what he says is so if asked for proof. However, if the critic is challenging the Christian, the burden of disproving lies with the critic. The closer the claim is to socially accepted knowledge, less proof is needed, while the further one moves from conventional knowledge, the more evidence is required. I believe that the legal burden of proof offers the best answers to the witnessing of others. It has been refined over the last 200 years to the point of evaluating a life that is held in its balance, just as everlasting life is held in the balance. Below we will list the levels of legal proof and some percentage and wording to indicate the degree of certainty needed. We have used different Bible objects for each one, but any criticism could be plugged into that particular burden of proof.

Problem of Evil

Without a doubt, the problem of evil is the most difficult Bible difficulty to answer. The problem of evil refers to the question of how to reconcile the existence of wickedness and suffering when there is an all-knowing, all-powerful loving God. The problem of evil is so serious that we can say, if a Christian is going to have doubts, this is the only issue it should take place because all other Bible difficulties are easily resolved in comparison. Under the burden of proof, the unbeliever who brings up the problem of evil is responsible for showing that this is a sufficient enough reason for not believing in God. The Christian apologist only needs to show that the problem of evil is not sufficient enough for not believing in God and need not provide an answer to the issue. Nevertheless, in GENESIS 3:1-6, 23-24 BDC: Why has God allowed bad things to happen when he has the power to stop them, we answer the problem of evil. We just need to show that there is a morally sufficient reason for God temporarily allowing evil to exist.

Positive Apologetics

Returning to our sports analogy, here in positive apologetics, the Christian is now playing offense, trying to score points, while the unbeliever is on defense, trying to prevent us from scoring points. Under positive apologetics, the Christian now has to own the fact that he or she is under the burden of proof. In other words, we are offering arguments, information, explanations, or evidence that will help the receptive person to accept biblical truths, with the eventuality of their accepting the Christian faith. We are trying to prove the existence of God, as well as that the Bible is the inspired, fully inerrant Word of God and that it is authentic and true. The unbeliever is trying to show that our arguments are not valid or not that effective.

We must understand that not all Christian apologetic augments are equal. Some arguments have liabilities when they are used. Now, understand, this author has written a book undermining the beliefs of the Jehovah's Witnesses, so this exercise below is only to demonstrate that some Christian apologetic questions are not effective and will backfire.

Wallace's 10 Questions

If I am to accept the teaching of the Jehovah's Witness religion, I am first going to have to trust the source of this teaching. But how can I trust someone who claims to speak for God when they have been wrong about prior predictions?

RESPONSE: The Witnesses will only say that under your logic, we would also reject Protestantism and all of their 41,0000 denominations because many Protestant leaders have predicted dates and were clearly wrong (**William Miller** (February 15, 1782 – December 20, 1849) was an American Baptist). They would also point out that the founding fathers of major Christian denominations of today, committed atrocious acts in their history, such as killing or having killed other Christians who dared to believe differently. During the Reformation the Calvinists had many arrested, tried, and executed by slow-burning for daring to believe differently. Calvin justified his actions in these atrocities by saying, "When the papists are so harsh and violent in defense of their superstitions that they rage cruelly to shed innocent blood, are not Christian magistrates shamed to show themselves less ardent in defense of the sure truth?" Will Durant, THE REFORMATION: A History of European Civilization from Wyclif to

Calvin, 1300-1564 (The Story of Civilization) (New York City: Simon & Schuster, 1980), 482.

Jehovah's Witnesses claim to be the only religious organization speaking for God, but don't the Roman Catholic and Mormon religions make very similar claims? Why should I trust the Jehovah's Witnesses?

RESPONSE: The Witnesses will only say that all Christian denominations believe that they are the truth and the way. There are 41,000 different denominations, all believing different from the others, even to the point of contradiction. Certainly, they can not all be right. This includes the so-called salvation doctrines as well.

The divisiveness would never work in an effort to fulfill the great commission of making disciples. What if we just singled out the Baptist church as our test case. There are over well 50,000 Baptist churches in the United States. There are literally 61 different Baptist divisions, i.e., subdivision denominations within the Baptist Church. Yes, they all believe differently as well. What if we just select one of this subdivision denominations, will we finally find a oneness of mind and teachings? No. Why? Because there exists yet another divisive problem, in that the Baptist churches as a whole are autonomous, which means that every individual church has the freedom to act independently and teach differently than the others. The irony is, they will argue that they are in agreement when it comes to the so-called salvation doctrines. Yet, this is not true because every one of the so-called salvation doctrines has anywhere from two to four different positions or views.

Zanesville, Ohio has eleven Baptist churches, in a community of 150,000 people. What if all eleven Baptist churches decided independently that they were going to go out and evangelize the community to make disciples? How could that even work? Suppose an unbeliever is visited by several different subdivision Baptist denominations and is told different views about the same doctrine? How is the unbeliever going to take Christianity seriously with such division as this? Moreover, we have other problems that we have not even addressed.

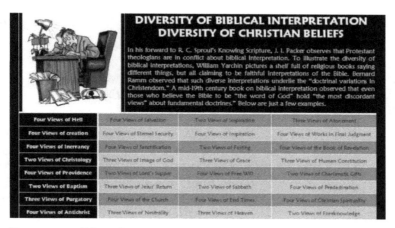

DIVERSITY OF BIBLICAL INTERPRETATION
DIVERSITY OF CHRISTIAN BELIEFS

In his forward to R. C. Sproul's Knowing Scripture, J. I. Packer observes that Protestant theologians are in conflict about biblical interpretation. To illustrate the diversity of biblical interpretations, William Yarchin pictures a shelf full of religious books saying different things, but all claiming to be faithful interpretations of the Bible. Bernard Ramm observed that such diverse interpretations underlie the "doctrinal variations in Christendom." A mid-19th century book on biblical interpretation observed that even those who believe the Bible to be "the word of God" hold "the most discordant views" about fundamental doctrines. Below are just a few examples.

Four Views of Hell	Four Views of Salvation	Two Views of Inspiration	Three Views of Atonement
Four Views of creation	Four Views of Eternal Security	Four Views of Inspiration	Four Views of Works in Final Judgment
Four Views of Inerrancy	Four Views of Sanctification	Two Views of Fasting	Four Views of the Book of Revelation
Two Views of Christology	Three Views of Image of God	Three Views of Grace	Three Views of Human Constitution
Four Views of Providence	Two Views of Lord's Supper	Four Views of Free Will	Two Views of Charismatic Gifts
Two Views of Baptism	Three Views of Jesus' Return	Two Views of Sabbath	Four Views of Predestination
Three Views of Purgatory	Four Views of the Church	Four Views of End Times	Four Views of Christian Spirituality
Four Views of Antichrist	Three Views of Neutrality	Three Views of Heaven	Two Views of Foreknowledge

Press on to Maturity

Hebrews 5:13-6:1 Updated American Standard Version (UASV)

¹³ For everyone who partakes of milk is unacquainted with the word of righteousness, for he is an infant. ¹⁴ But solid food belongs to the mature, to those who through practice have their discernment trained to distinguish between good and evil. **6** Therefore, leaving behind the elementary doctrine about the Christ, let us press on to maturity, not laying again a foundation of repentance from dead works and faith in God,

The problem of biblical illiteracy is well known but truly ignored. 90% of Christians are biblically illiterate in that they cannot explain the foundational doctrines of the faith or defend the Word of God as inspired, fully inerrant, and authoritative. Yes, they know some cute Bible stories and some Bible principles. This problem has existed for over a hundred years and nothing has truly been done to address it. Then, we couple biblical illiteracy with the fact that **almost no Christians are being trained** to make disciples in their churches. Thus, we have 41,000 different denominations all teaching differently, we have tens of thousands of churches in the same denomination broken off into different subdivisional denominations, and even a single subdivision has autonomous churches that believe differently, and the individual church has members that believe differently, with 90% being biblically illiterate and having no evangelism training. How do we fix that atrocious problem, so as to carry out the Great Commission? J. Warner Wallace continues,

The Jehovah's Witness translation of the Bible condemns false prophecy and says unfulfilled prophecy is an indicator God is not speaking thorough that Prophet and we should not, therefore, pay

attention to what that prophet is saying. So shouldn't this also apply to the teaching of the Watchtower?

RESPONSE: The Witnesses will only say this question is similar to the first one above. There have been many Protestant church leaders set false dates, predict false things. Thus, this argument like the other will only cause a self-inflicted wound.

Jehovah's Witnesses often talk about John 1:1 and argue the original Greek wording is more correctly translated "In the beginning was the Word, and the Word was with God, and the Word was ¬a god", rather than the orthodox rendering, "In the beginning was the Word, and the Word was with God, and the Word was God." But if this is true why do so many translators agree with the orthodox view?

RESPONSE: The Witnesses will only say I am not going to argue the Greek grammar because the Witnesses reason for translating John 1:1 as such is by following the Protestant religions grammar books, which all do not agree by the way. What I will point out Mr. Wallace is your last point. You asked, "*if this is true why do so many translators agree with the orthodox view?*" The majority of something does not in and of itself make something correct; otherwise, we would all be Catholic or Muslim.

Jehovah's Witnesses often argue God's true name is "Jehovah". But if this is true, why doesn't the word, "Jehovah" appears in the New Testament?

RESPONSE: The Witnesses would say, Wallace, Jehovah was used by Bible scholars up unto the 20th century. Look at the names in your Bible. Many Hebrew kings and others used by God personally in Bible times used part of the Father's personal name in their name, like **Jeh**oash, **Jeh**oram, **Jeho**iakim, **Jeho**iachin, **Jeho**hanan, **Jeho**ahaz, and even the wife of the High Priest **Jeho**iada; daughter of King **Jeho**ram of Judah, **Jeho**sheba, among many more. We notice that the beginning of the Father's personal name is used in every one of these cases. Does anyone find it a bit troubling that the Bibles (JB, LEB, HCSB), which choose to use the so-called scholarly "Yahweh" rendering still spell the above names with Jeho? Why do these same translations not spell **Jeho**ash "**Yah**ash"? Moreover, the 1901 American Standard Version uses Jehovah. Lastly, we do not have the original New Testament manuscripts so we can not say with certainty that the name Jehovah was not in there.

Jehovah's Witnesses say 144,000 people will be part of the "anointed Class' who will live with God in Heaven and will reign over the 'Great Crowd'. But doesn't the Bible describe this group in contradiction to what Jehovah's Witnesses believe?

246

RESPONSE: The Witnesses would say, All I can say here is the Bible makes it clear that not all good people are going to heaven. If the Witnesses are false over this misinterpretation, all Protestant religions have misinterpreted the Bible since the Reformation. The renowned Robert L. Thomas, Jr., professor of New Testament at The Master's Seminary in the United States, wrote, "The case for symbolism is exegetically weak." He added: "It is a definite number [at 7:4] in contrast with the indefinite number of 7:9. If it is taken symbolically, no number in the book can be taken literally." —*Revelation: An Exegetical Commentary,* Volume 1, page 474.

Why Do Jehovah's Witnesses feel the need to make obvious changes to certain passages of Scripture?

RESPONSE: The Witnesses would say, Your reference to the square brackets in the 1984 edition of the New World Translation is a mistaken notion. The square brackets [ ] enclose words inserted to complete the sense in the English text. This is done by all translations and in some these words are italicized. Moreover, again, it is your grammars that advocate for some of these additions. More importantly, you might be better focusing on the more than 50 dynamic equivalent translations where so-called true Christians have produced interpretive translations instead of the literal Word of God. CHOOSING YOUR BIBLE: Bible Translation Differences

Jehovah's Witnesses obviously deny Jesus is God, but how can they do this when Scripture repeatedly describes Jesus as Divine?

RESPONSE: The Witnesses would say, Divine, does not equal God. The Greek terms simply mean a divine person.

How Can Jehovah's Witnesses claim Jesus is a created being when Jesus created everything ever created?

RESPONSE: The Witnesses would say, Jesus was the first divine person to be created and then he became the master-worker of the Father and created all things.

1 Corinthians 15:27-28 Updated American Standard Version (UASV)

[27] For he [the Father] put all things in subjection under his [Jesus'] feet. But when he says, "All things are put in subjection," it is evident that he [God the Father] is excepted who put all things in subjection to him. [28] When all things are subjected to him [Jesus, the Son], then the Son himself also will be subjected to the One who subjected all things to him, so that God may be all in all.

If you are going to ask an apologetic question to undermine a belief or a translation, be certain that your side is also not guilty of the same things or it is not your grammars that they are depending on for their translation renderings.

I would also mention that the Jehovah's Witnesses are very misrepresented by the Christian apologists. The irony is, most Christian apologists are non-Jehovah's Witnesses and this is the field of apologetics that they have chosen, to deal with Jehovah's Witnesses, Mormons, Muslims, and so on. Because these Christian apologists are non-Jehovah's Witnesses, they tend to misunderstand much and are very eager to read other Christian apologist's books on the subject. So, if initial Christian apologists get it wrong in their books, it is a vicious circle that is created of repeating the same mistakes. Moreover, as I will repeat, if you live in a glass house; then, you should not be throwing rocks.

SOME GOOD THINGS ABOUT THE JEHOVAH'S WITNESSES

- The Jehovah's Witnesses **actually** go out and make disciples (Matt 24:14;28:19–20; Acts 1:8)

- The Jehovah's Witnesses **actually** live by the Bible when it comes to a lifestyle. They do not smoke, abuse alcohol or drugs, watch graphically violent movies, sexually explicit movies, dress morally, and they have the lowest divorce rate over adultery.

- The Jehovah's Witnesses **actually** study the Bible: The family studies it individually, then together as a family to prepare for the meetings, and then at the meeting itself.

- The Jehovah's Witnesses **actually** do not celebrate pagan holidays like Halloween.

- The Jehovah's Witnesses **actually** are one mind when it comes to teaching the Bible.

- Much more could actually be said.

SOME BAD THINGS ABOUT THE JEHOVAH'S WITNESSES ... HOWEVER, ...

- The Jehovah's Witnesses **actually** set four false dates of when Jesus was going to return.

- **HOWEVER**, it was actually a Baptist preacher, William Miller, who introduced the Witnesses to Bible chronology and end-times discussions. William Miller set two false dates. Also, if you go to Facebook groups that discuss end-times, you will find hundreds of thousands of so-called Christians on their talking about what they do not know. REMEMBER No **throwing rocks** when you live in a glasshouse.

- The Jehovah's Witnesses **actually** said it was a sin to get *immunizations* and Witnesses died. Then, they said they were mistaken and changed the teaching. The Jehovah's Witnesses **actually** said it was a sin to get *organ transplants* and Witnesses died. Then, they said they were mistaken and changed the teaching. The Jehovah's Witnesses **actually** said it was a sin to get *blood transfusions* and Witnesses died. Then, they said they were mistaken and changed the teaching slowly over many years until you can receive so much of a blood transfusion that the teaching is really moot.

- **HOWEVER**, it is not even really close. "Christians" have tortured and slaughtered millions of other Christians who dared to believe differently and tens of millions of other non-Christians in forcing them by the sword to convert to Christianity. REMEMBER No **throwing rocks** when you live in a glasshouse.

- The Jehovah's Witnesses **actually** had a sex-abuse scandal where leaders and some other men molested children. Because there must be two witnesses to a wrongdoing policy, they did not report the crimes and actually shunned and punished the wives. Very bad and I in no way rationalize this by saying what I must say now.

- **HOWEVER**, it is not even really close. The modern-day Catholic Church has allowed priest molestation for many, many decades, even protecting the molesters, allowing them to do it again and again. If you thought this was and is heinous study the history of Catholicism as Popes, Bishops and Cardinals were the chief sex-offenders. The other Christian denominations called out Catholicism on this, even the Baptist Church. Well, now the Baptist Church has been found to have the same child molestation scandal. REMEMBER No **throwing rocks** when you live in a glasshouse.

- The Jehovah's Witnesses **actually** have a bit of a mind-control problem, in that, you absolutely cannot think, believe, or teach anything different than what is being taught by the Governing Body of the Watchtower Bible & Tract Society, i.e., the Jehovah's Witnesses.

- **HOWEVER**, it is not even really close. Most of the 41,000 Christian denominations allow their members to believe a little different because there are many views on different doctrinal positions. Yet, the Trinity is the Holy Grail of their beliefs. If you reject any facet of the Trinity doctrine, you are rejected and are removed from being considered a Christian. You now become the anti-Christ, so to speak. It is not close because so-called true Christians have nor expelled those that dared to believe differently as the Witnesses do, they have actually tortured and killed them. John Calvin had Michael Servetus killed because he did not accept the Trinity doctrine. Martin Luther supported killing those that believed differently. These were not the only ones. REMEMBER, No **throwing rocks** when you live in a glasshouse.

Witnessing to the Jehovah's Witnesses

Yes, Jehovah's Witnesses are mistaken in a number of biblical doctrines but not on everything they teach. Moreover, so-called true Christians have also been mistaken on many Bible doctrines as well and over time with a better understanding; they arrived at the correct teaching. When you over exaggerate by calling the Jehovah's Witnesses a cult you only give them more fuel in their evangelism work because they will define a cult and show examples of real cults (Jim Jones, Charles Manson, David Koresh). This only makes it easier for the Witnesses to pull Christians away from the so-called true Christianity. In addition, many of the doctrinal positions that the Witnesses hold are actually borrowed from other denominations of Christendom within the last 2,000 years. The Christian evangelist needs to win Witnesses back into the fold of true Christianity, as well as protect the sheep currently within the fold. We do not do that by over-exaggerating our evidence or forgetting that our denominations taught similarly or that Protestant church leaders have made similar mistakes or trying to demean a religion by name-calling when they do not even fit the definition or characteristics of a cult.

The fact that I even uttered the above truths about the Witnesses will drive some to believe I am being an apologist for the Witnesses. Some readers will feel completely uncomfortable even uttering positive things about the Witnesses or admitting that Protestant denominations have made similar mistakes, some much worse. What does this sound like? It sounds like some so-called true Christian leaders have carried out a little mind control themselves. Most Christian leaders attempt to label the Jehovah's Witness, the Mormons, and the Seventh Day Adventists as cults for their "un-Christian" unorthodox beliefs. This is a wrong path to go down because while doing so, these leaders are forgetting the fundamentalist movement of true Christianity of late 19th and early 20th centuries that were trying to overcome liberal progressive Christianity apologetically and evangelistically. That battle for the Christian faith and the Bible was lost. Now, today the word "fundamentalist" is equivalent to the term "cult." When so-called true, genuine Christianity has had a far worse history, similarly many mistaken doctrinal positions, have done some mind control of their own, have divided into tens of thousands of denominations that all believe differently, it might not be wise to call other religious groups a cult. If you find these insights offense, it might be a little mind control at work, so ponder things objectively.

This is no easy task for most Christians. The Jehovah's Witnesses are well trained to defend their beliefs. They spend five meetings a week, much personal study and meeting preparation in taking in what they believe and learning how to defend their version of the faith. This is not said to scare anyone off from trying to approach the Witnesses, but rather to encourage you to prepare well. The irony is; we do not have to go out and find the Witnesses, as they come to us because they go house-to-house. The objective is not to be confrontational, as Witnesses are trained to abandon such conversations.

The best thing we can do is know what we believe very well and be accomplished at defending it. It is best to know what they believe as well and what Scriptures they use to defend such views. However, it is not that simple because they will know what we believe and what verses we use, and they will be prepared to undermine those verses. As was said, it is not going to be easy. It gets worse still if the average Witness cannot deal with our preparedness, but they believe we are sincerely interested, they will bring a pioneer[1] with them the next time they visit us. These ones have far more experience and knowledge. If that fails, they will bring the most qualified congregation elder. Do not be fooled; some Witnesses study secular books; they learn Hebrew and Greek, among many other academic fields. These latter ones are few in number, but I thought I would mention it in case they happen to be in your area.

If we want the Witnesses to visit us, all we have to do is write or call the main branch of Jehovah's Witnesses[2] and ask for one of their books, which will give us the basic beliefs they hold. They will not mail us the publication; they will have someone from the local Kingdom Hall (their church) deliver it. When they come, they will walk us through the book and look to start a study with us. If we want to win them over to our side, this is the best way, as we would have them all to ourselves in our home, going over doctrinal positions. It is best to make this stipulation, though, "I will study your book with you, but as you know, I believe differently, so along the way, I may raise objections, ask for more proof, as well as share how I see whatever we may be discussing." They will agree to this stipulation because they always believe they have the upper hand.

The best approach is to agree where there is an agreement because believe it or not; there will be more agreement than one might imagine. When we come to points of disagreement, have them make their case, letting them get through the entire presentation and then undermine it with Scripture from their New World Translation. We can be prepared because they will give us a copy of the book to prepare for the study; they will also provide us with a New World Translation if we ask for one. As we prepare for the study, be prepared to be surprised because the Witness literature is excellent at using verses based on isolated reading sound as though they do support what is being said in their publications. Thus, we need to look the verses up in three literal translations (NASB, ESV, and HCSB), we need to read the section of Scripture that the text is found in and look it up in a commentary volume. A superb, easy to read commentary volume set is Holman Old and New Testament Commentary Volumes. If there are translation issues, we need to investigate these. If there are textual issues, we need to examine these.

Once they arrive for the study, we should have our legal pad or our tablet right beside us with our information. Once we complete the study, let the Witness know that we take issue with some of the verses that they had used to support their position. Then, go through them one by one. It is as simple as that. If we share this information without asking them to defend against it, over the course of their study book (4-6 months), they will begin to doubt their position. One cannot sit through one correction after another over so many months and not begin to wonder about whether they are in the right religion. One thing that we do not want to do is what many of the cult books that undermine the Witnesses' beliefs recommend, i.e., shock and awe. They want us to sit there, accept a Witness belief, and methodically undermine it. This will not work; the Witness will not open, look in, or be a part of such a book. Even if we do not show them the book, they will walk out if the situation looks like an assault on their faith. I apologize for this analogy, but one can cook an animal alive if they turn up the heat slowly enough. If we walk through a couple of their books over an extended period, it will be so slow of an undermining that it will not be an affront, an assault.

PIONEERING AS A JEHOVAH'S WITNESS

The word "pioneer" itself refers to a person who is among the first to explore or settle a new territory, country, or area, making the way for others to follow. This is how the Witnesses view their work as an evangelist.

These are what Christianity would call evangelists carrying out evangelism. I will intertwine, compare, and contrast Christianity's 41,000 denominations with Witnesses.

Evangelism is the work of a Christian evangelist, of which Christians and Jehovah's Witnesses too are obligated to partake to some extent, which seeks to persuade other people to become Christian or a Jehovah's Witness, especially by sharing the basics of the Gospel, but also the deeper message of biblical truths. Today, very few from the Christian churches of any of the 41,000 denominations evangelize, while the Jehovah's Witnesses are very involved in this work. (Matt. 24:14; 28:19–20; Acts 1:8)

Preevangelism is laying a foundation for those who have no knowledge of the Gospel, giving them background information, so that they are able to grasp what they are hearing. The Christian evangelist, if there are any, are preparing their mind and heart so that they will be receptive to the biblical truths and the Jehovah's Witness is doing the same for what they believe to be true. In many ways, this is known as apologetics.

All Jehovah's Witnesses are evangelists and try to get out into their community for a minimum amount of hours each month. A pioneer is viewed as a parttime (auxiliary) and a fulltime (regular) pioneer.

THREE TYPES OF PIONEERS

Auxilliary Pioneer: It used to be that this person spent 70 hours each month in the evangelism of people in their communities by limiting their secular work to part-time. However, some time ago, the Witness organization lowered it to 30 and 50-hours.

Regular Pioneer: It used to be that this person spent 90 hours each month in the evangelism of people in their communities by limiting their secular work to part-time or no work at all. However, some time ago, the Witness organization lowered it to 70-hours.

Special Pioneers: This person spends 130 hours or more each month in the evangelism of people in their communities or other communities that the Witness organization assigns them to because they feel the need is greater.

All Jehovah's Witnesses as evangelists are more informed about what they believe than almost all Christians. Why?

- Because they have a personal Bible study every day

- Because they prepare for Christian meetings individually and then again as a family

- Because they then cover the material a third time at the meeting itself, where they participate as well

- When preparing they read the Bible study too, they look up all cited Bible verses, they use Bible encyclopedias (Insight on the Scriptures, vol. I & II) to dig deeper. They answer the paragraph questions by highlighting the answers. They write their personal answers in the margin

- They spend anywhere from 10 hours to 130 hours each month evangelizing about their beliefs.

Even though almost all of Jehovah's Witnesses are more informed about their beliefs than 99% of all Christians, they are not all informed equally amongst themselves. As one might expect, the Witness, non-pioneer can likely out conversate the Christian they meet in their evangelism work. And the parttime pioneers even more so but they are not capable of dealing with a well-informed pastor. The pioneer can likely hold his or her own against most pastors, priests, or ministers. However, likely not against a well-informed pastor. An elder (pastor)-pioneer could hold his own against a well-informed pioneer.

Almost all Jehovah's Witnesses are not aware of **a growing trend in their organization**. There are regular Jehovah's Witnesses, pioneers, ministerial servants (deacons), and elders (pastors), who are actually self-taught Bible scholars, or they have gone to Bible colleges or seminaries, and some even teach Bible classes. This is not even known by the so-called Christian apologists who write books about the Witnesses. Some of these even have PhDs. They are experts in hermeneutics, Bible translation philosophy and differences, biblical Hebrew and Greek, textual criticism, and so much more. There are literally thousands of these kinds of Witnesses. Their personal library is filled with hundreds, if not thousands of the same books used in Bible colleges and seminaries.

Bibliography

Aland, K. a. (1987). *The Text of the New Testament.* Grand Rapids: Eerdmans.

Aland, K. e. (1993). *The Greek New Testament, Fourth Revised Edition (Interlinear with Morphology).* Deutsche Bibelgesellschaft.

Andrews, E. D. (2016). *THE COMPLETE GUIDE to BIBLE TRANSLATION: Bible Translation Choices and Translation Principles [Second Edition]* . Cambridge: Christian Publishing House.

Andrews, E. D., & Wilkins, D. (2017). *THE TEXT OF THE NEW TESTAMENT: The Science and Art of Textual Criticism.* Cambridge: Christian Publishing House.

Arndt, W. F. (2000). *A Greek-English Lexicon of the New Testament and Other Early Christian Literature. 3rd ed.* Chicago: University of Chicago Press.

Beekman, J. a. (1974). *Translating the Word of God.* Grand Rapids: Zondervan.

Brand, C. e. (2003). *"Beast," Holman Illustrated Bible Dictionary.* Nashville: Holman Bible Publishers,.

Elwell, W. A. (2001). *Evangelical Dictionary of Theology (Second Edition).* Grand Rapids: Baker Academic.

Elwell, W. A. (2001). *Evangelical Dictionary of Theology (Second Edition).* Grand Rapids: Baker Academic.

Elwell, W. A., & Comfort, P. W. (2001). *Tyndale Bible Dictionary.* Wheaton: Tyndale House Publishers.

Hoffman, J. M. (2007). *AND GOD SAID: How Translations Conceal the Bible's Original Meaning.* New York, NY: Thomas Dunne Books.

Metzger, B. (2001). *The Bible in Translation: Ancient and English Versions.* Grand Rapids: Baker Academic.

Metzger, B. M. (1964, 1968, 1992). *The Text of the New Testament: Its Transmission, Corruption, and Transmission.* New York: Oxford University Press.

Metzger, B. M. (1994). *A Textual Commentary on the Greek New Testament.* New York: United Bible Society.

Owens, J. J. (1989–). *Analytical Key to the Old Testament.* Grand Rapids: Baker Book House.

Porter, S. E., & Boda, M. J. (2009). *Translating the New Testament*. Grand Rapids: Wm. B. Eerdmans.

Porter, S. E., & Hess, R. S. (2004). *Translating the Bible: Problems and Prospects*. New York: T&T Clark International.

Poythress, V. S., & Grudem, W. A. (2004). *The TNIV and The Gender-Neutral Bible Controversy*. Nashville:: Boardman & Holman.

Ray, V. (1982). The Formal vs Dynamic Equivalent Principle in New Testament Translation. *Restoration Quarterly 25*, 46-56.

Rhodes, R. (2009). *The Complete Guid to Bible Translations*. Eugene, OR: Harvest House.

Richards, E. R. (2004). *Paul And First-Century Letter Writing: Secretaries, Composition and Collection*. Downers Grove: InterVarsity Press.

Ryken, L. (2002). *The Word of God in English. Wheaton*. Wheaton: Crossway Books.

Ryken, L. (2008). *Choosing a Bible: Understanding Bible Translation Differences*. Wheaton: Crossway Books.

Ryken, L. (2009). *Understanding English Bible Translation: The Case for an Essentially Literal Approach*. Wheaton: Crossway Books.

Scorgie, G. G., Strauss, M. L., & Voth, S. M. (2003). *The Challenge of Bible Translation*. Grand Rapids: Zondervan.

Thomas, R. L. (1992). *Revelation 1-7: An Exegetical Commentary* . Chicago, IL: Moody Publishers.

Thomas, R. L. (2000). *How to Choose a Bible Version*. Scotland: Christian Focus Publications.

Printed in the USA
CPSIA information can be obtained
at www.ICGtesting.com
LVHW010221041023
759982LV00021B/129

9 781945 757785